I0589566

abbé Rivaux, Chestnut Hill Sisters of St. Joseph

Life of Rev. Mother St. John Fontbonne

abbé Rivaux, Chestnut Hill Sisters of St. Joseph

Life of Rev. Mother St. John Fontbonne

ISBN/EAN: 9783744659444

Printed in Europe, USA, Canada, Australia, Japan

Cover: Foto ©Lupo / pixelio.de

More available books at **www.hansebooks.com**

Rev. Mother St. John Fontbonne,

Foundress and First Superior-General

OF

THE CONGREGATION OF THE SISTERS OF ST. JOSEPH

IN LYONS.

Translated from the French

OF

THE ABBÉ RIVAUX,

Honorary Canon, Author of "Cours d'Histoire Ecclésiastique."

Look, and make it according to the pattern that was shewed thee in the mount.—EXOD. xxv, 40.

Who shall find a valiant woman? the price of her is as of things brought from afar off and from the uttermost coasts.—PROV. xxxi, 10.

NEW YORK, CINCINNATI, AND CHICAGO:

BENZIGER BROTHERS,

Printers to the Holy Apostolic See.

Copyright, 1887, by Benziger Brothers.

𝕬𝖕𝖕𝖗𝖔𝖇𝖆𝖙𝖎𝖔𝖓.

His Eminence CARDINAL CAVEROT, Archbishop of Lyons, having cordially recommended the Life of Rev. Mother St. John, the Foundress and first Superioress of the Sisters of St. Joseph of Lyons, we hereby give our *Imprimatur* and recommendation to the translation of the same work, assured that whilst it will prove of special interest to the spiritual daughters of this saintly Mother, it will be found also a source of edification to the members of all religious Communities and to the devout laity.

The world is ruled not by ideas but by ideals, and pious biography,—the Gospel and counsels of perfection realized in actual life—is a most powerful motive to " go and do likewise."

✠ PATRICK JOHN,
Archbishop of Philadelphia.

Given at PHILADELPHIA,
FEAST OF ST. AGNES, Jan. 21, 1887.

CONTENTS.

—BOOK I.—

Origin of the Congregation of the Sisters of St. Joseph.—Mother St. John before and after the Revolution of 1789.

CHAPTER I.

CHAPTER II.

CHAPTER III.

CHAPTER IV.

CHAPTER V.

CHAPTER VI

—BOOK II.—

Mother St. John after the Revolution.—Foundation, Unification, and Organization of the Sisters of St. Joseph of Lyons.

CHAPTER I.

CHAPTER II.

CHAPTER III.

CHAPTER IV.

CHAPTER V.

—BOOK III.—

*Mother St. John's administration and direction.—Wonderful in-
crease of the Congregation of Lyons.—Its numerous and glorious
spiritual offspring.*

CHAPTER I.

CHAPTER VI.

–BOOK IV.–

Closing years of Mother St. John's life.

CHAPTER I.

CHAPTER II.

CHAPTER III.

Preface

To the American Edition.

The desire to render generally accessible to the Sisters of St. Joseph some of the records of our beloved Congregation, at present available only to those conversant with French, has prompted the translation of the present work. All the English-speaking communities of our Institute treasure a special reverence for Rev. Mother St. John Fontbonne, for to the Congregation of Lyons they, with but very few exceptions, can trace their origin. The interest, then, that attaches itself to whatever concerns one's religious family, will, we trust, secure a welcome for our book, whatever may be its faults and shortcomings.

We have rendered the Abbé Rivaux's " Life " somewhat freely, taking the liberty to add or curtail where fuller and later information seemed to render it necessary. The sketches of Foundations in various parts of the world, which are not to be found in the original, were introduced at the suggestion of one whose wish we regard as law. Brief and defective as they necessarily are, we feel confident they will render the work more acceptable to our Sisters in both the Old and the New World.

'To the dear correspondents, who from our different communities so promptly forwarded us the asked-for data, we return our grateful acknowledgments :—without their co-operation, our researches would, in many cases, have been fruitless.

Should our labors have the coveted result of making our Blessed Father St. Joseph more loved, the grace of our holy vocation more fully appreciated, we shall have been repaid far beyond our deserts.

THE SISTERS OF ST. JOSEPH.

MT. ST. JOSEPH, CHESTNUT HILL, PHILADELPHIA,

Feast of Our Lady's Immaculate Conception, 1886.

AUTHOR'S DECLARATION.

I declare that in relating in this book some extraordinary facts, established by well-authenticated testimony, and in giving the name of Saint or Blessed to persons whom the Church has not beatified or canonized, I intend it only in the measure authorized by the decrees of Pope Urban VIII.

I declare, moreover, that I submit this work to the infallible authority of the Sovereign Pontiff, disavowing sincerely whatever therein may be found not conformable to the teaching of the Holy Church, my Mother, whom I wish to love and serve until my last sigh, and in whose obedience it is my hope to live and die.

𝔇𝔢𝔡𝔦𝔠𝔞𝔱𝔦𝔬𝔫.

To His Eminence Cardinal Caverot, Archbishop of Lyons and Vienne, and Primate of the Gauls.

My Lord:

Deign to accept from your children, the Sisters of St. Joseph, the Dedication of the Life of Rev. Mother St. John, their Foundress in Lyons.

It is from the pen of the holy and learned Abbé Rivaux, to whom we are already indebted for the Life of Rev. Mother M. of the Sacred Heart of Jesus. Death has, to our great regret, prevented his giving to the work the development he had intended ; but, through respect to his memory, we refrain from adding anything thereto. In the second edition, if such be called for, we hope to complete it with notes already collected.

In publishing the lives of our Foundresses and Mothers, it is our intention that, by reading and meditating on them, we may become more thoroughly imbued with their spirit, may enter more closely into their interior life, and thus renew the primitive fervor of our beloved Institute.

History shows us these venerable Mothers constantly sustained, encouraged, and directed by holy Prelates and illustrious Princes of the Church. But in this respect we need not envy them, since Divine Providence, which apportions righteous men along the course of ages, according to the necessities of His works, has deigned to give us, in the person of Your Eminence, a support proportionate to our weakness and to the dangers of an epoch in which evil is ever on the increase.

Venerable Prelate, so worthy of your illustrious predecessors, permit us, then, to lay at your feet this volume, as a tribute of our profound veneration and filial piety. Your blessing, my Lord, and your approbation will be an additional mark of the paternal goodness and benevolent protection you have ever lavished on the Sisters of Saint Joseph.

Accept, we beg, the expression of our lively gratitude. We supplicate the Sacred Heart of Jesus to render to you a hundred-fold all the good you have done to our Congregation, and to preserve long to the Church a Prelate who causes her to be so much loved and honored.

Deign, my Lord, to bless your numerous family of St. Joseph, and, in particular, I humbly pray, her whose honor it is to be

Your most respectful and humble daughter,

Sr. Marie Emilie Blaffard,

Superior General.

Approbation

Of His Eminence Cardinal Caverot.

Rev. Mother and Daughter:

I have just received the Life of Rev. Mother St. John, the dedication of which you have so kindly asked me to accept.

By adding this interesting biography to that of the holy Mother of the Sacred Heart, his previous work, the venerable Abbé Rivaux has deserved well of your Congregation.

Thanks to his labors, you now possess an exact and detailed history of your origin : you can gaze on the portraits of your first Mothers, those whom God raised up for the reorganization of your Institute ; for their labors, their sufferings, and their virtues are renewed in these pages consecrated to their memory. Herein you will find your religious archives, those treasures precious to you beyond all price.

I can well understand, Rev. Mother, how eager you are to place in the hands of your religious daughters the Life of her whom they so justly venerate as their Foundress. You have every reason to believe that the work will tend greatly to their edification ; for what more profitable or delightful to the members of a religious family than to go back to the early days of their foundation, days superabounding in the benedictions of Heaven !

May God, then, deign, Rev. Mother and daughter, to hear your prayers, which my heart re-echoes, by preserving in your dear Congregation the spirit which influenced its birth and development; that spirit which, even until now, has drawn down upon it such abundant benedictions.

Yours wholly in our Lord,

✠ L. M. CARD. CAVEROT.

PAGNOS (Jura), Aug. 26, 1885.

INTRODUCTION.

THE venerable servant of God of whom we are about to write had been a religious of St. Joseph previous to the Revolution of 1789. Expelled from her convent by revolutionary impiety, immured in a prison, and condemned to death, she owed her life only to the fall of Robespierre.

Ardently desirous of martyrdom, she, with tears, bewailed her loss, when the jailer who was to have led her to the scaffold came, instead, with the tidings of her deliverance. While the most lively emotions of joy thrilled the hearts of her fellow-prisoners at the prospect of freedom, sadness overwhelmed her, who, like the great Apostle, burned with desire to be immolated for God and to be with Jesus Christ.

Retiring, then, to the bosom of her family, she there lived so holily, so faithful to her religious vocation, as to merit the honor of becoming, after the Revolution, the instrument of Divine Providence for the re-establishment of her beloved Congregation, and for giving it, with a new constitution adapted to the exigencies of the times, an extent, a unity, an amplitude, a brilliancy, which it had not previously known.

Her long life of more than eighty-four years was wholly spent in loving, practising, extending, and propagating the religious life, as well as in founding and directing numberless houses of the Congregation. Hence she has left, in both hemispheres, a numerous posterity of souls consecrated to God by the holy vows of religion.

No one, even the most unobservant, can be ignorant that in our day is raging a tempest of error and falsehood, in which the religious Orders are calumniated and attacked with the utmost virulence. Not only is the supernatural phase of their existence misunderstood and misrepresented, but their social influence is systematically ignored. Even when men cease to regard them as malefactors, they fail not to arouse public opinion against them.

In view of such hatred,—explicable only as the effect of passion or ignorance,—it seems useful, nay, even necessary to present here some serious considerations on the private life, services, sanctity, and rights of monastic institutions and of religious, the holy militia, living by renunciation and devotedness, fulfilling day and night their sublime ministry of public prayer and perpetual self-immolation for the salvation of the world.

I.

The monastic and religious life is, as it were, a flower indigenous to the Catholic religion and inseparable from it ; nevertheless, it has not always existed ; at least, not in the form it has assumed since the early persecutions. A tree has existence before it bears its blossoms ; these, even when they do appear, may be killed by time, frost, or storm, the robust trunk retaining. meanwhile, that life and sap destined to produce new blossoms.

So, likewise, the germ and principle of the religious life is contained in the Gospel ; the evangelical sap tends, necessarily, to its development. As long as this fruitful tree lives, in what climate soever it may be, the divine sap will bud forth and adorn it with flowers of the religious life. "It is certain," says Balmes, "that religious Orders will spring into being wherever religion herself exists. One is the effect ; the other, the cause."

Some climates and seasons are, undoubtedly, more favorable than others to their full and vigorous growth. Persecutions, too, must be encountered : they are their winter and their storm ; but when peace and serenity return, they, too, will reappear as surely as flowers spring forth to greet the return of May.

" You have seen," says Montalembert, "a forest ravaged and destroyed by the woodman's axe : on every side reign death, devastation, sterility. The grand old oaks are fallen, and their withered foliage lies heaped on the surrounding soil ; their giant branches are stripped and dismembered, their mutilated trunks bestrew the ground ; nothing has been spared, and the very saplings that flourished beneath the shade of the ancestral boughs seem included in the common ruin. And yet, nothing has perished ! From those very stumps which the axe has discrowned, strength and life shall spring forth anew. Clothed in a second growth, they will bud and blossom with additional splendor. In like manner, nay, with still more marvellous fecundity, from the mangled yet inexhaustible womb of the Church, shall be brought forth the invincible race of the servants of God."

Such is the richness of that interior sap which descends from Heaven to nourish the religious life, that it must, necessarily, surmount every obstacle, and, like a vigorous plant, make its way in spite of every impediment.

Artisans of nothingness, *the woodmen of Atheism* set themselves eagerly to destroy the works of God ; but He, the indefatigable Creator, ceases not to reanimate what has proceeded from His hands. The religious life is inseparably united with the life of the Church ; it shall end only when she ceases to exist.

II.

The end of the religious life, then, is to raise the soul to Christian perfection by the practice of the evangelical counsels, which, no less than the precepts, are a part of the Gospel and of religion. The whole moral doctrine of the Gospel rests, as we know, on the incontestable fact that there exist in man three great concupiscences or disordered passions, whence proceed all the vices and evils of the world : *pride,* or immoderate love of honors ; *avarice,* or unbridled search after riches ; and *lust,* or the ill-regulated love of sensual pleasures.

To these passions our Lord Jesus Christ opposes the contrary virtues of humility, disinterestedness or poverty, and chastity. In a common and ordinary degree, these virtues are binding upon all, and by their practice alone is assured to society any peace or happiness that can be enjoyed here below. In their extraordinary and perfect sense, humility or obedience, poverty, and chastity are simply of counsel, and constitute the religious life or state of evangelical perfection, so bitterly calumniated, and, at times, regarded as an institution, not only useless, but positively injurious to society—as if the practice of perfect virtue could bring ruin on the world !

"Public utility," writes the great Leibnitz, "requires that there be men given to the ascetic or monastic life, who, treading pleasures under foot, may devote themselves wholly to divine contemplation and perfect virtue. This is not one of the least beautiful prerogatives of the Catholic Church, in which alone we find reproduced so many eminent examples of the ascetic life."

"The contemplative life is the most divine of all," writes Plato, that almost inspired philosopher of antiquity. On this "summit of practical Catholicity," to use the expression of Mgr. Dupanloup, flourish the most exquisite blossoms of humanity.

III.

Invincible and divine by its evangelical origin, the religious life responds, like the Christian life, to the most intimate requirements of the human soul and society. He, indeed, must be unacquainted with human nature, who does not recognize that amidst the vast number of souls whom Jesus calls into His sheep-fold, there are some who vehemently hunger and thirst after Christian perfection, and that the ordinary path of virtue, leading though it does to Heaven, is not enough to satiate their desires. "There are, it is true," says the learned convert Hurter, "other routes by which souls may journey to Heaven ; but shall we esteem as a fool him who chooses the steepest and most rugged, because it is at the same time the most direct, most certain, most heroic, and most favorable to wisdom and perfection ?"

"Again," he says, "as the hart pants after fountains of living water, so to the religious life have ever tended the aspirations of those grand souls thirsting after God and perfection, such as the Pauls, the Anthonys, the Brunos, the Francises, the Clares, Theresas, and hosts of others. Such exquisite fruits ripen only on the choicest stock, take root in none but the richest soil."

Besides these souls of the highest order, there are many others who desire solitude. Natural attraction ; disgust or dread of the world ; a desire to secure one's virtue and salvation ; a yearning for peace, tranquillity, and recollection ; a taste for prayer and study ; love of solid and holy learning ; all these different motives act irresistibly on a vast number of souls.

Debar them from the monastery and the convent, you deprive them of their element ; you render them useless, nay, it may sometimes be, even injurious, to society.

There is a third class for whom the monastery and the

religious life become a necessity : for penitents. for the unfortunate. The world, as is often truly said, is a sea bestrewn with shipwrecks. What hopes deceived, what affections blighted, what illusions dissipated ! What bitter regrets, what frightful remorse—remorse, happily often the first step towards salutary repentance ! Leave no such asylum to those souls, weary of life and of themselves, and often despairing, and what a tempest of crime will desolate the world ! As dislocated, suffering, dangerous members, those victims of vice or misfortune will become the scourges of society. Gather them, on the contrary, into a convent as into a bark of safety ; under kind and gentle influence they will be consoled, encouraged, and instructed ; and that desperate soul which might have become the terror of its fellows, will, in that asylum, be transformed into a useful and edifying member of society, it may be, even, into a Saint.

This is what M. Augustin Thierry means when he says that " A convent is not only a place of meditation and prayer, but often an asylum opened against the invasion of barbarism in all its forms."

" Compare," says Victor Hugo himself, " the convent with the prison ; the expiation of crime, forcible and full of rage, with the expiation of love and recovered innocence ! "

The world and its maxims make men wicked and vicious : the convict's cell consummates their vice or despair : the convent alone has power to convert and transform.

IV.

The convent and monastery owe their power of sanctifying and rehabilitating souls to their life of innocence and perfection, to their life of prayer, of mortification or expiation, and of charity. For in these four things lies the essential end, the supreme object of the existence of monks and religious.

Now, as has been before remarked, the religious life is a flower of the grand and glorious tree of the Church ; and Christian perfection, itself the richest fruit of the Gospel, is the sole reason of its being. Nay, the religious life is, properly speaking, only Christian perfection realized according to time and place, by divers means, but always based on those three vows of religion, diametrically opposed to the three great concupiscences which ravage the earth.

By his vow of obedience, which subjects him to a rule conformable to the Gospel and represented by a wise superior, the religious sacrifices his pride and self-love, and with them, the vices and errors of which they are so fruitful a source.

Thanks to his vow of poverty, the religious is preserved from the excesses, disorders, and injustices which, through all time, have been the result of avarice and the love of wealth. So fatal is this passion that the Gospel, in all things else so calm and moderate, fulminates against it a terrible anathema : " Woe to the rich ! " *Væ divitibus!*

By the vow of absolute chastity or virginity, the religious rises above what is merely natural and becomes angelic. " Some sages and philosophers," cries out St. John Chrysostom, " have, indeed, vanquished anger or despised riches; but as to virginity, it has never bloomed with them. On this point they grant us the victory, acknowledging it as something superior to nature."

Hence the Church is so enamored of virgins, that she surrounds them with the most tender solicitude, and considers them the most illustrious portion of her family, her crown of glory, her most precious jewel. Her greatest Doctors have, in their regard, been prodigal of admiration and the flowers of their genius. Virgins, says St. Cyprian, are angels among men. Virginity, exclaims St. Ambrose, has Heaven for her country : here she sojourns as a lovely and illustrious foreigner : on high she dwells as princess in her palace, and the angels call her sister !

Virgins, according to a pious author, form, as it were, a pleiad of pure stars, a milky way in the firmament of the Church, a phenomenon wholly unknown outside her pale.

V.

The monastic and religious life not only sanctifies and edifies, but the monk, the religious, prays and expiates. Humanity is overwhelmed with miseries, wants, and infirmities. What optimist dare deny it ? Now the logical language—rational as well as Christian—of want and misery is prayer. Can we conceive a being as loving, suffering, thinking, or even desiring, without giving utterance to prayer ? But prayer is the very office of the religious.

Let us again cast our eyes upon the earth: it is covered with crime and disorders. Now sin calls for expiation. Hence the custom of sacrifice, which, universal as it is mysterious, has existed everywhere and always: in the Old and the New World; amidst savages and civilized nations, bearing ever the same characteristics,—a chosen victim, an innocent victim substituted for the guilty one and satisfying for him. It is, as Cicero says, a law of nature.

Are not, then, the religious, whether male or female, who pray, who suffer in expiation of sin, the saviours of society, the benefactors of the human race? Hence men free from the dominion of folly or prejudice regard them as innocent victims, serving as a counterpoise to the iniquities of the world. "It is necessary that some should pray for those who never pray," acknowledges Victor Hugo. "The Saints bear up the world," writes St. Jerome, "and by the power of prayer ward off its imminent ruin."

The Emperor Constantine begged the prayers of the

humble St. Anthony, and the great Theodosius, on the eve of his victorious expedition, recommended himself and his army to the intercession of a poor hermit.

Let us remember Sodom and Gomorrha, which would have been preserved from destruction had they contained ten just men. "Go about through the streets of Jerusalem," said the Lord to Jeremias, "and see, and consider, and seek in the broad places thereof, if you can find a man that executeth judgment: and I will be merciful to it." Is it not, then, incontestable that the Saints, being expiators, are saviours?

He who prays for the people, says the Scripture, is a lover of his brethren: *Hic est fratrum amator, qui multum orat pro populo.*

Read the History or Constitutions of any religious Order; you will find that one of its chief ends is to pray for the world, to expiate its crimes. Then, in leaving the world, the religious does not abandon it; he separates himself from only that he may become more useful to it. He departs, it is true, from the ranks of society, but it is to immolate himself for its conservation. In this there is something superior to the most beautiful instances of self-devotion recorded in history. It is an imitation of Jesus Christ, who suffers death "because it is expedient that one man die for the people." The last day alone shall reveal how, by the prayers of religious, storms have been prevented, tempests dissipated, and chastisements warded off, even from those very persons who have most despised them!

Like those magnetic rods which we place on the summit of our buildings to preserve them from lightning, the peaceful domes of convents rise towards Heaven to deprecate its wrath by continual supplications of love. Yes, we have said it; they are veritable lightning-rods!

VI.

Dwellings of saintliness, of prayer and expiation by mortification, convents and monasteries are also houses of charity, almsgiving, and all good works.

Whatever certain volumes, in which ignorance rivals prejudice, may pretend, the history of religious and monastic institutions is a monument as heroic as it is sublime. It has been read, recounted, celebrated, admired by the greatest Saints and the grandest geniuses of the world, the Athanasiuses, Jeromes, Augustines, Gregorys, and others. Such names compel respect; they cannot be overruled by a shrug of the shoulders or a shameless lie. "It has not been sufficiently remarked," says a grave author, "that all, or nearly all the Fathers of the Church, the grand Doctors of primitive times, were members of the monastic order."

Monks and religious were the models of humanity, the fathers and benefactors of the poor, the civilizers of barbarians, the defenders of the weak and of true liberty, the introducers of agriculture, the example of laborers, the preservers and propagators of study and science. This is the true, irrefutable history of monks, whether in the East or the West. On which account, Mgr. Plantier has said that, in attacking the monastic institution, one cannot escape an odious alternative : he must either calumniate what he knows, or blaspheme what he knows not.

VII.

In every epoch, the religious and monastic institution has proved an inexhaustible source of benefits, infinitely diversified, according to time and place.

It originated, as we know, in the East, not far from the banks of the Nile, in the scorching solitudes of the Thebaid. The distinctive sign of the Oriental monk was absolute seclusion. Whether hermit or cenobite, he isolated himself from the world, and retired into the desert, there to pray, labor, and practise fasts and austerities, the very thought of which affrights our delicacy. One might say that to him the body was nothing; the soul, everything.

To judge wisely of any institution, one must consider it amidst the circumstances attending its development, and have regard, also, to its providential end. Now, the society from which the Oriental monk withdrew was a society enervated by luxury and the abuse of all material delights. The land from which he fled was a land of pleasure. Everything tended to self-gratification: the delightfulness of the climate; the perfumes that filled the air; the beauty of the heavens: a civilization which had exhausted all the refinements of voluptuousness, and consecrated sensual pleasures themselves to the divinity; effeminated arts; an emasculated literature; in a word, everything that could be seen, heard, or felt, invited men to pleasure, to luxuriousness. And yet, such a society was to be subjected to the law of the Gospel, was to be permeated with its spirit. Heroic undertaking, for the accomplishment of which the Oriental monk was the instrument chosen by Divine Providence!

It would be a grave error, writes Balmes, to imagine that so many thousands of solitaries failed to exercise great social influence. In regard to morality, the power of their example was immense. People ran to the desert, gathered around the monks, questioned them, listened to them. What a preaching was theirs! How could exhortations, enforced by such example, fail to have effect? How could people disregard the soul and its destiny, when they beheld men, for the sake of salvation, condemn themselves to such rude privations, such rigid penances? Reflection and emotion triumphed over the most careless, often over the ill-disposed ; so that many who went thither to mock, yielded to the spell of an influence which retained them in the desert.

How often might be seen poor wanderers, second Magdalens, returning thence to astonish and edify the world by their austerities, as they had previously disgusted it by their debaucheries.

Of the crowds that daily flocked to visit those holy solitudes, it could truly be said that none returned unbroken to the haunts of society ; each left in the desert its quota of holy penitents, who, allured by the charms of its heavenly atmosphere, sought admission among the fervent votaries of penance and prayer.

VIII.

Nor is this a problem difficult of solution:—the sophisms of worldly wisdom, the prejudices of ignorance were totally vanquished. Men could not regard as foolish, or above the power of nature, a life which produced men so wise and calm, so reasonable and just, so saintly and so happy; a life whose supernatural character was frequently attested by stupendous miracles to which the Doctors of the Church have borne witness.

Could men declare the accomplishment of the Gospel precepts to be impossible to nature, aided by grace, when they beheld in the daily lives of the monks the heroic realization of the evangelical counsels? And that, too, beneath the scorching tropical sun; within sight of cities the most voluptuous, such as Alexandria and Antioch; on the classic soil of pagan softness ; in lands the very atmosphere of which seemed an incentive to pleasure? Thus it was that from the deserts of Nitria, the Thebaid, and others was wafted over the world the perfume of grace, sanctity, and edification. To the farthest bounds of the empire the salutary impression spread. communicating to society something of the monks' own life of innocence, temperance, prayer, penance, and unselfishness. This was their mission; its accomplishment is their glory.

IX.

To contemplation, prayer, and expiation the Eastern monks added manual labor, estimating, even, by one's diligence in the latter, his progress in perfection. St. Hilarion's address to his body became a proverb in the desert: "If thou wilt not labor, neither shalt thou eat; and if thou eatest, it is only that thou mayest be the better able to labor."

By labor they were enabled not only to supply their own wants, but also to exercise hospitality and bestow abundant alms; it helped, also, to subjugate the body, and removed the dangers of idleness. St. Augustine assures us that, in his time, wherever there were any poor, there also were to be found monks ministering to their necessities. They seemed, indeed, to consider themselves the farmers of the poor. Admirable farmers, exclaims Balmes, who, denying everything to self, cultivated the desert and made the very rocks fruitful, to provide revenues for those who had nothing !

When the poor man went to the monasteries of the desert, he was received as a friend, nay, as a master ; the most affectionate care was lavished on him ; the monks disputed for the honor of serving him, of preparing his bed, of watching over him if he was ill. Orphans were most tenderly received. We must, writes St. Basil, the great legislator of the religious life in the East,—we must care for and educate the orphan with the utmost charity, as the child of the religious family.

Such exquisite charity towards the neighbor contrasts wonderfully with the frightful austerity which the monk exercised on himself. It would seem that the first end of his providential mission was to carry moral energy to the highest degree of heroism ; and mortification of the senses to its farthest limits ; to arouse, excite, and encourage souls in lands where indolence, effeminacy, pagan corruption, and climatic delights seemed to render impossible the simple practice of the Gospel precepts.   Surely, under such circumstances, we may well exclaim, How wonderful is God in his Saints ! *Mirabilis in sanctis suis Deus !*

X.

Nor was the Western monk less strongly animated by the love of God and desire for his own salvation.   Like those of the East, he sacrificed everything to this supreme interest : family, friends, fortune, honors, rest, comfort, and pleasure ; he became poor and chaste ; he died to the world.   Like them, he was an angel of prayer and expiation, but he was less severe to his body ; and his fasts, although almost continual, were not so rigorous.   Difference of climate and constitution in the North had to be taken into account, and St. Benedict, the monastic legislator of the West, wisely arranged for this.

The Western monk, exerting his strength less in corporal mortifications, reserved it for labor, which, by his rule, was made a rigorous obligation ; and this labor was, principally, the cultivation of the soil.   Herein we must again admire the wonderful dispensations of Divine Providence.

The excessive Roman taxes, as well as the great barbarian invasions of the fifth and sixth centuries, had led to the almost total abandonment of agriculture ; there remained but few farmers, and those were half savage and idolatrous.   The druidical forests, which still existed, extending themselves so as to meet on all sides, covered immense tracts of country.

Bands of monks, writes a grave author, went forth, not only into the fields, but into the most distant and impenetrable forests, which they disputed with the wild beasts, at that time so numerous and daring that they might often be seen prowling, in broad daylight, through the Gallo-Romanic towns.

The monastery once established and the land brought under cultivation, people gathered around it to find assistance, protection, security. A village, a town sprang up, and solitudes, until then uninhabited, became peopled with numerous families. "Soon," says the learned Mabillon, "to the ordinary cultivation of the soil, the monks added gardens, orchards, parterres." Happy, indeed, was the country in which a peaceful colony of St. Benedict's children arrived! Happy the soil wherein they took root! Happy the surrounding population! How did those at a distance envy them!

The clearing and cultivation of the woody and swampy lands of the North—Germany, Belgium. Holland, England and others, even to Scandinavia and the ice-bound coasts of Greenland—was almost exclusively the work of the monks.

As to France, it has been estimated that the culture of one-third of her territory is due to them, as is also the existence of nearly one-half of her cities and towns. In Lombardy, the monks, chiefly the sons of St. Bernard, taught the peasants the arts of irrigation, and made it the richest and most fertile land of Europe.

In Spain and Portugal, all candid travellers, even Protestants and Free-thinkers, have recognized monastic cultivation as the principal origin of the national agriculture. Germany, in particular, says Cardinal Pacca, is, so to say. the *creation* of the monks. Hence, even Michelet called it the *Daughter of the Popes*, because it was the popes who sent the monks thither, and directed and encouraged them in their painful toils. The Benedictines, says Guizot, have been the cultivators of Europe. Now, according to

Cantu, it is by agriculture alone that man establishes himself in a country, and attaches himself to it by all those sentiments which render sacred the name of Fatherland. Whence it follows that the monks have been truly the founders of European civilization.

XI.

While the Benedictine agriculturist watered with his sweat the soil of Europe, which he fertilized by his toil alone, without the resources of modern civilization, the Benedictine scholar collected, preserved, and copied ancient manuscripts : thus preparing the materials destined to restore human learning.

Abbeys, says M. Granier du Cassagnac, have been the nursery of modern civilization. They have cultivated ideas as well as the soil ; and sown, in *their* time, the harvest we reap in ours.

That the Benedictines, during several centuries, enlightened and nurtured Europe, is, says M. Lenormant, a fact acknowledged by all historians, whatever their origin or opinions. Without the monasteries, writes Leibnitz, all the ancient manuscripts would have been lost, and science with them. As copyists of books and manuscripts, the nuns rivalled the monks. Neither sarcasm nor falsehood can do away with the fact that conventual libraries were, in Europe, the first archives of knowledge and literature.

Besides the *Scriptorium*,[1] which was the printing-office of that epoch, every monastery had its school, wherein were studied the Sacred Scriptures, the works of the Greek and Latin Fathers and Christian poets. It seems to us that biblical literature and philosophy, the literature and philosophy of St. Augustine and St. John Chrysostom, were well suited to such superior minds.

---

[1] The Scriptorium of a monastery was a hall of solid stone walls, with iron doors and windows, in which manuscripts could be preserved from the ravages of fire or barbarians It was there, also, that the copyists pursued their labors.

XII.

On the Western monk was imposed another gigantic and superhuman task,—the conversion and civilization of the barbarian hordes that had overrun Europe. Barbarism without the monks, says Montalembert, was chaos; with the monks, it has become Europe Christianized and civilized, the leader of the world.

Sent, directed, sustained, and encouraged by the Papacy, they, with invincible perseverance, carried out, in a great measure, the heroically holy work of moulding and forming the diverse elements of those barbarian conquerors, in order to civilize and sanctify them.

Thus, under religious and monastic action in Gaul, the Visigoths, Burgundians, Franks, Aquitanians, Normans, and ancient Gauls formed the first and most glorious kingdom of the world, the "Most Christian" monarchy of France, "The Eldest Daughter" of the Church.

Beyond the Pyrenees, from the commingling of Goths, Vandals, Suevi, Cantabrians, and Celtiberi came forth the "Catholic kingdom" of Spain; while the remnants of the Huns, Vandals, Heruli, Ostrogoths, and Lombards formed the transalpine kingdom of Italy, under the glorious domination of Charlemagne.

In Great Britain the Saxons, Britons, Picts, Scotch, and Irish, united by religion despite their natural and national antipathies, won for their country the immortal title of "The Island of Saints."

In Germany, hordes of fierce and idolatrous barbarians became so transformed as to merit that their nation should be called "The Daughter of the Popes."

That such social regeneration was superhuman, no one can deny. Man would have failed, acknowledges M. Villemain; religion alone had the power. The great agent of social salvation in the fifth and sixth centuries, says M.

Littré, was the Church, acting by her missionaries. Whatever there was of civilization at that time, was, of necessity, with the Church, and with the monks, the militia of the Church.

XIII.

That colossal, humanitarian, and international work of transformation, union, and sanctification, which gave birth to the society known under the beautiful name of Christianity, has never ceased to be continued, developed, and perfected.

The children and disciples of St. Dominic, St. Francis, St. Ignatius, and other holy founders, sprang up, in the course of time, at the moment designed by Providence; and, in conjunction with the sons of St. Benedict, seconded their Christian and social work; with this difference, however, that instead of living in the desert, they established themselves in the midst of society, the better to understand and provide for its wants.

Never has Christianity known more devoted, more intelligent preachers. They are instructors of youth, indefatigable apostles, scholars, *literati, savants,* theologians, historians, controversialists, missionaries, martyrs, laborers in every Christian work, intrepid soldiers of God and His Church, declared adversaries of vice and error; and, on account of these two latter titles, honored with the bitterest hatred of heresy, unbelief, and human depravity. But we shall not recount here the unjust attacks and iniquitous measures of which they have been the object during modern times: nor shall we relate how they have been ignominiously proscribed, expelled from their peaceful homes and consecrated sanctuaries. We prefer to pass over in silence those sad events; events, moreover, so recently renewed.

To the services rendered to the Church and society by religious men have been added, from century to century, those of numerous Congregations of religious women; devoted, some to the care of the sick, others to prayer, the greater number to the education of children of all ranks and conditions. It would be impossible to tell the good which those Congregations have done on this point to the Church and the family. If France, despite its errors and misfortunes, is still one of the most Catholic nations of the world, it is because its women, generally speaking, remain Christian. It is woman who preserves that religious atmosphere which still pervades France; and this social benefit is due to the fact that, up till now, the education of women has been almost exclusively confided to religious Congregations.

Hell and impiety are well aware of it; hence their desperate efforts to obtain control of education. It is to obtain this end that they are expelling the religious, God, the crucifix, catechism, and prayer from the primary school; and have established, for secondary instruction, lyceums for girls, in which neither prayer nor religious instruction is permitted.[1]

Behold how the free-thinkers and free-masons wish to replace the Visitandines, those angels of prayer, who recall the name, renew the spirit and sweetness of St. Francis de Sales; the pious Ursulines; the Dominicans, Sisters of the Angelic Doctor; the Daughters of the Seraphic St. Francis; the Daughters of St. Teresa, whom a Saint has styled *the St. Paul of women;* the children of St. Vincent de Paul, who, to the sweetness of a virgin add the tenderness of

---

[1] This undertaking is so absurd and immoral that M. de Rochefort himself calls it "one of the blindest follies it is possible to commit." The Catholic regards it as more than folly; as an evil action, a crime. "Piety in a young girl is so touching, and impiety, above all in a woman, is contrary to nature," writes Talleyrand. "Atheism in a man saddens me; in a woman, it repels me," says M. Legouvé, of the French Academy.

a mother and the courage of a soldier; the Religious of the Sacred Heart, who are at the very Source of light, sweetness, and pure love; the Religious of St. Joseph, who claim as father, patron, and model him to whom God confided the care of His Beloved Son, of His Immaculate Mother, and, in latter times, of His Church.

In all these Congregations live angelic creatures, who have nothing to do with the world save to shelter under their wings and bring up their young sisters destined to live in the world. Formed in their school, the latter learn the love of sacrifice; virtue becomes their brightest ornament; their charm is innocence, and the love which they inspire has in it something of religious veneration.

Devotion to the Blessed Virgin, the glory, the model, the liberatrix of woman, incessantly reanimated and intensified by religious education, renews among women, with the love of purity and self-sacrifice, the truest and deepest piety, and crowns their very weakness with an aureola of glory which wins respect for even their tenderest years. By the resplendent halo of Christian modesty, woman is dignified, she is exalted from that state of abjection and degradation into which paganism has ever forced her; from that glorious virtue she receives her right to equality with man, to his protection and veneration, and to that exquisite delicacy by which, wherever the reign of the Gospel prevails, man yields to woman the precedence. Let, then, the women of our time be on their guard. They do not sufficiently realize that by godless, irreligious education the descent is paved to that pagan degradation, that shameless slavery, in which the female sex was held everywhere, prior to the advent of Christianity.

XIV.

In presence of the ingratitude shown for the benefits of religious Orders, the lies and calumnies heaped upon them, and the infamous war declared against them by denouncing them to the people and the state as their principal enemy, their greatest danger, their members find themselves under like circumstances with St. Paul, as recorded by the pious author of the Imitation :

"Though Paul endeavored to please all in the Lord, and become all to all, yet he made little account of being judged by men. He labored abundantly for the edification and salvation of others, as much as lay in him, and as much as he could ; but he could not prevent being sometimes judged and despised by others. Therefore he committed all to God, who knoweth all, and defended himself by patience and humility against the tongues of those who spoke unjustly, as well as those who devised vain and lying deceits, and who, according to caprice, made acquaintance of whatever they wished. However, he answered them sometimes, lest his silence might give occasion of scandal to the weak."[1] For the same reason the Apostle wrote to the Corinthians : "I am become foolish; you have compelled me. For I ought to have been commended by you."[2]

In view of the forgetfulness, contempt, ingratitude, and calumnies which are their portion, religious Congregations do well to defend themselves, like the Apostle, "lest their silence be a cause of scandal to the weak." Hence, honest men, friends of truth and religion, delight in seeing hagiography flourish, and Lives of the Saints multiplied everywhere.

What happiness is it, moreover, to know the Saints, to publish what one knows of them !

For a long time the Jesuits, Dominicans, Franciscans, and secular clergy, the Visitandines, Ladies of the Sacred Heart, and others, have been enriching hagiography and

---

[1] Imit.. Bk. III.. ch. 36.   [2] II. Cor. xii. 11.

edifying the world by their pious recitals, their instructive annals, or the Lives of their Saints. Pious laics, even, have eagerly joined in the movement, because, as one of them says, " God saves souls and the world by the Saints." Under the present circumstances, especially, one must bless God for this defensive movement, at once instructive, edifying, legitimate, necessary, and conformable to the practice of the Apostle of Nations.

Up to the present time the Sisters of St. Joseph have formed an exception to this general movement. We can understand it : simple, modest, humble, silent, after the example of their holy Father St. Joseph, who is the great Model and Patron of the interior life, " hidden in Christ," according to the expression of the Apostle, they have lived by this Divine attraction, as if the heritage of tradition sufficed for them.

But times have changed—" There is a time to speak and a time to be silent," says the Holy Spirit. The Church, moreover, has spoken, by proclaiming St. Joseph Patron of the Universal Church. That interior life in which his daughters loved to remain hidden is attacked as it has never previously been. It is held up to the people not only as folly, but as injurious, dangerous, nay, even criminal ; and it is pursued and unmercifully beaten down as such.

Formerly, when pagan tyrants accused the martyrs of odious crimes, they responded : " No, no ; no crime is perpetrated amongst us. We are Christians, and our faith forbids not only the act, but the thought, the very shadow of evil."

In like manner, religious, male and female, may and ought to say to those sectarian persecutors who accuse them of being the enemies of modern states and society : That is not true ; we are enemies to no one. Our whole life, our religious vocation is inspired, directed, and regulated by a dual love : the love of God and the love of the people, whom we call *the neighbor,* because our faith tells us that all men, even the most wicked, the most erring, are *neighbors and brethren.* Read the Lives, the sincere and candid histories of our Fathers, our models, our masters, our authors, our founders, and you will see that we are the children of the Saints : *filii sanctorum sumus.* To thus give light and truth to the blind and the evil-minded is one of the ends of modern hagiography.

XV.

On the other hand, St. Paul says to all Christians : "Remember your prelates, who have spoken the word of God to you : whose faith follow, considering the end of their conversation." And again : "We beseech you to know them who labored among you, and are over you in the Lord and admonish you, that you esteem them more abundantly in charity for their work's sake," which you are called to continue. Question your ancestors, says Moses, and they will declare to you that you are the portion of the Lord, His people, His inheritance. [1]

These recommendations of the Holy Spirit are of great importance and sovereign utility, particularly to religious Orders and Congregations, whose ancestors or founders were all Saints, the majority of them great Saints. To converse with them is to converse with Heaven, according to the words of St. Paul ; and one is sure, in their school, to learn how to serve God, love the neighbor, and sanctify one's self. "O Philothea," says St. Francis de Sales in his Introduction to the Devout Life, "let us unite our hearts with those blessed souls : for as the young nightingales learn to sing with the old, so by the commerce we have

---

[1] Heb. xiii. 7 ; I. Thess. v. 12, 13 ; Deut. xxxii. 7, 9.

with the Saints, we shall the better learn to pray and to sing the Divine praises."

Wise and adapted to all times as are these counsels of the amiable Saint, and conformable to those of the Holy Spirit, they are especially suitable to ours, wherein that which is know as the *modern* spirit, as full of softness and infirmity as of self-sufficiency and fatuity, laughs at the past and thinks itself superior in all things to bygone days. It is the case of the sick man, all the more seriously ill because he denies and is not sensible of his disease.

The Congregation of St. Joseph, then, gives proof of a wisdom blessed by God, in returning to its past, so as to put before its young religious the lessons and example of its venerable founders and restorers.

Good sense is the great master of human life, says Bossuet.

Now, Mother St. John possessed this precious gift in an eminent degree from her very youth. At twenty-five years of age, "she had the wisdom of the aged," wrote Mgr. de Gallard, Bishop of Puy, a holy prelate, confessor of the faith, who knew her perfectly.

There is nothing truly great save goodness, says Bossuet again ; and with this characteristic, Mother St. John was supereminently endowed. A mother in the truest and deepest sense of the word, her maternal affection won its just response in the extraordinary and universal filial love which animated her daughters, a love surpassed only by their feelings of veneration and confidence.

One word of hers, whether spoken or written, decided any point, calmed all difference and smoothed away difficulties. For her children were convinced it came from a heart that loved, a mind just and upright, a soul whose will was subject to the will of God, and moved by the inspirations of grace.

Her humility, resignation, and confidence in God rose

to heights attained only by Saints. Modelling her life on that of St. Joseph, she labored earnestly, indefatigably, yet silently, peacefully, without parade or show, united heart and soul with God in a spirit of faith and simplicity truly patriarchal.

The obedience due to the authority of her office was rendered light and easy by the esteem, confidence, and respect inspired by her example ; for, like her Divine Master and Exemplar, she practised before she taught or commanded : "Jesus," says St. Luke, "began to do and to teach." [1]

This life, as simple as it is solid and profound, reminds us of that of St. Joseph, whom Mother St. John chose as her Father and Model ; and it is our most earnest hope that it may lead to an increase of devotion to this great Saint. This is what our Holy Mother the Church invites us to by the new and ineffable splendor she has thrown around the name of the Saint of Nazareth, by taking refuge herself, as did Jesus and Mary, beneath his protection and guardianship, as is shown by the Pontifical decree declaring St. Joseph the Patron of the Universal Church.

The days of Herod are renewed, and an impious sect tries, as far as possible, to kill Jesus by destroying the faith and souls of children.

Let us, then, go to St. Joseph with the venerable Mother St. John, and, like her, under the protection of this great Saint, labor unceasingly to preserve the faith, knowledge, love, and reign of Jesus, not only in our beloved and unhappy France, but wheresoever we may be called.

"Who will find," says the Holy Spirit, "the valiant woman, more precious than diamonds ?"

We have found her ; let us study, meditate, love, and follow the example she has given during her long and

---

[1] Acts i. 1.

saintly career; *fac secundum exemplar quod tibi monstra-tum est.*

Now, more than ever, is it necessary that weak and enervated souls should inhale the odor of good example, and breathe in an atmosphere of moral greatness.

As the life of Mother St. John was the link which bound the new Congregation of the Sisters of St. Joseph of Lyons with the primitive foundation of Le Puy, a brief sketch of the latter seems a necessary preface to the account of its restoration after the Revolution of 1789.

On this account we here insert, regarding the birth of the Congregation, what has been given to the public, in our previous Life of Rev. Mother of the Sacred Heart of Jesus, second Superior-General of the Congregation of St. Joseph of Lyons.

Origin of the Congregation of The Sisters of St. Joseph. Mother St. John before and after the Revolution of 1789.

CHAPTER I.

Origin of the Congregation of the Sisters of St. Joseph.—Its Founders.—End and Mission of the Institute.—Rev. Father Médaille's Instructions to the first Sisters.—Approbation of the Congregation.—Its development.—The Community at Monistrol.— Designs of Providence in regard to its Superior, Mother St. John.

THE pious Congregation of the Sisters of St. Joseph, in our time so flourishing, so useful, both to the Church and society in every quarter of the globe, has had a double origin : the one before, the other after the Revolution of 1789. That revolutionary cyclone which overthrew the very pillars of the sanctuary respected not this humble Congregation, but assailed and dispersed it with a host of other grand and holy institutions, the offspring of faith and charity ; only a few scattered remnants found refuge in the mountain fastnesses of Forez and Velay.

This Institute, predestined to bear the blessed name of Joseph, name so dear to the hearts of Jesus and Mary, was founded in the middle of the seventeenth century ; its regular canonical erection dates from March 10, 1651.

Beside the cradle of the new religious family which came to adorn and rejoice the Church, history shows us, as the authors of its existence, an eminent and holy prelate, Mgr. de Maupas. Bishop of Le Puy, and Rev. Jean-Paul Médaille, a saintly missionary of the illustrious Society of Jesus.

Henry Cauchon de Maupas du Tour's parents were Charles Cauchon de Maupas, Baron of Tour, Counsellor of State under Henry IV., and Anne de Gondi, a member of that illustrious family de Gondi, which attached to itself, as friend and spiritual father, the great St. Vincent de Paul. He was born at the Chateau de Cosson, which still exists, two leagues from Rheims, between Sermiers and Chamery.

The noble child was held at the sacred font of baptism by Henry IV. himself, after whom he was named. The godson of the great king received a most brilliant education under the direction of his mother—a woman endowed with every grace and virtue suitable to her rank and sex— and his father, a nobleman as remarkable for his literary attainments as for his religious principles and the signal services he rendered his country and his king.

Endowed with most happy dispositions, the young Count de Maupas responded admirably to the enlightened care of his illustrious parents, and gave evidence, at a very early age, of a decided inclination to the ecclesiastical state.

Faithful to the inspirations of grace, he generously renounced all those worldly advantages which his birth and the favor of the king would have assured him in the world, and gave himself wholly and entirely to God and His Church.

While yet young he was nominated to the Abbey of St. Denis at Rheims; and his conduct, amidst ecclesiastical dignities and the favors of fortune, reminded men of the great St. Charles Borromeo; for, despite his youth, he administered his rich benefice with the zeal, prudence, and charity of a truly apostolic man.

The Queen Consort, Anne of Austria, well aware of the Abbé de Maupas' extraordinary merit, wished to retain him at court, and, with this view, appointed him her Grand Almoner. The preference of this august queen was in itself a proof of his worth and talent, for she was possessed of rare gifts of discernment, so that for Bossuet she testified esteem and admiration worthy his powerful genius. Daughter, sister, wife, and mother of kings, she, says one of her biographers, was fully able to sustain gloriously the dignity of such titles.

Belonging, through his mother, to that illustrious family de Gondi, whose children were educated, whose mother was directed by the great St. Vincent de Paul, the Abbé de Maupas had the happiness of frequent intercourse with that glorious Apostle of Charity, and was united with him by bonds of the closest friendship.

Under the influence of such a mother and such a friend, it is not surprising that the young Abbé dwelt amidst what Tertullian calls "the poison of the court," without detriment to either his modesty or his virtue. On the contrary, the dangers that encompassed him served but to render his holiness the more remarkable, and the good example of one so distinguished by birth and talents was productive of most happy results.

A more extensive field, however, was to be opened to his zeal; for the see of Le Puy becoming vacant in 1641, King Louis XIII. nominated as its Bishop the Grand Almoner of his august wife.

The Abbe's humility, however, so long resisted the appointment, that he took possession of his see only on January 10th, 1644, from which time he gave himself up wholly to the labor of the apostolate. Emulating the example of our Lord Jesus Christ, who said, "I am the Good Shepherd; I know my sheep, and my sheep know me." Mgr. de Maupas visited constantly and assiduously the flock confided to his pastoral care. For seventeen years, that is to say, until 1661, he was, to use the words of St. John, " the angel" of the happy church of Le Puy. A great admirer, a faithful imitator of St. Francis de Sales, whose biographer he became, he was distinguished among the prelates of his time by his eminent piety, vast erudition, and apostolic zeal. Every year of his administration was signalized by some important acts, tending either to the reformation and sanctification of his clergy, the religious instruction of his people, or the alleviation of human misery. Among the works to which his zeal and charity gave birth, the most remarkable, the most fruitful was, undoubtedly, the foundation of the Congregation of the Sisters of St. Joseph, at once contemplative, educational, and devoted to works of charity. Teaching, although but lightly touched upon in the primitive constitutions, seemed, in some sort, necessary to associate the new institute to the Divine apostolate, and confide to it, in the mystical body of Jesus Christ, the united duties of Mary and Martha. Thus, by its threefold mission, it has embraced both the active life and the practice of evangelical perfection in all their plenitude.

The admirable qualities of the Bishop of Le Puy drew around him magnanimous souls capable of seconding his arduous labors in the cause of God, among whom none was more closely united to him in heart and mind than Rev. Jean-Paul Médaille, of the Society of Jesus, the apostle of Velay, the evangelizer, not only of Le Puy, but of Clermont, Saint-Flour, Rhodez, and Vienne. This holy religious suggested to Mgr. de Maupas the happy idea of establishing the Sisters of St. Joseph. In his apostolic journeys he had met many pious widows and young girls anxious to retire from the world, in order to devote themselves, in a special manner, to prayer, the practice of virtue and their own sanctification, while, at the same time. consecrating themselves to the service of their neighbor.

This had been the first conception, the early inspiration of St. Francis de Sales, who, in founding his dear Order of the Visitation, " his joy and his crown," had intended it to be a congregation of women, who, to the ordinary exercises of the religious life, should add the visitation of the sick and poor, and, in general, all those labors which tend to promote the temporal or spiritual welfare of " the dear neighbor," as this amiable and devoted servant of God himself expresses it.[1]

His plan, carried out in 1612, the first year of the new Institute, was modified five years later, at the urgent request of Mgr. de Marquemont, Archbishop of Lyons, who regarded cloister as essentially necessary for the stability of the religious state among women. St. Francis de Sales, on the contrary, wished to unite the duties of Martha and Mary: the exterior works of charity with the repose of contemplation. Thinking of the human nature of Jesus, the former busied herself in preparing for His natural wants, while the latter, contemplating the hidden Divinity, sat at His feet in an ecstacy of love and adoration. " My design," said St. Francis, " has always been to unite these two states in so just a proportion, that, instead of destroying, they should aid each other; that one should sustain the other, and that the Sisters, while laboring for their own sanctification, should, at the same time, contribute to the comfort and salvation of their neighbor. To

---

[1] Rev. P. Helyot, in his *History of Religious Orders*, writes the historian of our Congregation in Clermont, attributes our foundation to Rev. Father *Pierre* Médaille or Médailhe, who, in 1650, was only fourteen years old. This error, which is easily proved by consulting the mortuary registers of the Society of Jesus, is explained by the zeal with which this later Father Médaille propagated our Institute wherever he exercised his apostolate. He did not create, but he powerfully sustained the work of his namesake, and to his memory, also, the gratitude of our Congregation is due.—The Translator.

prescribe cloister to them now would be to destroy an essential part of the Institute; to deprive the neighbor of precious aid and good example and the Sisters themselves of the merit of those works of mercy so strongly recommended by the Gospel, and authorized by the example of our Lord Jesus Christ Himself.

Despite the force of this reasoning, the Saint finally yielded and cloister was enforced by the Constitutions of the Visitation approved by Paul V. in 1618; which led the holy Bishop of Geneva to say afterwards, with amiable wit and admirable humility: "They call me the founder of the Visitation! Could anything be more unreasonable? I have done what I did not wish to do and have failed in what I wanted to do."

But the idea of a mind so great, of a Saint so perfect as St. Francis de Sales, could have been but the inspiration of Heaven, and was not to prove abortive. Consequently, we see that, only a few years after his death, there sprang up, on all sides, communities of women destined for the solace of all human miseries: uniting prayer and contemplation to the external works of charity, and thus adding another jewel to that glorious crown of the religious life, which is at once the ornament, the honor, and the strength of the Catholic Church. The composition of that essence, so strong and yet so delicate, which renders those sublime virgins brave as soldiers, tender as mothers, pure as angels, with hearts as immense as misery, as strong as love, is a secret communicated by Heaven to Catholicity alone, since it alone has been able to produce them.[1]

---

[1] We find at the same epoch the secular Sisters of the Society of St. Joseph established at Bordeaux in 1638; and the Hospitalières of St. Joseph, founded at La Flèche in 1642.

But we must not confound these with the Sisters of St. Joseph of Le Puy, restored afterwards in the Sisters of St. Joseph of Lyons, which, in its turn, has been the Mother of the Sisters of St. Joseph of Belley, Bordeaux, Chambéry, America, etc.— The Sisters of St. Joseph of Cluny, founded in 1807, are also distinct from the preceding. (Life of Mother St. Joseph.)

But up to that time many holy and learned persons, like Mgr. de Marquemont, were unable to conceive that the flower of virginity could be preserved secure and inviolate without the safeguards of solitude and the cloister-grate. In their opinion, the cloister, with its holy ardors, was, as it were, a shelter, a conservatory, necessary to the growth of that pure blossom, foreign, indeed, to our cold earth, yet transplanted hither from the glowing regions of the seraphim.[1]

The founders of the Sisters of St. Joseph, on the contrary, thought, with St. Vincent and St. Francis de Sales, that the fear and love of God were infallible antidotes against temptations and worldly seductions; and that, wanting this holy love and fear, the closest grates would prove but feeble barriers. With St. Augustine they said : "Love God, and do what you will." *Ama, et fac quod vis.* For nothing is as strong as love, writes the pious author of the Imitation ; and according to the Holy Spirit, it is stronger than death. Instead, then, of devoting the new Congregations of virgins to a life wholly cloistral, their founders threw them boldly into civil and military hospitals ; sent them as mothers to the bedside of the sick, the attics of the poor, into isolated huts and garrets; on far distant missions ; among savages, even to the soldiers' camp, "with the city streets and highways for their convent, obedience for their enclosure, the fear of God for their grate, and holy modesty for their veil."

Such are, literally, the simple precautions pointed out,

---

[1] The contrary idea terrified Mgr. de Marquemont, a prelate eminently pious, but somewhat timorous and opposed to every innovation. Immutable in her dogmas, the Church is not so in her discipline and institutions. For the rest, the new religious form was not without precedent, as Bellarmine declared when consulted by St. Francis de Sales on this subject.

As to the dreaded inconveniences, the Sisters of Charity, the Sisters of Mercy, Sisters of St. Joseph, Little Sisters of the Poor, and a thousand other such Congregations, answer it to-day, by shedding abroad over the Church and the world such a perfume of virtue as to leave no cause for envying even the most strictly enclosed Orders.

the new discipline inaugurated by St. Vincent de Paul for his heroic daughters. "I have experienced," says St. Francis de Sales, "a special delight in founding a Congregation wherein charity alone, and the loving fear of God, shall serve as enclosure."

It would seem that these great Saints, and those who shared their sentiments, foresaw, from afar, the needs and exigencies of our times, " without faith, without God, without affection," wherein that charity which occupies itself with man's corporal wants would alone have power to gain his heart and lead him back to religion.

To such a work the patronage of St. Joseph was marvellously suitable. For our Lord Jesus Christ, in His infinite and ineffable goodness, having willed to leave, as His representatives on earth, the afflicted, prisoners, the sick, the hungry, naked, and homeless poor, declaring with His Divine lips that whatever is done unto the least and the last of the unfortunate is done unto Himself, it follows that it is He whom we tend in the suffering members of humanity.[1] The poor man is another Jesus Christ hidden beneath those rags, and continuing, under that veil which faith alone can penetrate, His life of humiliation.

Should not, then, St. Joseph, who guarded, protected, cared for, and clothed the Sacred Humanity of our Saviour, become the model and patron of souls who devote themselves to the service of the miserable, raised by the Gospel to the dignity of Jesus Chirst ? " They should serve their neighbor with the same care, diligence, charity, and love with which this glorious Patriarch served his reputed Son, Jesus Christ, and the Blessed Mary, his most pure Spouse."[2] This way of regarding the poor cannot but be an incentive to the most sublime works of charity. It explains the heroic acts of the Saints who saw Jesus Christ begging

---

[1] St. Matth. xxv. 35.   [2] Rule of the Sisters of St. Joseph.

in the poor, suffering in the sick, weeping in the afflicted, and captive in the prisoner.[1]

The interior life and manual labor were equally sanctified by the Foster-father of Jesus, the Spouse of Mary. It is not, then, surprising that the new form which grace developed in the religious spirit tended to model itself on the life of the glorious Patriarch, to place itself under his protection and to assume his name. When God wills to sanctify and to save an age, and when His Church needs to be glorified and avenged, He exhales a Divine breath, and the "face of the earth is renewed." Such a Divine breath swept over the world at the time of which we speak.

At the head of this providential movement were the Sisters of St. Joseph of Le Puy, for Mgr. de Maupas, whose ambition was to follow in the footsteps of St. Francis de Sales, entered eagerly into the project of Rev. Father Médaille, to establish a congregation to fill the place left vacant by the Sisters of the Visitation when they embraced enclosure.

Acting on the Bishop's suggestion, Rev. Father Médaille assembled his spiritual daughters in the house of a pious widow, Mme. de Joux, whose hospitable dwelling became a veritable *cœnaculum,* and the cradle of the new Institute.[2]

---

[1] If there exists here below a doctrine which elevates man, it is, most assuredly, Christianity, which is only, when defined, the dogma, the law and fact of the deification of creatures. What more calculated to develop human dignity and morality, than our communion with the Divinity, by the Incarnation and the Eucharist so prolonged and multiplied?

When the world calls faith an abasement, it is either ignorant, foolish, or lying. "Catholicity," says Hutchinson, "has been the belief of the most powerful and enlightened European nations, and of the most illustrious personages that have ever honored the name of man."

[2] It was then that our founders set about drawing up rules that should assure the stability of the new Society. These were prayerfully elaborated, and decided upon little by little; the foundation being those first writen by St. Francis de Sales for the Visitation, and which Mgr. de Maupas called *the best guarantees for the future* of the new Institute. Rev. Father Médaille added thereto some regulations of St. Ignatius, especially in regard to the vows, which were to impose the same obligation as the simple vows pronounced at the end of the novitiate in the Society of Jesus.

This truly Christian lady constituted herself the Sisters' adoptive mother ; and until her death ceased not to labor with all her strength, and contribute, to the best of her power, towards the establishment and development of the new-born Congregation. No work is more difficult, none costs more labor and toil, or more maternal care, than the foundation of a religious Order.

During the first days of this spiritual birth, Rev. Father Médaille wrote to one of his cherished daughters[1] a letter, in which, speaking of the spirit that ought to animate the new Congregation, which he calls " his little design," as St. Francis de Sales called the Visitation his " little Institute."[2]—he gives it as its model the poverty, purity, obedience, humility, and charity of our Lord Jesus Christ in the Sacrament of the Altar.

" God," he writes, " has, if I do not deceive myself, revealed to me, in the Holy Eucharist, a perfect Model of our little design. Jesus is wholly annihilated therein. We also, my dear child, must labor to establish an annihilated Institute. It must be nothing in the eyes of the world ; and, before God, it will be whatever He, in His infinite mercy, will deign to make it. It must be lowly and hidden, like Jesus Christ in the Most Adorable Eucharist, wherein He is so concealed as to be wholly invisible. O my God ! how blessed will be our Institute, if it maintain this spirit of lowliness, humility, annihilation, and a life hidden from the world and even from its own eyes ! What comparison

---

To these fundamental principles the founders added some personal ideas, which we might better call the breathings of the Divine Spirit, so great are the piety, strength, and supernatural wisdom which they exhale. (*Hist. of the Cong. of St. Joseph in Clermont-Ferrand.*)

Through the providence of God, the original MSS. of this Rule, written by Father Médaille's own hand, and by him given to our first Mothers, was saved from the general destruction of the archives in 1793, and is still preserved with religious veneration in the Mother-House of Le Puy. (*Annals of the Cong. of Le Puy.*)

[1] Doubtless to her whom he had appointed to govern the Sisters.

[2] St. Jane Frances called it "a little March violet, having no brilliancy of color."

can there be between our nothingness and the annihilation
of our Saviour-God in His Divine Sacrament !

"In It we have a perfect Model of poverty, chastity, and
obedience. In the eyes of the world, what so poor as the
species under which the great God conceals Himself; not
even the reality of bread, only its form and appearance !
What detachment does He not show in things devoted to
his use ? The altar and its ornaments, the tabernacle,
sacred vessels, and all that surrounds Him in the Sacrament of His love, may be rich or poor, it matters not;
whether given Him or taken from Him He makes no resistance ; He is equally content when stripped of all. In
our poverty, we, likewise, should be so stripped, so de-
spoiled of all that we have consecrated to God and the
foundation of our little design, or to be equally content to
have much, to have little, or to have nothing ; for our
little design requires perfect detachment.

"As to chastity and purity, in this mystery our beloved
Saviour, the Virgin-Spouse of virgins, has eyes and heart
for souls alone. In it there is no exercise of the senses:
everything tends to purity and the purification of hearts.
Ah, should not we be happy if the same were true of us ?
If we had neither eyes, ears, tongue, nor heart save for this
dear Saviour ; and if every exercise of our senses tended to
purity and the sanctification of souls ? This, with the help
of God, will be the chastity of our little Institute.

"But is not the holy obedience of this Divine Saviour
truly miraculous ? Has He ever had a thought or uttered
a word contrary to the will of the priest, a weak and often
sinful man, who handles Him, and carries Him whithersoever he wishes ? Has He ever refused to descend, when
the priest so willed, into our hearts so wretched and so
poorly prepared ? Ah, this reflection would melt my
heart, were it not as hard as marble. Let us never lose
sight, my dear daughter, of the marvellous perfection of

this Divine obedience. May the Divine Goodness grant that ours may wholly resemble it, since we are members of an *Institute of annihilation.* May we never have a thought, a feeling, a word, contrary, in the slightest degree, to obedience. Let us, in imitation of our dear Saviour, obey as children, without reasoning or troubling ourselves about anything ; letting ourselves be guided by Divine Providence as a tender Father who knows what is necessary to us, and who, after all, absolutely governs His creatures lovingly annihilated in His bosom, such as should be, especially, the souls composing *our little design.*

O cherished and most humble obedience, the certain mark of solid virtue ! Would that thou mightst be ever truly perfect in the members of our new religious body, if, indeed, I may call it such, since, truly, it seems to me it is only the shadow and not the reality of a body, so great should be its spirit of annihilation.

" And if we desire a Model of love for God and charity to our neighbor, where shall we find a better one than in the Adorable Sacrament ? This mystery is 'the Love of loves;' for it reveals the extent, the perfection, the duration, the immutability, the grandeur of holy love. Our cherished Congregation,—each of whose members should always have the plenitude of holy love in her heart,—professes to be a Congregation of most perfect love ; it will find herein enough for imitation. Moreover, this sacrament is a mystery of perfect union. It unites creatures with God, and by the title of *Communion* which its bears, unites the faithful among themselves by a common bond, of which our Lord speaks in such ravishing terms, when He prays His Father that the faithful ' may be one,' that they may be consummated in one, as the Father and He are but one.

" Behold, my dear Sister, the end of our Congregation of annihilation ! It tends to procure this double union, entire, of ourselves and our dear neighbors with God ; of ourselves with our neighbor in general, and our neighbor with us, but all in Jesus and in God His Father.

"May the Divine Goodness deign to show us the excellence of this end, and assist us in becoming fit instruments to succeed therein. I have called this union *entire*, because the word expresses all the perfections comprised in the nature and exercise of the love of God and our dear neighbor. God grant we may be able to contribute, as feeble instruments, in re-establishing in the Church this entire union of souls in God and with God.

"Finally, our dear Institute ought to be all humility; it should love and choose what is most humble in everything. It must be all modesty and sweetness, all candor and simplicity, wholly interior, in a word, void of self and all created things, and replenished with Jesus and God, by a plenitude which I am unable to explain, but which the Divine Goodness will make you comprehend. Are not all these virtues found in a most wonderful degree in the Blessed Eucharist? What more humble than our Divine Saviour in this mystery? What more modest, more benign and gentle, more simple and sincere, more replenished with God and void of all things else? Behold, my dear Sister, the Model of our Institute!

"It seems to me that herein we shall also find its character and employments. In food and clothing our Sisters should observe great modesty and frugality, accommodated, however, to diversity of circumstances. This, again, may be noticed in the species of the Blessed Sacrament, which, although everywhere alike, yet present differences in taste and color, according to the diversity of quality in the bread and wine.

"Our houses should, like the tabernacle, be always locked; and our Sisters, in imitation of Jesus Christ, should leave them only through obedience or charity, returning, as soon as may be, to their different employments.

"As our dear Saviour in the Holy Eucharist lives not for Himself, but entirely for God His Father and the souls redeemed by His precious blood, so, my dear Sister, must our little design, and those who compose it, live not for self, but be wholly lost and annihilated in God and for God; be everything for the dear neighbor, nothing for self. Deign, O my God, to operate these marvels, according to Thy good pleasure. Amen."

Such were the instructions which the pious and lowly family of the Sisters of St. Joseph received at its very beginning. They express the character, and delightfully breathe the spirit of their Father; they reveal the virtues that shone in his first home of Nazareth: humility, simplicity, poverty, a life hidden in God, purity, obedience, the sweetest union, and the most exquisite charity. At Nazareth, the source and model of these virtues was the mystery of the Incarnation there operated: the Holy Eucharist, which is a continuation of the same, should likewise produce them in the bosom of St. Joseph's new family. Emulating the example of their Father, the Sisters should keep the abasement of Jesus ever before the eyes of their soul; and as St. Joseph was inspired and actuated by the annihilation of the Incarnation, so should they be instructed and animated by the humiliation of their Eucharistic God. For the Saint and his children there is the same Exemplar, Jesus our Lord, the Son of God, lowly, humble, and concealed.

What an honor, but, yet more, what an obligation does this blessed similarity impose upon the Institute of St. Joseph, which, like its Patron and Father, should be as exalted in contemplation as it is elevated in love and abased in humility!

The first years of a religious Order are like the first days of the novitiate. There is about them the freshness, the glow, the buoyancy, the *élan* of love in youth: something undefinable, yet ever reminding us of the ravishing and inimitable glory of the dawn. And, at the same time, how little, how lowly, how unperceived, for, to use the expression of de Maistre, "Nothing great has had a great beginning." "If you wish to be great, begin by being lowly," writes the great Doctor of Hippo.

On the 15th of October, 1650, the Feast of St. Teresa, the Bishop assembled the little community in the Orphan Asylum of Le Puy, which he confided to their care.[1] After having addressed them in words full of the spirit of God, he solemnly invested them with the religious habit, and gave them rules for the direction of their life. He concluded the pious ceremony by placing the humble Institute under the protection of the glorious St. Joseph, declaring that it should be known thenceforth as the Congregation of the Sisters of St. Joseph. A short time afterwards he confided to them the Asylum of Montferrand also ; and, being daily more edified by their zeal and charity, he, by an episcopal ordinance of March 10, 1651, solemnly and formally authorized the new congregation.[2]

Not content with this authorization, Mgr. de Maupas strove to obtain for the new Institute the favor and protection of his colleagues. "The bishops,"[3] he says, "are most humbly entreated to have for this Congregation a paternal charity, and special care for its maintenance and advancement, in consideration of the great St. Francis

---

[1] Rev. Father Médaille, himself so perfect an observer of rules, and so well versed in the conduct of souls, had charged himself with the training necessary to prepare his spiritual daughters for their new life. With such a Master of Novices, and under the vivifying action of the Holy Spirit, they advanced with rapid strides in the way of perfection. After some months of silent and energetic formation, Father Médaille decided to open the door of the *cœnaculum* and close a retreat which superabundance of grace and generous fidelity had rendered fruitful, by presenting his spiritual children to the Bishop of Puy, that they might receive at his hands the religious habit. (Extract from the History of the Congregation of St. Joseph in Clermont.)

[2] The almost complete destruction, during the French Revolution, of the Records of the Congregation of Le Puy, was an irreparable loss to the Sisters of St. Joseph, depriving them, as it did, of those traditions dearest to every religious Order,—those relating to the first members, their early struggles and difficulties.

[3] See the Constitutions of the Sisters of St. Joseph.

de Sales, whose spirit and views in the institution of the Sisters of the Visitation it is the object of this Congregation to perpetuate."[1]

This holy and venerable prelate having, in 1661, been translated to the see of Evreux, Mgr. Armand de Béthune continued his good work, and lavished the most paternal care on his Institute, which he reconfirmed by an ordinance of September 23, 1665. One year later the civil power lent its aid to the increase of a society so useful to the public weal, and Louis XIV., by letters patent, authorized and confirmed, in 1666, the first establishments of Le Puy, Saint-Didier, and other places in Velay.

Thus, loved and blessed by both God and man, the modest Institute of St. Joseph spread rapidly, like the grain of mustard-seed. When scarcely fifteen years in existence, its beneficent branches overshadowed not only the diocese of Le Puy, but those of Clermont, Viviers, Usès, and others. "Everywhere," says the *Dictionnaire Universel*, "the Sisters of St. Joseph are engaged most successfully in the instruction of children of their own sex, in the care of the sick, and in procuring for the neighbor all the spiritual and temporal helps of which they are capable."

In 1668, Henry de Villars, Archbishop of Vienne, established them in the great Hotel Dieu of his archiepiscopal see ; and, by a pastoral letter of September 2d of the same year, recommended them to his whole diocese.

Lyons, the City of Mary, could not but lovingly adopt

---

[1] In his Preface to the Life of St. Francis de Sales, written by Mgr. de Maupas in 1659, he says: "For more than twenty-five years that I have been engaged in public offices, I, despite my unworthiness, have been brought into close communication with very many religious Orders. I respect, I honor them ; my heart has been profoundly moved by their holy practices, yet, I must confess, I have found in the Visitation I know not what of blessed predilection for the exact observance of the holiest laws of humility and charity. It is on this account that, without in the least failing in the esteem I owe to others, I have decided to institute the humble Congregation of the Sisters of St. Joseph on the model and in the same spirit as the Sisters of the Visitation, before they adopted enclosure."

the Daughters of St. Joseph. To them she confided the greater part of her charitable works, and the alleviation of the numerous miseries that groaned within her vast bosom. The education of children; the instruction of deaf-mutes; solace of the poor; care of incurables and sick of all kinds; attendance in the prisons; charge of a House of Correction in the Rue Saint-Jacques, a Place of Detention at Perrache, and the great Hospital in Saint-Nizier:—such were, up to the Revolution of 1798, the works, at once humble and grand, patient and generous, heroically accomplished by the Sisters of St. Joseph. In the ardor of charity, in sublime self-devotion, they rivalled the dear and heroic daughters of St. Vincent de Paul.

We have seen the Institute of St. Joseph in its origin and its early years. Not in vain did it bear the name of Joseph, for its increase was truly wonderful.

When, before being gathered to his fathers, the Patriarch Jacob blessed his children, to Joseph, his best-beloved, he said : " Joseph is a growing son, a growing son and comely to behold. The God of thy Father shall be thy helper, and the Almighty shall bless thee with the blessings of Heaven above." This prophetic blessing had been merited by Joseph's innocence and purity, as well as by that generosity which made him the saviour of his brethren. By the like sanctity and charitable devotion did the new Institute merit to share in the same blessing.

With the glorious name of St. Joseph, it possesses two other privileges very dear to its heart : the right to claim St. Vincent as the friend and director of its founder, and the inappreciable advantage of having realized the ardent desire of St. Francis de Sales ; for the Institute of St. Joseph was, so to speak, the first flower of the mind of that great prelate, the spontaneous fruit of his heart.

Have we not heard the Bishop of Le Puy presenting his dear Congregation of St. Joseph to the other bishops of

France as having been established to perpetuate the spirit of *the first Institution* of the blessed Bishop of Geneva? In the first Chapter of the Constitutions we find the following recommendation: "The Sisters of St. Joseph shall endeavor, in their entire conduct, to imitate the customs, spirit, and life of the Sisters of the Visitation founded by St. Francis de Sales. They shall always entertain the most sincere veneration for the founder of that religious Order, and shall do all in their power to acquire the spirit with which he inspired that Order in its institution."

The Constitutions, throughout, tend to lead the new Institute to a triple end: the sanctification of its members by prayer and union with God, the Apostolate by teaching,[1] and charity to the neighbor by external works. It is the sweet and ardent spirit of St. Teresa, fused with the apostolic zeal of St. Ignatius, and the charitable spirit of St. Vincent de Paul, who said to his daughters: "My intention is that you should treat the sick and infirm as a tender mother cares for her only son." Thus the Institute, as we have already said, embraced both labor and evangelical perfection in their full plenitude.

The Constitutions, at first in manuscript, were, in 1693, printed by order of Mgr. de Villars, Archbishop of Vienne; and in 1729, a second edition, issued at Lyons, was approved by Mgr. de Neuville de Villeroy, Archbishop of that city.

The costume then worn by the Sisters was a dress of coarse stuff, like a long tunic, plaited in at the waist by a wide cincture, which, being carried to the back, hung down like the ends of a basque. Around the neck was a large

---

[1] In modern times, female education has become more and more a social necessity, and the greatest benefit religious communities can confer. The solace of human miseries is but secondary, for the reason, so little understood in our days, that all that tends to the health of the soul is to be greatly preferred to that which relates to bodily comfort.

white handkerchief, afterwards replaced by the guimpe. Their head-dress,—that used by widows of the time,—resembled the present *coiffure* of the Sisters, to which they added a hood or bonnet of black silk, called a *calèche*, like that now adopted by the Tertiaries of Instruction of Le Puy. When they went abroad, they wore a scarf about two and a half yards long, which, being thrown over the head and shoulders, was then knotted on the breast. Their distinctive sign was a small brass crucifix, which hung upon the breast.

Up to the Revolution of 1789, the Institute of St. Joseph, following that law of progress which its name symbolizes, increased and diffused itself in a wonderful manner, without, however, having any common administration. Like the monasteries of the Visitation, each house was complete, distinct, and independent, recognizing as its first Superior the bishop of the diocese in which it was located. The bishop usually named a Spiritual Father, who exercised jurisdiction as his vicar over one or several houses; he also appointed a place for the novitiate, and had the power of transferring Sisters from one establishment to another. The communities were, to use the simile of St. Francis de Sales, as so many distinct hives, each having its queen or mother, but all influenced by the same spirit, having perfect resemblance in life and action; subject, in a word, to the same Rule, and thus presenting a beautiful picture of unity in variety.

" Our daughters," wrote St. Francis to St. Jane de Chantal, " are the daughters of the clergy of each diocese, and the clergy form the first Order of religion."

These hives—to continue the simile—swarmed from time to time and sent forth new colonies out of their superabundance, which in their turn became the parents of new foundations.

Of the spiritual hives of St. Joseph existing at the time

of which we write, one of the most edifying and flourishing was that of Monistrol, in the Department of Haute-Loire. In the designs of Providence, the Superior of that little community was the Nehemias who was to reconstruct, or, rather, re-found the second Congregation of St. Joseph on the ruins of the first. As Nehemias, after the destruction of the Holy City, placed the sacred fire in a cistern where it was extinguished in the slime, so, during the revolutionary tempest which destroyed the religious houses of France, the spirit of the Congregation of St. Joseph was to be hidden in the heart of the Superior of Monistrol, not indeed to become extinct, but to shine forth pure and resplendent when God should arise and bid the waves " Be still ! "

She of whom we speak was the Rev. Mother St. John, a soul at once grand and simple, prudent and gentle : a soul whom God, according to the sacred simile, had fashioned like unto a strong and solid ship that should bear its precious cargo, safe and untouched, through its voyage over a rough and tempestuous ocean.

CHAPTER II.

JEANNE FONTBONNE—known later in life as Rev. Mother Saint John, Foundress and Superior-general of the Sisters of St. Joseph of Lyons—came into the world on the 3d of March, 1759, at Bas-en-Basset, a little town of Velay. She was the youngest child of Michael Fontbonne and Jeanne Theillère, a couple as remarkable for the depth of their Christian faith as for their true and solid piety. God blessed them with four daughters and one son, who, responding to the care lavished on them, fulfilled in after life the words of the Holy Spirit : "Train up a child in the way in which he should go, and when he is old he will not depart from it." Catherine, the eldest daughter, died a short time after her marriage and previous to the Revolution, leaving to her native place the remembrance and example of all those virtues that constitute a truly Christian matron. Her death was a sensible blow to all her relatives, but every one remarked the depth of grief evinced by little Jeanne, whose tender and sensitive heart preserved, throughout life, the remembrance of this beloved sister, who was, as it were, the first fruit rendered to God from a blest parental tree.

A second daughter married M. Teissier, a most edifying Christian, and in her family was renewed the lively faith and profound piety that had blessed the paternal hearth. After the death of their only son, the pious couple devoted themselves wholly to the practice of their religion, consecrating their wealth to the promotion of charitable works, especially those under the charge of the Sisters of St. Joseph, after that Congregation had been restored by their sister, Mother St. John.

Claude Fontbonne, the only son, inheritor not only of the name but the virtue of his parents, having married Mlle. Marie Plainay, of one of the most honorable families of Bas, there remained at home only Marguerite and Jeanne, the two youngest children, in whom were centred all the hopes and wishes of their fond parents, of whose declining years they seemed destined to be the support and consolation. Most carefully, then, did they endeavor to cultivate those precious blossoms, all unconscious, meanwhile, that God was but moulding them to His designs; that He had in reserve for their children, Jeanne, especially, one of those extraordinary vocations by which a soul is destined to become the light and ornament, not of one hearth alone, but of the Church itself, by enriching her with a new spiritual family, a religious Congregation destined to give legions of virtuous souls to earth and Saints to Heaven—a vocation similar to that of St. Clare, St. Teresa, St. Jane F. de Chantal, and, in our own times, of Mother Emilie, Foundress of the Sisters of the Holy Family, and Ven. Mme. Barat, Foundress of the Ladies of the Sacred Heart. Of such grand souls, mothers of a glorious and immortal progeny, has the Holy Spirit declared that "they are the most beautiful of the daughters of Israel."

Led, then, by Divine inspiration, the parents instilled into the tender hearts of their children the most sublime lessons of virtue, instructed them with special care on the principles of the Catholic faith, and inspired them with sentiments of profound respect for the ministers of God, and all that pertained to Divine worship.

We are accustomed to say that something seems lacking

to children who have not been reared under maternal care :
they remind us of plants deprived of necessary sunlight.
In this respect Marguerite and Jeanne had nothing to desire, for their holy mother made them her companions in
prayer and works of piety. In her company they attended
the Church Offices, and, by her example, became so permeated with the spirit of faith, as to make it, according to
the words of Scripture, the mainspring of their life and
actions. Jeanne's soul seemed to respond almost naturally to the influence of grace. Wise and thoughtful beyond her years, her questions, remarks, and conversation
often revealed germs, as rich as premature, of the beautiful
qualities that were to adorn her later life. The noble
Christian, the valiant woman, the saintly religious,—all
were revealed in that child of benediction ; and the blossom of her early youth gave promise of richest fruit in its
maturity. The childhood of every life, says Mgr. Dupanloup, is the flower giving promise of the fruit. "It is true
that every flower," continues he, "does not bring forth
fruit, but, incontestably, if there are no flowers, there will
be no fruit, and lives the most prolific of good have always
had a promising springtime."

Now the springtime of Jeanne's youth was so beautiful,
that her relatives and friends, delighted at the characteristics revealed in her, often quoted the words of the Gospel regarding the great Saint whose name she bore :
"What an one, think ye, shall this child be ?" *Quis putas
puer iste erit?*

A man of the world, more remarkable for statesmanship
than for virtue, has said : "The presence of a holy
maiden purifies, sanctifies the place wherein she dwells, and
her innocence excites either to virtue or self-condemna-
tion those who come in contact with her."

Stronger still is the power of virtue and innocence, when
with it we find the seal of Divine election, marking the

soul for higher things.   Hence, whether at home or abroad, with kinsfolk or with strangers, Jeanne possessed great ascendency over others, and won for herself extraordinary esteem.   Her sister Marguerite, especially, looked up to her with the deferential affection usually accorded to the older sister, nor could she bear separation from her. Always together in their childish amusements, or more frequently still, kneeling before the statue of our Lady on the little altar they so delighted to arrange, it seemed as if their souls, like those of David and Jonathan, were knit together ; even the prison or chains could not part them, death alone had the power.   It might be said that they were twin blossoms on one stem, mingling their perfume. or, more justly, two bodies animated by the same soul.   Piety does not exclude tenderness ; grand and holy souls are always possessed of tender feeling ; and if St. Teresa calls the spirit of evil " The one who cannot love," may not we also say that a Saint is "one who loves " ?

When old enough to attend school, the two girls were confided to the care of the Sisters of St. Joseph at Bas, which community was under the direction of two of M. Fontbonne's sisters,—Mother St. Francis, Superior, and Sister M. of the Visitation, Mistress of Novices.   We can readily understand with what an affectionate welcome they received their little nieces, of whom their father said :   " It has been my most earnest wish to confide them to you, that you may make them like yourselves.   They have a great attraction for prayer, and we have never had to urge them to that duty.   Our most ardent desire is to see their naturally good qualities improved and developed."   Loving their relatives in God and for God, the aunts' first care was to encourage the virtuous dispositions of the children, who, on their part, endeavored to obey them as Jesus obeyed Mary and Joseph in Nazareth. Marguerite entered, almost immediately, on her preparation for her First Communion with the greatest joy and fervor; and when, on one occasion during the instruction, Mother St. Francis endeavored to impress her with the thought that she could never become worthy enough to receive our Lord, she burst into a flood of tears. Then her little sister began to console and encourage her, saying : "Ah, what would not *I* give to be in your place ! But I too, ere long, shall share your happiness." When, in truth, her own time came, Jeanne seemed, in her fervor, to be more like an angel than an inhabitant of earth ; and she would lovingly exclaim : "Oh ! when shall I receive Him whom I love ? How I would wish to die when He enters my heart, so as never more to lose Him ! "

When the long-looked-for day arrived, Jeanne, accompanied by all her family, approached the Holy Table with such awe and reverence, that she seemed like a little angel prostrate before the face of her God. Dead to earthly sights and sounds, she saw only the Altar and her Beloved ; the Sacramental Presence of her God brought Heaven into her heart, and, inundated with grace, she hesitated not to devote herself body and soul to the promotion of His honor and glory. Thenceforth the sisters "advanced in wisdom and age, and grace before God and man," and their lives revealed daily the all-powerful influence of grace.

To Jeanne's solid virtue and good qualities was united a singular attractiveness, so that her elder sisters and brother strove with their parents for her society. Cheerful and joyous in temperament, she was the soul of her class exercises and enjoyments, and such was her influence that her companions used to make her the referee of their little disputes, and it was a common saying among them : " Let us tell Jeanne about it ; she will settle everything."

After some time, their parents sent the girls to complete

their education at the *Pensionnat* of the Sisters of St. Joseph at Le Puy, in which were brought up the children of the principal families of Velay. Amiable, obedient, and industrious as at Bas, the young girls soon won the affection of their teachers and companions, and long after their departure, they were remembered as models of regularity and perfect deportment.

Jeanne's superiority in intellect and virtue, and that rare good sense which seemed her dominant characteristic, exerted at Le Puy, as at Bas, an indescribable charm. Thus did that little plant gather around it many innocent doves, who in later years were to find safety and shelter in its beneficent shade ; in other words, the companion so loved in youth had the happiness of welcoming many of them in after years, as their Mother, in the Congregation of St. Joseph.

CHAPTER III.

THEIR education completed, the young girls returned to the bosom of their family, and such
was their holy and edifying demeanor, that it was
remarked by the entire parish, for the just, says the
Holy Spirit, bloom like the lily and shed a heavenly perfume all around them.

Rising early in the morning, the pious girls assisted at
the Holy Sacrifice, and then, returning home, tried to
share and lighten the burden of their mother's household
duties. As soon, however, as these had been completed,
they used to beg permission to go to the convent, to pray
with the Sisters and to hear the spiritual lecture. " It is the
Sisters' hour for prayer, mamma," Jeanne would say coax-
ingly. " Let us go and join our aunts, for you know,
mamma, the more numerous we are, the more likely we
shall be to gain our petitions. There we can pray for you
more effectually to God and His Blessed Mother." And
in these words Jeanne did but repeat the idea of the greatest Doctors of the Church. " What one cannot obtain in
prayer," says St. John Chrysostom, " may be won by the
prayers of many." " When prayers said in common,
blending together in unison, ascend to Heaven, it is im-

possible that they remain unanswered," says St. Thomas. " Where two or three are gathered together in my name," says our Lord, " there am I in the midst of them."

Smiling at the little artifices of her children, the happy mother would grant their request with a tender embrace.

At the convent they met with an affectionate welcome, and when, as is the custom among the Sisters of St. Joseph, at the termination of the lecture, all present were required to make some reflections on the subject, Mother St. Francis used to question her nieces and lead them to express their ideas simply and candidly. Their wise and enlightened reflections often astonished the Sisters, and of Jeanne, in particular, they felt that the Spirit of Wisdom dwelt in her soul.

As, at that time, each community of the Sisters of St. Joseph received and trained its own subjects, the ceremonies of reception and profession were sometimes held at Bas, on which occasions Marguerite and Jeanne never failed to be present. Since their return from Le Puy each had felt herself called to the religious life, and had revealed her secret to the other. Eager to draw the blessing of God on their first inspiration, they agreed to make trial in the world of the life of the Sisters of St. Joseph : to obey their parents and relatives as fervent novices ; to practice self-renunciation, humility, and poverty as far as practicable, and perform the visitation of the sick and poor in the company of their mother. The love of God thus filling their hearts left room for no other love, and their angelic purity and modesty avoided everything that could interfere with it.

Afraid to speak of their vocation to their parents, knowing the anguish it would cause them, they desired to make Mother St. Francis the confidante of their hopes and aspirations. She heard the news with great but secret joy, and, to try their resolution, drew an unattractive picture of the religious life ; representing it as beyond their feeble virtue, she urged them to pray, to reflect, to try themselves seriously, and to distrust the imagination, which often leads the young astray in even their best intentions.

After leaving the convent, they entered the church, where, prostrate before our Lord, they implored Him to enlighten them, and open some way for their entrance into religion, if such were His holy will. Consoled and strengthened they left the church, and Jeanne said : " We are not good enough to be religious, Marguerite ; that is why my aunt spoke as she did. Let us agree to redouble our pious exercises, our fervor and submission, in order to merit so great a grace. When I do wrong, you must remind me ; and if you forget, I will do you the like service." God, who loves the simple-hearted, could not but respond to their holy endeavors.

Mother St. Francis, in the meantime, had imparted the news to Sister M. of the Visitation, to whom God had given special graces for the discernment of religious vocations. " Mother," answered she, "that does not surprise me. I have very closely watched our nieces, and have been fully persuaded that the grace of God is acting sensibly in their souls. We have every reason to hope that the Divine Master calls them to His service. But who is to break the news to their parents ? They are becoming old ; they have only these two girls. They will never give them up; Jeanne, especially, who is so inexpressibly dear to them." It would seem, nevertheless, that the parents were not wholly ignorant of what was passing in their children's souls, for Mme. Fontbonne had, but a short time previous, said to her husband : " If God were to demand the sacrifice of either of these girls, we should have to be resigned. He is the Master ; His claim is greater than ours. But," she added, "I pray with all my heart He will not choose our darling Jeanne." Little did the tender mother dream that He was about to demand a double sacrifice ; to exact the return of the sacred deposit she had so admirably guarded ; to cull from the home-parterre those tenderly-nurtured blossoms which He alone could bring to perfection. The Divine election, through which their little Jeanne was to become the future restorer of her Congregation, demanded means of spiritual culture different from those available to her holy and excellent mother.

Mother St. Francis and her sister continued, meanwhile, to observe their nieces more closely, and lost no opportunity of putting their virtue to the test. Far from representing the religious life as agreeable or holily advantageous, they always held up its difficulties, sacrifices, renunciations, and asperities ; and in their intercourse with the young girls became grave, not to say severe. Far from being disheartened, the young aspirants did but redouble their fervor, humility, and sweetness ; they frequented the convent with ever-increasing attraction, and left it but with regret.

On the 19th of March, the Feast of St. Joseph, a reception and profession of more than ordinary solemnity and edification were held at the convent, at which Marguerite and Jeanne were present. Mgr. de Gallard, Bishop of Le Puy, who presided at the ceremony, was struck by their piety and modest recollection, and on leaving the chapel asked Mother St. Francis who those " two angels " were. The Superior replied that they were her nieces, whereupon the Bishop added : " They, also, will become religious." Delighted at this confirmation of her hopes, she said : " Such, indeed, is their ardent desire." The Bishop expressed a wish to see and converse with them, and, after the interview, assured their aunt that he was charmed with their excellent dispositions. Speaking of Jeanne, in particular, he said : " Train that child most carefully, for she is destined to be, one day, the light and glory of your Congregation." We can imagine with what joy the aunts thus heard from the mouth of so holy a prelate a confirmation of the favorable judgment they themselves had already formed. Thus was the Divine call continually revealing itself with that progress and perfection which characterizes the works of God, who, according to the Prophet, "ordereth all things mightily and sweetly;" *fortiter suaviterque disponit omnia.* "But the God of all grace," writes St. Peter,[1] "who hath called us unto His eternal glory in Christ Jesus, after you have suffered a little, will Himself perfect you, and confirm you, and establish you." The first step towards the accomplishment of this vocation we are now about to see revealed under the dispensations of Divine Providence.

Mgr. de Gallard had not visited Bas merely to preside at a religious ceremony, but to reveal to Mother St. Francis his intention to found at Monistrol, a little town in Haute-Loire, where he usually resided during the vacations, a community of the Sisters of St. Joseph, for whose Superior he had chosen Mother St. Francis, thoroughly convinced of the good that could be there effected among the young by Sisters imbued with her truly religious spirit.

He begged her to set out for Monistrol as soon as possible, promising, however, in response to the earnest prayers of her community, who were inconsolable at the loss of such a Mother, that she might return to them as soon as the new establishment should be fully organized.

When about to take his leave, Mgr. de Gallard said to Mother St. Francis:

"I wish you to bring with you some of your holy daughters from here, and your two nieces also, who will become religious in the community of Monistrol. There also you will find some good subjects, so that a novitiate can be

---

[1] I. Pet. v. 10.

opened at once. I will always be the father and protector of that house."

Then blessing and consoling the Sisters in the most paternal manner, the Bishop departed, greatly edified by their truly fervent spirit.

Mother St. Francis, like a good religious, set herself immediately to accomplish the will of him who was at once her Superior and the Angel of the Diocese. The most difficult part, however, was to take her nieces with her; nor could she bring herself to ask of their parents so great a sacrifice. Jeanne, herself, with supernatural courage, undertook the painful office, imitating Isaac, who carried the wood destined for his own sacrifice.

She spoke to them first of the vocation of Marguerite, her elder sister, and the parents, truly Christian as they were, resigned themselves to it. But when she went on to beg the same permission for herself, the news fell upon them like a thunderbolt. Breaking forth into sobs and tears, they cried: " Alas, we are old ; we had counted on you to be the support of our declining years. You are our only hope. If you leave us, you will hasten our death." Every means was employed to shake her resolution, and her tenderly sensitive heart suffered most acutely. But, thanks to this blessed child so wonderfully filled with the spirit of God, everything was accomplished " mightily and sweetly." More closely united by the very violence done their vocation, the two sisters, night and day, incessantly implored the Lord to strengthen them, and, at the same time, change the intense but natural grief of their beloved parents into calm and holy resignation. Their prayers were answered. Faith triumphed over nature, and with many tears, the good father and mother blessed them, saying: " Since He who gave you to us demands you from us again, may His holy and adorable will be accomplished in you, beloved children, for He is the Father and Master of all." Mother St. Francis and Sister Mary of the Visitation, who were present at this heart-rending scene, tried to console the bereaved parents, promising to be mothers to their children.

Everything being thus arranged, the sisters left Bas, July 1, 1778, at which time Jeanne was nineteen years old.

At Monistrol, Mgr. de Gallard received them with the kindness of a father, and conducted them to the little house in which they were to reside until the development of the community should call for a larger and more commodious dwelling. The fame of Mother St. Francis' sanctity had preceded her, and she was received not only with sympathy but veneration. Parents esteemed themselves happy in confiding their children to her. Many young ladies of the city, also, petitioned for entrance into the community ; and the novitiate which she opened, being manifestly blessed by God, increased rapidly. Marguerite and Jeanne Fontbonne were truly the ornaments of that novitiate, in which their fervor took new and admirable growth. Employed in the lowest offices of the house, they performed them with a humility, exactitude, and joy which edified the whole community, for Jesus in Nazareth was their Model, and they obeyed the Sisters without distinction, as He obeyed Mary and Joseph. Jeanne's modesty, fervor, exemplary fidelity to the least rules and practices of the novitiate, her gentle sweetness and amiability, made her the very angel of that little *cœnaculum ;* and her solid virtue, clear and upright judgment, well-balanced mind— as decided and practical as it was refined and delicate— won the admiration of the Sisters. All agreed that both were ripe for the religious life, and they were accordingly received to the habit in 1779. As the records of the place were burned during the French Revolution, the precise date of either their reception or profession is not known ;

but both ceremonies were held at the proper time, and conformably to the rules of discipline then in force. Mgr. de Gallard presided, giving Marguerite the name of Sister St. Teresa, and Jeanne that of Sister St. John. The act of profession consummating the sacrifice, put, as it were, the seal on their hopes and aspirations.

Casting aside joyfully the crown of roses that wreathed her brow, and loosening her beautiful hair, Sister St. John exclaimed : " Cut off, Mother, cut off this vain adornment, and cover me with a thick veil, that henceforth I may be separated forever from the world and its pomps."

The new spouses of Jesus slackened not in their fervor, and thenceforth to the professed as previously to the novices, they were models of perfect regularity and true religious obedience. Their wise Superior spared them no trial that could prove and strengthen their virtue ; and her direction, especially as regarded the younger, was almost always severe; for to her strong and saintly soul the truest love was love for their perfection. Hence she endeavored so to chisel that pure and beautiful marble, as to engrave deeply thereon the image of Jesus Christ, in that form, especially, which was so dear to the great Apostle,—the image of Jesus crucified, *et hunc crucifixum.*

Deeply skilled in the spiritual life, Mother St. Francis knew that as gold must be refined and purified in the furnace, so Jeanne's soul must be tried in the crucible, out of which it would come forth only the more resplendent. It may be, also, that she feared the influence of flesh and blood in her relations with her nieces, or dreaded to arouse in her community feelings and susceptibilities always injurious to discipline and the religious spirit. Be that as it may, Divine Providence, the Disposer and Ruler of human events, had His own august designs in her manner of direction. Even at that time might be heard, in the distance, the faint rumblings of that terrific storm which, a few years later, was to burst on France, directing its fury mainly against religion and its Divine works. God, in the meantime, willed to prepare for her future mission the young religious destined to steer her little community through the first hours of the tempest, and, in after years, reconstruct her Congregation from the shattered remnants spared by revolutionary fury. Such a destiny called for a strong, valiant, soldier-like soul, such as can be trained only by severe and vigorous discipline ; and Mother St. Francis was the instrument employed by Divine Wisdom for this end.

Treated with outward coldness and severity by one whom she loved both as natural relative and spiritual Superior, our poor Sister St. John suffered exceedingly. She trembled involuntarily when she went to ask her permission to do anything, and when, during the hour of recreation, she would give herself up to innocent mirth, she tells us. that if she chanced to meet her aunt's glance, she did not venture again to open her mouth. Her affection for her Superior was not, however, lessened by this apparent harshness, and until the end of her life she entertained the most profound veneration and filial love for Mother St. Francis.

Having been placed, some time later, at the head of the schools at Monistrol, Sister St. John displayed qualities that won for her the love and veneration of her pupils and their families. On Sundays and Thursdays she was accustomed to assemble the young girls of the parish, read them a spiritual lecture, and speak to them so wisely and sweetly of the things of God, that she drew their hearts to the love and practice of virtue. So great was her success, that Mother St. Francis, without relaxing her external severity, could not but bless God for the good operated by her niece.

The community at Monistrol was, indeed, a veritable *cænaculum*, in which the Holy Spirit seemed to delight in shedding His gifts. The Bishop, marvelling at the extraordinary fervor of the Sisters, thanked God for having inspired him to choose so holy a Superior. The Sisters at Bas, however, continually reminding him of his promise to restore Mother St. Francis, compelled him finally to acquiesce in their desires, and allow their beloved Mother to depart.

So wisely and so well had she established the work, that the Bishop felt certain the blessing of God would rest upon it, and assure its success. The better to preserve and perpetuate its spirit, as well as to give the venerable Superior a testimony of his satisfaction and gratitude for all she had done at Monistrol, he told her that the work should be carried on by her whom she had so thoroughly trained, her niece, Sister St. John, whom he intended to appoint Superior. At this unexpected news, Mother St. Francis ventured modestly to expostulate, saying that Sister St. John was inexperienced, and was, moreover, the youngest of the community. But the prelate replied that though young, she possessed that wisdom and judgment usually found only in the aged.

This honorable, spontaneous, and almost inspired testimony, rendered by that wise prelate to the youthful Superior, confirmed the hopes already entertained as to her virtue and efficiency. In this way was our Lord, according to His custom, gradually preparing and consolidating the designs of His infinite wisdom in her regard.

CHAPTER IV.

Mother St. John as Superior at Monistrol.—Works undertaken by
her.—Breaking out of the Revolution.—Mgr. de Gallard refuses
to take the oath and is forced into exile.—Apostasy of the Curé
of Monistrol. Persecution of the Sisters.—First attack on the
Convent.—Dispersion of the Sisters.—Second attack.—Mother
St. John and the remaining Sisters take refuge in her father's
house.

THE premonitory symptoms of the Revolution, to
which we have before alluded, grew daily more
threatening, and the new Superior of Monistrol was
destined to meet and heroically resist its attacks, in which
many, even, of the stones of the sanctuary should be broken.

According to the Bishop's wish, the election took place
on the 5th of October, the day after the departure of
Mother St. Francis.

Dear and venerable as this Superior was to the people
and Sisters, they could not but mourn her loss ; but to her
nieces, especially to the one on whom the burden of superiority now fell, it was most bitter ; to use the Scriptural expression, it was like a division of the soul. At Bas, on the
contrary, there was the greatest rejoicing, and the people
united with the Sisters in welcoming Mother St. Francis'
return. We cannot do better than transcribe here the
words of a venerable priest, her compatriot, who writes :
" Mother St. Francis was absent from Bas for seven years,
superintending a foundation of the Sisters of St. Joseph at
Monistrol. After having satisfactorily accomplished that
mission, she returned to her former home. She was a person

of extraordinary merit, endowed with exquisite tact, correct judgment, and unbounded zeal ; and it is not surprising that her works were crowned with great success. She remained at the head of the community in Bas until the Revolution, which in France has always been anti-religious, dispersed the Sisters and closed the doors of the convent."

Her successor at Monistrol, then only twenty-six years old, set herself zealously to carry on the work so well begun.

In every emergency she displayed prudence, tact, and administrative talents far beyond her years and experience; at the same time, she lost nothing of that simplicity, amenity, and equality of disposition which had always characterized her. Broad in her views and unbounded in her charity, she understood and practised religious life in its fullest perfection, and her Sisters were accustomed to say that they had never heard the vows of religion explained so well as by Mother St. John. She had the grace of procuring union of hearts; her wish was that her Sisters, like the early Christians, should have but one heart and one mind.

Her delight was to take part in the recreations ; and often seated on the grass, surrounded by her spiritual family, she would spend the hour in joyous, intimate, and pious conversation, which she was accustomed to end by exclaiming, like the Beloved Apostle John: "O my Sisters ! let us love one another ; it is so sweet, so good to love ! And then it is the law of our Lord."

Charmed with the spirit that animated that house, Mgr. de Gallard found great consolation in visiting it, and, after the example of St. Francis de Sales in his dear little *beehive* of the Visitation, in instructing his children on the religious life, and the spirit and obligations of their state. When, during these pious conferences, the Sisters asked him questions on the subject, he would sometimes refer to

Mother St. John, saying : "Let your Mother here reply to that question." The excuse of ignorance which she pleaded being of no avail, she would, with the humility and simplicity of a child, express her thoughts and opinions, begging the Bishop to rectify her errors. Thus it was that the prelate took pleasure in revealing to others the rare wisdom, prudence, and judgment of the young Superior.

On one occasion, he, under more solemn circumstances, gave public proof of the high esteem in which he held her. Having undertaken to build at Monistrol a hospital to be under the charge of the Sisters of St. Joseph, the Bishop, at the laying of the corner-stone, desired Mother St. John to bless it after him. Terrified at the command, yet constrained to obey, she was overwhelmed with confusion, and suffered much, as she herself says, at seeing "one so mean and unworthy standing beside His Grace, and associated with him in so holy an action."

The zeal, devotedness, charity, and wisdom displayed in the new work under her direction won for her community the confidence and affection of the townspeople, and in the accounts then written we find her spoken of as "the Mother of the whole city." Mme. de Chantemule, a lady ennobled even more by virtue and charity than by blood, had consecrated part of her fortune to the beneficent work undertaken by Mgr. de Gallard. By frequenting the hospital she became acquainted with its Superior, and conceived the highest veneration for her wisdom and sanctity. Virtue effaced all social distinctions, and throughout life, the noble lady and the humble religious were linked in a close and holy friendship.

To increase the good operated by this foundation, Mother St. John undertook to assemble in one of the halls of the hospital the pious young girls of Monistrol; that, under her supervision, they might work for themselves, their families, or the poor; and that thus she might draw them from the dangers of the world, and form them to solid piety. The more effectually to compass her end, she used to read to them spiritual works, which she supplemented by pious exhortations on the duties of their state. By such means, coupled with her talents for direction, the young Superior was, with the blessing of God, enabled to do much good, and the town soon became filled with pious, fervent Christians; so that with St. Teresa she might have said: " I have seen the grace of God, as a mighty eagle with outspread wings, seize upon these young souls to drag them from evil and the world, and raise them up even unto Heaven."

But the year 1789, the fatal epoch of the Revolution, broke on unhappy France. Religion and its beneficent but calumniated works were to pass through the fiery ordeal, submit to every species of outrage and persecution, and sustain irreparable losses. The storm speedily assumed frightful proportions, and its hellish fury found vent in the wildest excesses. Having overthrown the Church in France, it sought to take her place and exercise her powers, in which view it framed the infamous "Civil Constitution of the Clergy," a confused and absurd medley of Jansenism, Protestantism, and impious laicism. Declared obligatory on the 4th of January, 1791, it was imposed on all the clergy, who were required to swear before the revolutionary municipalities that they would conform thereto ; the penalty of refusal was, first, deprivation of all salary, and afterwards, deportation, exile, or death. Like his venerable colleagues, the Bishop of Le Puy refused the impious oath, and expressed his reasons for that act in the following address to the municipal authorities:

" I have already told you the truth, gentlemen; I have told it respectfully, yet, at the same time, with that zeal and freedom to be expected from your Bishop. But, O the depth of the judgments of God! the holiest of my duties is, perhaps, about to become for me, your chief pastor, the inexhaustible source of sorrow and of tears. By obeying the voice of God and my own conscience, I shall, perhaps, dig the abyss which is to separate me from my people. I shall, probably have made the torch of faith shine more brilliantly in their sight, only to hasten the moment when it shall be torn from my grasp. Yet a few more days, and my only consolation may be to weep, like Rachael, over my children, whom I shall vainly call by that name, once to me so sweet: 'my people, my beloved flock;' for such you shall ever be, until the Church, our common Mother, breaks the links, the sacred bonds that unite you to us in Jesus Christ.

"Whatever may be the painful consequences of the duty I am about to fulfil, I call on the God of our fathers to witness that, whether absent or present, my heart shall remain ever in the midst of you. Exiled in a foreign land, far from this new country to which Heaven has called me, which my heart has adopted, and to which I have sworn a fidelity which nothing has been able to change or to shake, I shall weep at the remembrance of Sion and my Beloved Spouse. O ancient and venerable Temple, heretofore the witness of my joys, to-day the depositary of my grief, may my tongue cleave to my palate ere I ever forget thee ! Holy ministers and faithful counsellors in my pastoral cares, and you, indefatigable co-laborers in the work of Jesus Christ, if I can no longer direct and share your labors, I will, at least, associate myself thereto by my vows and prayers. Chaste spouses of Jesus Christ, Christian virgins, though unable to console myself with you in the trials that are common to us, I will at least strengthen my constancy and fidelity by the remembrance of yours. Poor ones of Jesus Christ, in lamenting your bitter lot, there will remain to me, at least, the sad consolation of knowing that, before God, I am innocent of your sorrows and your sufferings.   What a heart-rending prospect !   May God, so fruit-ful in resources and so rich in mercies, spare me the chalice so filled with bitterness !   May the charity of Jesus Christ dwell in our midst, and may the peace of the Church soon restore happiness to us all !"[1]

But these tender and sublime words were powerless to touch or soften the wolves of the Revolution.   On the con-trary, they won for him the more speedily their bloody at-tentions.   Ere long he was grossly insulted and even fired at in his carriage ; and to such extremities did they pro-ceed, that he was compelled to take refuge in Switzerland.

Poet as well as orator, he has expressed in verse the he-roic sentiments of his magnanimous soul in the hour of trial. We subjoin the hymn of his resignation, which shines as a gleam of light through the sorrows and dark-ness that overwhelmed him.

> Wilt choose the oath or indigence ?
>   My heart, oh, answer me !
> Farewell, forever, honor, wealth ;
>   Let God my portion be.
>
> Shall not the bark that bears not **gold**
>   Attain the wished-for port ?
> More speedy still, from burden **free**,
>   'Twill enter Heaven's court.
>
> Around me swells the angry sea,
>   It roars with threatening voice ;
> I laugh to scorn its impotence,
>   And, calm in God, rejoice.
>
> O sea, beat o'er me in thy wrath !
>   Though tossed still to and fro,
> The Bark of Peter shelters me
>   Which ne'er shall shipwreck know.

Before his departure into exile, when Mother St. John

---

[1] Given at Puy, Jan. 13, 1791.

went to bid him farewell, and to receive for the community his parting benediction and advice how to act amid the assaults which she foresaw the Revolution would raise against them, he gave her his own portrait in testimony of his veneration for her, and as a token which might soften somewhat the bitterness of separation.'

This sad parting interview was but the prelude to heavier trials. The position of the community became daily more painful and critical, as the Curé of Monistrol, a man of considerable learning and talent, permitted himself to be seduced by the Revolution, and endeavored, by every means in his power, to make his flock sharers in his fall by dragging them into the Constitutional schism.

What a dangerous temptation, what a sorrowful trial for those religious! Nevertheless, they were neither seduced nor terrified. They courageously refused to assist at a procession of the Blessed Sacrament presided over by the apostate ; and, despite all the efforts of their erring pastor, who went so far as to rouse the parish against the community, the Sisters of St. Joseph remained firm and unshaken in the faith, directed and sustained by their holy Superior.

It was not long ere the emissaries of the Revolution came, armed with hatchets and axes, to attack their peaceful dwelling, and force them to take the impious oath exacted by the convention, and already taken by their unfaithful pastor. But calm and serene, Mother St. John presented herself before them, alone; and, in the name of her daughters refused the required oath, saying with admirable dignity and firmness: "It is unnecessary to bring the community before you: here, the head answers for the

---

' The Sisters of St. Joseph at Lyons still preserve, with love and veneration, the portrait which this confessor of the faith gave Mother St. John ; as also a magnificent cross of gold, enriched with many precious relics, which Cardinal de Bonald gave to the same dear Mother as a token of esteem.

members." Disappointed and abashed at her holy courage, the miscreants withdrew, exclaiming: "What a woman that is! There is nothing to be gained from her."

Changing their tactics, they returned to the charge later on, and by various artifices, tried first to separate, and afterwards to weaken the union of the community with that "head" whom they could not hope to vanquish. All was useless; the vigilant sentinel was not to be taken unawares; she sustained her community, encouraged the timorous, and consecrated the time allowed them under the circumstances in imploring that help from God which they so sorely needed; pouring meanwhile, into the Heart of Jesus alone, the anguish that filled her own.

Finding, however, the tempest was not likely to abate, and dreading for her daughters inexpressible misfortunes, she advised them to seek shelter, for the time being, in the bosom of their own families.

The last embrace was given amid sobs and tears of anguish, and the Sisters separated, imploring our Lord to shorten the bitter days of exile. Mother St. John, however, with Sister Teresa and Sister Martha, a lay-sister devotedly attached to her, remained at her threatened and dangerous post, despite the tears and entreaties of her aged father, who wished her to seek safety beneath the paternal roof.

But at last the dreaded hour arrived. An infuriated mob besieged St. Joseph's Convent, broke open the doors, and forced into the street the three religious, taking possession of the establishment in the name of the Commune. Sheltered at first by some pious persons, they found means later to get to their father's house, which they made a solitude, another convent of St. Joseph.

Thanks to the pious customs of the faith preserved in that patriarchal home, such a transformation was very easy. It was even its inestimable privilege, during the

Revolution, to shelter under its roof the most Blessed Sacrament, preserved in a secret room of the house, in which sacred oratory the family were accustomed to meet for night and morning prayers. There, too, it was that Mother St. John and her two religious companions mingled their tears for the woes that afflicted the Holy Church of Jesus Christ; there they prayed for the beloved Sisters whom the persecution had dispersed; there, too, they encouraged to perseverance in their faith those faithful Catholics who came secretly to adore their Eucharistic God.

Mother St. John, by her holy and inflamed discourses, increased the ardor of love in their hearts, and throughout those days of mourning and weeping, that blessed home, happy in possessing the spouses of our Lord, became a sanctuary whence prayer and praise ascended daily unto God.

Very frequently, too, they had the joy of welcoming some persecuted confessor of the faith. for M. Fontbonne had caused several secret hiding-places to be constructed, to which they could fly in case of emergency. The advent of the priest meant, to the holy inmates of that home, a feast of joy, an opportunity of approaching the Sacraments of Penance and the Eucharist, and assisting at the Holy Sacrifice—graces all the dearer because of the danger that attended them. It was a renewal of the Church of the Catacombs; and from those secret sacred mysteries the assistants came forth, replenished with zeal and ardor for the cause of religion, and more strengthened to suffer, nay, if necessary, to die for Christ. But how cautious soever they might be, such a mode of life could not escape discovery; suspicions were aroused and the house was often searched by the municipal authorities, in hopes of finding therein some faithful minister of Christ whom they could drag thence to prison, to exile, or to death.

But M. and Mme. Fontbonne, like vigilant sentinels ever on the alert, were not to be taken by surprise. Fearless of personal danger, they met their unwelcome visitors with imperturbable coolness, and, more than once, succeeded in disarming their fury and calming their suspicions.

When, on one occasion, the search had been more than ordinarily rigorous, one of the officers noticed a little secret door in one corner of the house, and demanded whither it led. Terror thrilled every heart, for it was the entrance to the hiding-place where, at that moment. the object of their search was concealed. "Open this door immediately," cried the officer. "I must know what it is." "Oh, most certainly, citizen," cheerfully responded Mme. Fontbonne, apparently all eagerness to comply with his request. Completely deceived by her manner, he resumed : " Well, never mind it. We are sure of your loyalty."

The priest was saved, and with hearts overflowing with gratitude to God, that happy household chanted the canticle of thanksgiving.

Thus did the home of the Fontbonnes, bearing a likeness to the primitive Church, win for itself benedictions like those which, in those early days, hallowed the homes of Priscilla, Aquila, Chloë, and others that had the honor of sheltering the Apostle of Nations, whose gratitude has handed their name down to the veneration of succeeding ages.

CHAPTER V.

EANWHILE, the fury of the Revolution, far
from abating, was ever on the increase: and
with the triumph of the Convention and Robespierre, the late Superior of Monistrol and her sister became, no less than the priests, the objects of search. A
price was even set upon their heads; and God, whose designs are impenetrable, but who, doubtless, wished to
enhance their glory and their crown, permitted their retreat to be discovered.

Breaking tumultuously into the house, the emissaries of
Satan demanded the religious sheltered therein. To ward
off the danger that thus menaced the priests hidden there
at that very time, Mother St. John, Sister Teresa, and
Sister Martha appeared before them. "What do you
want, my friends?" asked Mother St. John, in a calm and
dignified tone. "We want," answered they, "to take you
and your companions to the Mass which the patriot priest
is going to say in this parish." "Never," exclaimed the
heroic Mother; "never will we consent to communicate
with a faithless priest, an apostate!" "We would rather
die than renounce our faith," added the religious unanimously.

Enraged by their refusal, the men seized them by force,
and dragged them towards the church, beating the drum

meanwhile and crying aloud : " Make way for these three citizens, whom we are taking to church." Kneeling benches had been placed for them in the choir, that they might be more easily seen by all the people. But, firm and undaunted, the Sisters stood erect, to show their abhorrence of the sacrilegious ceremonies so tumultuously celebrated before them. On bringing them forth from the church, their persecutors again loaded them with every species of insult, until they reached the house of M. Fontbonne ; but the dirt and slime of earth cannot sully the wings of angels. Before entering the house, Mother St. John, desiring to protest against the impious violence of which she and her Sisters had been the object, addressed herself to the surrounding crowd, exclaiming : " My friends, know that by force alone have we been carried to the sacrilegious Mass of an apostate priest. Our hearts and our wills have had no part therein ; we remain inviolably attached to the true faith, the Catholic and Roman faith, and no violence shall ever be able to separate us from it." Her courageous words were received with furious vociferations by the maddened crowd. Nor was it long before the victims were torn from the arms of their parents, handcuffed, loaded with chains, and thrown into the prison of Saint Didier, to await the sentence of death.

Their aged father, broken-hearted at the sufferings of his children, used to go four leagues on foot, and brave every danger, to carry them a little food in their horrible prison. The Sisters had been incarcerated but a few days, when they saw the prison doors open to receive other captives, among whom they recognized their aunt, Mother St. Francis, the late Superior of Bas. At the dispersion of her community she had not been able to return to her own family, but continued for some time to wander, with several of the Sisters, through the hamlets and forests of the surrounding country, seeking, sometimes at night, hospitality and shelter from isolated Christian families. But amid such trials she had the ineffable consolation of being allowed to carry about with her the Most Blessed Sacrament,—a privilege like that granted to the early Christians in the time of persecution. Assembling around her her Sisters, in some little hut or hidden recess in the depth of the forest, she would lay on the corporal her Sacred Treasure ; and there, long prostrate before Him, who was homeless like themselves, they would adore and bless Him for thus condescending to console their sorrows, and accompany them in their wanderings, wherever, by the force of the tempest, they were compelled to flee.

Unable to find a safe asylum, Sister Mary of the Visitation, like her Sisters, wandered from one hiding-place to the other, meeting them in their sad but holy reunions whenever she could do so without danger to them or herself. Having on one occasion found refuge with a friend of her family, some one ran, breathless, to warn her that the *Sans-culottes* were coming to make their customary search. She had barely time to throw herself into the nearest bed ; and the mistress of the house, pretending to be occupied in the care of a patient, excused herself for not being able to receive the men as she desired, but begged them to take some refreshment. The ruse was successful : Sister Mary of the Visitation was saved.

At Easter, Mother St. Francis and her companions made their way over mountains and through forests, at the cost of indescribable dangers and fatigue to the Shrine of Louvesc, that they might receive the Sacraments of Penance and the Blessed Eucharist from a true priest. So great were the trials which had to be undergone in this holy pilgrimage, that faith and love alone could have surmounted them ; but the example of their saintly Superior inspired the Sisters with courage like unto her own.

Their Paschal duty accomplished, they returned to their

wandering life in the vicinity of Bas, where it pleased God Mother St. Francis should be discovered by the *patriots*, arrested and dragged to the very same prison in which Mother St. John and her companions were confined. Sister Mary of the Visitation again escaped the persecutors.

The little troop of captives, meanwhile, were calmly awaiting their fate, and preparing themselves for martyrdom ; and their prison, the scene of sufferings and privations of every kind, was the scene also of sanctity, courage, celestial joy, and holy magnanimity like to those of the first champions of the faith. Separation from the world had no sadness or terrors for those to whom the whole world was a prison, and to Mother St. John it seemed rather release from a dungeon than entrance therein.

" The world," said Tertullian, speaking of the ancient martyrs, " is a thousand times more gloomy than the prison: its darkness blinds the heart. The chains of the world are much heavier ; its fetters bind the soul. The world exhales a more poisonous miasma, which arises from the passions of men. The world encloses many more guilty wretches ; of its superfluity the prisons are filled. The martyrs live in a gloomy dungeon, but they are themselves a light ; chains bind them, but they are free before God. They breathe an infected atmosphere, but shed around them a perfume of Divine sweetness. Let us, then," concludes the African Doctor, "let us not use the word *prison;* rather call it a retreat. Though the body be chained and the flesh captive, the heart and mind are free."[1] "As for me," writes St. Jerome, " my prison is a castle, and my desert, a paradise."[2] As if to them had been addressed these powerful exhortations, the Sisters transformed their prison into a place of retreat, a convent, a house of prayer. The heart of Mother St. John, above all, overflowed with

---

[1] Tertullian, Ex. to Martyrs.   [2] St. Jer., Ad. Ruf.

joy; her cell was her palace, the vestibule of Heaven; and her chains, jewels and bracelets of inestimable price; the nakedness of the prison, the hardness and humidity of the plank that served her as a bed, dear and blessed means presented for the practice of religious poverty and mortification. Deprived of the happiness of assisting at Mass and receiving the Sacraments, she visited in spirit the closed churches, desiring to water with her tears and blood those desecrated sanctuaries; and offered her life daily in expiation of the sacrileges that had stained them.

Like the young virgin Blandina, whom the Acts of the Martyrs represent as a noble mother, *tanquam nobilis Mater,* because of her courage and sublime exhortations to the other martyrs, the young Superior of Monistrol, about the same age as the great martyr of Lyons, was also the noble mother of her companions in captivity, by communicating to them something of her strength and fortitude.

"The just," says the Holy Spirit in the Book of Wisdom, "shall hold themselves with great firmness against those who torment them, and despise their holy works. At the sight, the wicked shall be troubled." So, by her heavenly serenity and ready answers, Mother St. John confounded her jailers. They commanded her to work on Sundays and holydays, and to observe the Decade which they had substituted therefor. "If I had been willing to do that," she replied, "I should not now be here." When, disconcerted, they threatened her with a deeper dungeon, "Come, let us go," she answered. "Which way leads to it?" When they wished to force from her the cry *Vive la Republique!* she cried louder still, *Vive Jesus! Vive Marie!*

After a long detention, in the course of which they had seen many of those in the prison summoned to the scaffold, the executioner at last entered their room, and cried aloud: "Citizens, it is your turn to-morrow." Trembling with joy and not with terror, they, with St. Cyprian, responded, *Deo gratias!* "To-morrow!" said the prisoners among themselves, "oh, to-morrow will be the happiest day of our lives; let us, then, prepare our garments." Mother St. John remembered that she still possessed a small piece of money, and it was unanimously resolved to spend it in having their clothes washed the best they could, for the grand festival of the morrow.

Thus prepared, with lamps aflame with the light of faith and love, those wise virgins eagerly awaited the coming of the Bridegroom, that with Him they might enter in to the wedding-feast of the Lamb. Suddenly the door was thrown open. Starting to their feet, they were preparing to go forth to that scaffold which they regarded as the stepping-stone to Heaven, when they heard the words: "Citizens, you are free. Robespierre has fallen; your chains are broken." At this news, which to so many of their fellow-captives was "tidings of great joy," Mother St. John exclaimed, sorrowfully: "Ah, my Sisters, we were not worthy the grace of dying for our holy religion. Our sins have been the obstacle to so great a favor."

When, in her after life, the Sisters used to allude to this holy period, she would adroitly turn the conversation from herself to her fellow-sufferers, whose glorious martyrdoms she delighted to recount.[1]

Thus snatched from the claws of the revolutionary tiger, and freed, to their regret, from their chains, the religious

---

[1] Mother St. John has left us a list of twenty-one persons of her acquaintance, chiefly ecclesiastics, who were then immolated for the faith. Their names are inscribed in her prison note-book. While the above-mentioned Sisters were immured in Saint-Didier, five other Sisters of St. Joseph were imprisoned in Feurs, twenty in Clermont, and others in various parts of France. To some of these Sisters was granted the glory of dying for their faith and vocation, as is shown by the following extract from the Annals of the Congregation of Le Puy: "Our Congregation has had its martyrs; the condemnations of the Civil Tribunal record the names of some religious of St. Joseph.

"A judgment delivered by this fatal tribunal on the 16th of June condemns to death—the sentence to be carried out on the same day—seven persons, among returned to the bosom of their families. It was not long before Mother St. Francis and her daughters had the opportunity of presenting to Citizen Pierrot, who then represented the people of France in Haute-Loire, a claim for the restoration of their property, which, through the goodness of God, having been accepted as valid, the Sisters reassumed possession of their beloved convent. Mother St. Francis presided over this community until 1802, when, attended by her relatives, Sister Mary of the Visitation, Sister Teresa, and Mother St. John, she rendered up her pure soul to her Divine Spouse, for whom she had so zealously labored, so gloriously suffered. Her name and memory are still held in veneration in those places sanctified by her zeal and virtues.

Sister Mary of the Visitation survived her eight years,—years wholly consecrated to labors of charity. To visit the poor in their miserable dwellings; to obtain help for them by every means in her power; to lead them to make good use of their trials and privations, was the labor of her life, so that she was known as the Mother of the poor, the consoler of the afflicted, to whom, under God, many souls owed their eternal salvation. In 1810 she was called to her reward, and in death was attended by her two nieces, who had ever gratefully regarded her as the angel guardian of their religious vocation.

But to return to our subject. On their release from prison, Mother St. John and her sister were met by their

---

whom we find two priests and two religious of St. Joseph, Sister Anne Marie Garnier and Sister Marie Aubert. The Author of *The Martyrs of the Revolution in the Haute-Loire* thus recounts their bloody execution: 'The numerous spectators who congregated to see the condemned walk from their prison to the scaffold, beholding their calm and recollected demeanor, could scarcely restrain the evidences of their emotion. On the way, the priests chanted the *Miserere*. Sr. M. Aubert, the first to die, was followed by Sr. Garnier, Marie Best, Marie Roche, Barthélemy Best, and lastly by the two priests, M. Mourier and M. Abeillon, who seeing the bloody tragedy drawing to its close, intoned the *Te Deum*, and rendered up their own lives in the act of chanting: *In te, Domine, speravi.*' "

brother, Claude Fontbonne, who, at the news of their approaching execution, had hastened to Saint-Didier, in the hope of receiving their parting words, and of recommending himself to their prayers, concealing, in the meanwhile, from his aged father the impending crisis in the fate of his children.

On his way he met a friendly notary of Bas, who told him of Robespierre's fall, and the probable deliverance of his aunt and sisters, but hope had died within him.

When, therefore, he arrived at Saint-Didier and found that, instead of bidding them farewell, he could congratulate them on their restoration to freedom, the sudden transition from deep grief to heartfelt joy was too much for his strength, and he fell senseless to the ground. The shock brought on a violent fever, during which Mother St. John never left him, until, by her care, her prayers and tears, she had restored him in health to his family.

Nor was this the only blessing by which God rewarded the Christian devotedness of the true brother. All his children having in their infancy been recalled, one by one, to the bosom of God, the desolate parents felt most acutely the loneliness of their childless hearth. In 1803, another son was born to them, and a Franciscan who lived with M. Fontbonne—his convent being still closed—seeing that he dreaded the loss of this child also, said : " Have confidence; this boy will not die. Get him baptized at the altar of St. Thyrsius. He will one day be a priest of the Church, and a zealous missionary." The words proved prophetic ; the child was baptized by the name of James Fontbonne, and when grown up and ordained to the sacred ministry, consecrated himself to the missions of America, as we shall see later on.

This boy was to Mother St. John a child of predilection ; and when afterwards Providence fixed her at Saint-Etienne, she loved to have him near her, that he might grow up, under her own eyes, in piety and the fear of God.

The first use Mother St. John made of her liberty was to try to reassemble at Monistrol her dispersed community. The religious life was her element, and with her usual prudence and address, she applied to the municipality for the restoration of that house in which had been invested the dowries of herself and Sisters. A claim so just could not be ignored, but the convent had been sold by the Commune, and the proprietor refused to restore it at any price. The municipal finances were at the lowest ebb, and the officials all hostile to religion, for the revolutionary spirit had been carried farther in Monistrol than in other places ; as the pastor himself had greatly favored it, the torrent, meeting no check, had swept before it everything good, whether moral or physical. According to the remark of Taine, it is characteristic of revolution, when unrestrained, to go on blindly, devouring all before it, and leading to bankruptcy the countries under its rule. A report addressed to the First Consul by the Prefects of France sets forth that "a universal degradation, physical and moral, brought about by the reign of anarchy and impiety, was then imprinted on the face of France." It is not our task here to prove that assertion ; it is a historical fact. Hence, Monistrol lent itself less readily than Bas to religious restoration ; and while awaiting better days, Mother St. John, with her sister and her faithful companion, returned home. With a joyful heart M. Fontbonne received them, exclaiming : "How happy I am to see you again ! He who gave me means to care for you in your childhood is ever good and powerful. Now that you have suffered in His cause, He will not let you want for anything. You will draw down His benediction on this house and on your aged parents."

"Yes, dear parents," responded Mother St. John, "do not be uneasy : we shall not want anything while we dwell with you ; and later on God will know how to provide for our necessities. We will work in order to second Divine Providence ; and then, have we not made a vow of poverty ? We will practise it after the example of our Divine Master, and it will be sweet to suffer something for His love, since we have not been found worthy to die for Him."

Thus did parents and children,—rivals in faith and virtue—render their common abode a veritable sanctuary of perfection. So great was the odor of the sanctity practised therein by the religious, that its remembrance was transmitted from father to son as a most precious family inheritance. " I remember well," says one of Mother St. John's nieces, " that when we were very young, our father used to tell us often about Mother St. John and her rare virtue. Hearing those recitals, our hearts were deeply touched and filled with a desire to please our saintly aunt by our good conduct, for he made us feel that she was watching us from her throne in Heaven. Such a thought had great influence over us ; our prayers were better said, our tasks more readily accomplished, and our obedience more prompt and cheerful."

Happy those families who possess Saints ! Happy the parents who, after the example of Anna, the mother of Samuel, delight in consecrating their children to God, at least by rearing them in a Christian manner ! The pious Catholic child is the glory, the consolation, the crown, the perfume, the benediction of home. Now this Christian education, as we know, is what hell unmercifully attacks at present, by its impious or atheistical agents who have the upper hand. Their end they disguise under the name of secular or unsectarian education. But when they do away with the idea of God, they not only *secularize* the soul of the child, they pervert, they degrade, they kill it.

Let us hope that the spirit of Christian France will resist such a crime. "Christian feeling," exclaims Father Felix, "is the natural respiration of France." May its enemies fail in their attempts to stifle that which has made her heretofore so strong, so grand, so beautiful !

CHAPTER VI.

HIDDEN from the world, Mother St. John and her companions spent their days of exile in religious austerity, prayer, and continual union with God, praying incessantly for the Church and unhappy France. Her heart, to use the words of a Saint, was an altar whereon the flame of Divine love was never extinguished. Faithful to the spirit of her Institute, with prayer she united action, catechising children and the ignorant, visiting the sick and prisoners, and procuring for the dying the last rites of the Church. This latter work, as precious as it was difficult in those times of persecution, seems to have been her favorite employment.

By such means—as the ark of the ancient covenant guarded the tables of the law—did her faithful heart, in view of the new alliance for which she so longed and prayed, preserve silently and carefully the traditions, zeal, and spirit of the Institute in which she had consecrated to God the flower of her youth. The heart which had so ardently longed for the immolation of martyrdom, became, by the ardor of its desires, as the altar of holocausts, whereon, according to the law, was to burn, undying, the sacred flame. Hence, when peace was restored to the Church of France, and the hour for reopening the sacred temples, and re-enkindling with the lamps of the sanctuary the torch of the religious life, had dawned,

Mother St. John possessed within herself, living and pure, that flame which was to enlighten and adorn the reconstructed Congregation of St. Joseph. She was, to use the expression of the Sisters of St. Joseph in America, " the vessel of election, pre-ordained by God for the re-establishment of the Congregation."

Dispersed as then was the Institute of St. Joseph, it was not wholly forgotten by its absent Pastor and Father, who preserved, even amid the sorrows and trials of exile, a lively remembrance of his persecuted daughters, whose works of zeal and devotedness had given them a lasting claim on his esteem and affection.

In 1798, they had the inexpressible consolation of receiving from Mgr. de Gallard, the banished Bishop of Le Puy, a letter conveying encouragement and direction under the trials they had to encounter. We subjoin, in its entirety, this document, worthy of the apostolic times, and so honorable to the Sisters of St. Joseph :

" My beloved Daughters:

" You have such sacred rights to my thoughts and affections, you have merited them on so many glorious titles —your virtues and my obligations ; your examples and my desire for good ; your tribulations and my sympathy ; your hearts and mine—all speak to you of my tenderness, all warrant my lively and continual solicitude in your regard.

" As the eyes of the Lord are always fixed upon the just, and the ears of His mercy ever open to their prayers, so I dare also to say, my beloved children, my eyes are incessantly turned towards you, and my sorrowful heart hears, ever, the cries that proceed from yours. I remember (and, oh, how could I forget ?) that you are that precious portion of my inheritance, always so dear to me and ever so worthy of my affection. You are, in my eyes, the chosen race, the holy people, object of the complacency of Heaven, since in dragging you forth from your sacred retreats, impiety has not been able to rob the God of all purity of His true sanctuaries, that is, your hearts consecrated by virginity.

" Up to this time, the enemy of virtue and all good has failed in his efforts to shake your constancy. Worthy Spouses of Jesus Christ, like Mary you remain standing at the foot of the Cross, nor have you ever recoiled from the chalice of sorrow and opprobrium which Jesus has incessantly presented to your lips. O my beloved daughters, rejoice in the Lord and praise Him for all those sorrows which render you like unto your Divine Spouse, for all those triumphs by which Heaven crowns your invincible firmness !

" Jealous of your glory, dismayed at the strength of your virtues, humbled by your courage, the spirit of lies and deceit again assails you. By his efforts to annoy you and weary out your patience, he believes he has almost exhausted it ; and he seems to have given you over, during these times, to all the suffering and horrors of want, only to force you to bend the knee to the idol of crime and impiety, and compel you to sacrifice to him the immortal fruits of all you have had to undergo ; for one cannot be deceived as to the views of the powers of darkness : they have themselves torn aside the false veil that sometimes covers their artifices.

" All these means tend but to one end ; it is always the same : to efface from souls every trace of virtue and religion. As the wicked can find no rest, they can give none ; if they flatter, it is to destroy ; if they promise, it is to deceive ; if they give, it is to corrupt. Ah, could you believe that the voice of justice and humanity would be heard in those hearts hardened to every noble sentiment, as well as to remorse ?

" See how they have treated, how they still treat those strong ones of Israel, who, by degenerating from their first fervor, have had the weakness to yield to their promises or threats! What has been the result of their complaisance? They have increased the boldness and strength of impiety, brought division into the camp of Israel, and scandalized the little ones of the faith. Behold what have been the fatal effects of those acts, whose perfidy was concealed by either avarice or terror!

"The chief pastors have constantly revealed it; and what remains to those who have preferred their own lights to those of our guides and chiefs? The bitter regret of having increased the woes of religion and their country, under the vain pretence of lightening them, and the shame of having trusted more in the lying promises of the deceiving spirit, than in the oracles of those who have received from Heaven the mission to unmask and confound him.

"Instructed as you are, my dear children, by these fatal examples,—the subject, we doubt not, of your tears as of ours,—far from me be the thought that you would allow yourselves to be deceived by the new snare which is spread before you by the enemy of your virtue and happiness! What attraction in your eyes could there be for a gift offered you by hands as perfidious as they are sacrilegious, and which you could accept only at the expense of your conscience? Who, better than you, knows what St. Paul said to the early faithful: "You cannot be partakers of the table of the Lord, and of the table of devils: you cannot drink the chalice of the Lord, and the chalice of devils"?

"The state of distress in which I see you, my dear children, pierces me to the heart, and in my personal indigence, I feel only the powerlessness in which it leaves me to succor you; but habituated as you are to privations and sacrifices of every kind; accustomed to contemplate our Divine Model, who had not whereon to lay His head;

penetrated with love and confidence in our Heavenly Father, who feeds the birds of the air, you will cast yourselves into the vast bosom of His Providence, and will expect from His infinite goodness alone the reward of the sacrifices you have already made, and are still ready to make for His great glory and the sanctity of your state.

" How holy and profound, my beloved daughters, are the designs of God over us, when He permits the impious to violate the sanctuaries of virginity, and scatter their stones in the midst of a perverse world ! Heaven has willed to make you a spectacle to angels and to men. You are as the seeds of flowers caught up by the wind and dropped in city, in country, even into the bosom of your own families, that you may bear everywhere the good odor of Jesus Christ.

" Called to a mission so sublime, and proved so worthy of fulfilling it, can I fear from you any weakness ? No, my beloved children ; the true glory of virgins is " to follow the Lamb whithersoever He goeth." You have had the happiness of following Him in the path of His sorrows and humiliations ; the greater number of you can, like the Apostle, glory in bearing on your innocent flesh the stigmata of Jesus Christ : you all envy the fate of your blessed companions who have followed the Divine Spouse even unto Calvary, and who, after His example, have consummated thereon their sacrifice, praying for their persecutors and the executioners who murdered them. Ah, I have the firmest confidence that I shall yet share with the Spouse of your souls the inestimable consolation of having in you my crown and my glory !

" Persuaded that impiety seeks only a pretext to enkindle against you the fires of another persecution, I am not affrighted at the new dangers that threaten you. There is no question of *danger* for you ; but, while groaning in all the bitterness of my soul over the additional sufferings that may be heaped upon you, I dare to congratulate you on being always judged worthy to suffer for justice' sake, and I congratulate myself on being the pastor of so many heroic souls, called to the double crown of virginity and martyrdom.

"I unite myself, my cherished children, to your combats and your victories, your tribulations and your favors. Let us humble ourselves beneath the almighty hand of God who visits us. Let us leave to Him our cares and our solicitudes, and even in the very midst of suffering, we shall find our surety, our protection, and our strength in the God of all grace, who has called us to His eternal glory in Jesus Christ our Lord. Amen.

"Given at the place of our exile, July 19th, 1798."

Does not this letter, so replenished with faith, wisdom, and holy sweetness, remind us of the admirable epistles of St. John? Nothing can equal the paternal tenderness of apostolic hearts for the spiritual children whom they have "engendered in faith and the Gospel." "O Corinthians," wrote St. Paul to his beloved spiritual family in Corinth, "our mouth is open to you, our heart is enlarged. You are not straitened in us, but in your own bowels you are straitened . . . . I speak to you as my children . . . . . Great is my confidence with you, great is my glorying for you. I am filled with comfort."[1]

The great hearts of John, Paul, and the other apostles were the golden channels of that Christian charity whose source is on Calvary and which is to flow through the apostolate and the Tabernacle until the end of the world, to purify and save it.

In the relations that existed between the venerable Bishop of Le Puy and the Sisters of St. Joseph, we see revived, in a very atmosphere of selfishness and hate, the spirit of

---

[1] II. Cor. vi. vii.

apostolic times, when Christians had but "one heart and one soul," so that the pagans, ravished at so beautiful a spectacle, cried out, " Behold how these Christians love one another !"

This apostolic letter of Mgr. de Gallard, like that of Rev. Father Médaille, is as honorable as it is instructive to the Sisters of St. Joseph. Both breathe eloquently the spirit of the Congregation,—its humility, zeal, and devotedness. Let us, then, here remind its members of those words of the Holy Spirit : " Remember those who were placed at your head. My son, forget not the discipline of your fathers." " Follow the examples of the Saints," says the Imitation, and listen to the words of the aged.

Second Book.

Mother St. John after the Revolution.—Foundation, Unification, and Organization of the Sisters of St. Joseph of Lyons.

CHAPTER I.

The time designed by Providence for the restoration of the Congregation of St. Joseph arrives.—Mother St. John is called to Saint-Etienne.—Community of the Rue de la Bourse.—The Sisters resume the religious habit.

S we have already seen, the paternal home to which the revolution had restored, or, rather, exiled Mother St. John, became for her a place of retreat, where, by persevering and inviolable fidelity to her obligations as a true religious and daughter of St. Joseph, she was, unconsciously, fitting herself to be the worthy instrument of Divine Providence for the great work of the restoration of her beloved Congregation, a restoration which was to be, in truth, a re-creation by the new form and admirable extension given to it. In her hands and under her supervision and direction, but humbly and quietly, without any outward show, the Congregation of St. Joseph was to become one of those great spiritual families which " rejoice, enrich, honor, perfume, and make fruitful the Church," as the glorious Bride of Christ herself sings in her office for the festivals of canonized founders of religious Orders.

After twelve years of prayers and tears, and of ardent holy longings, the moment marked out by God came at last. In 1807, God called Mother St. John to the city of Saint-Etienne, in Forez, where, as formerly in Puy, He had sown the little grain of mustard-seed, which she was to cultivate and increase.

This germ of the Congregation of St. Joseph consisted of some pious young girls and former members of religious Orders, who had assembled together to consecrate themselves to the service of God, to aid and mutually animate one another in the practice of perfect virtue, and to devote themselves, night and day, to the alleviation of human miseries, multiplied a hundred-fold by the ravages of the Revolution. They had established themselves at Saint-Etienne, in the Rue de la Bourse, where they were known as the *Black Sisters*, from the color of their secular dress ; or *Sisters of a Good Death*, as the care of the sick and dying was one of their favorite works. Rev. Claude Cholleton, curé of the principal parish of Saint-Etienne, who, in 1804, had been appointed Vicar-General, approved their pious and charitable design, and seconded it to the best of his power. Having consulted His Eminence, Cardinal Fesch, then Archbishop of Lyons, on the subject, that prelate strongly advised him to transform the little association into a house of the Sisters of St. Joseph, not by creating a new Congregation, but by restoring, as far as might be, that founded at Le Puy, but destroyed by the late tempest. That zealous and powerful prince of the Church promised to further the design as far as lay in his power, and he became, in reality, one of the greatest protectors and benefactors of St. Joseph's Institute.

Acting on the Cardinal's suggestion, Father Cholleton, with his consent, invited to Saint-Etienne Mother St. John, whose signal merit and rare qualities had been made known to him by Rev. Father Imbert, a Franciscan, her former director at Monistrol, who was then preaching the Lenten sermons at Lyons. Her parents, greatly enfeebled by age, could not bring themselves to sacrifice a second time her who, like the young Tobias, was "the light of their eyes, the staff of their old age, and the consolation of their life." Anxious at all hazards to keep her treasure, the aged mother tried to lessen the esteem in which her daughter was held, telling the priest that she was not at all capable of doing what he desired, since she was very deficient in judgment ; but this little ruse of maternal love rendered desperate, was easily seen through ; it was well known that. on the contrary, common sense and sure and solid judgment were the dominant characteristics, the distinctive traits of Mother St. John.

Nor was the daughter, on her part, willing to undertake the work thus urged upon her. She resisted, partly on account of the sorrow and loneliness such a separation would entail on her aged parents, but more, because her humility dreaded the title and responsibilities of re-storer, or foundress, which, she foresaw, would be the necessary consequence of the task imposed on her. Obedience, however, finally triumphed, and submitting to the will of God, revealed through her ecclesiastical Superiors, she went to Saint-Etienne on the 14th of August, 1807, accompanied by her faithful Sister Martha. To lessen, as far as in her power, the anguish of the separation, she left her beloved Sister Teresa to be the consolation of her parents, and the staff of their declining years.

At Saint-Etienne she was received as an angel from Heaven by the little community which so eagerly longed to greet her as their Mother. With indefatigable zeal she set her-self to train her religious in the manner of life of the first Sisters of St. Joseph, and to impart to them that primitive spirit which she had so sedulously cultivated within her own breast. And worthily did the fervent subjects respond to the wishes of their Superior. Nothing could be more edifying than the spectacle presented by the newly-organized community, in which were revived the austerities and heroic traditions of the early days of the faith. Each occupied herself, according to her skill and aptitude, in some of the works to be found in a manufacturing city, observing, meanwhile, the most absolute silence, the most perfect regularity. Prayer was continual, fasts frequent and severe, the discipline and cilice in daily use. As in the ancient Thebaid, or at Citeaux in the days of St. Bernard, they practised the evangelical counsels in their utmost rigor. Wine and everything that could flatter the appetite was banished from their table, and Mother St. John, to whom the use of snuff had become a necessity and very beneficial, sacrificed it also.

Mme. Teissier (Mother St. John's sister) and her husband were then living in Saint-Etienne. Perfect Christians, as they were, they knew and appreciated the merit, value, and supernatural advantages of Christian mortification ; they themselves embraced suffering in the most edifying manner, because, beneath its gloom and shadow, they recognized the beauty of Divine love, so that they admirably understood the words of St. Teresa : "To suffer or to die."

Nevertheless, they were surprised and terrified at the austerities practised by the religious. "O my sister," Mme. Teissier would say ; "you do not eat enough here to live ; your health will never be able to bear such privations," to which Mother St. John would answer gayly : "Oh, don't be at all uneasy ; one must suffer something, you know, for the love of our Lord, who suffered so much for us." And though these charitable friends strove by their gifts to lessen somewhat the austerities of the Sisters' table, the poor became the greatest gainers thereby.

Not content with fasts, the Sisters used to sleep on the

floor, on pallets, or on boards, some, indeed, on planks studded with iron nails; they prolonged far into the night their painful vigils, and rose before the crowing of the cock. Mother St. John was often obliged to moderate her daughters' thirst for mortification and penance; and when, later, the ecclesiastical Superiors judged it necessary to modify their manner of life, and restore the simpler primitive observances of the Congregation, she took from the Sisters an extraordinary number of iron bracelets, cinctures, chains, disciplines, and all sorts of instruments of penance. Surprising as it may seem to those who know not the hidden sweetness of the cross, that life of privation and self-immolation was one of delightful peace and joy : a life of continual gladness, the very remembrance of which soothed the declining years of those who had spent their youth therein. "Oh, how happy we were!" exclaims, later, one of those voluntary victims; "how happy we were, wearing that coarse habit, which so often won for us the contempt and insults of the passers-by ! Our humble, penitent, and mortified life concealed treasures of benedictions and celestial joys not to be found elsewhere." She who spoke thus was a lady endowed with the rarest gifts of nature and grace, who, in 1805, at the age of twenty, had embraced that life crucified and hidden in Jesus Christ. At her reception to the religious habit, in 1808, she was given the same patron as her venerable Superior, and under the blessed name of Sister St. John, founded afterwards the Congregation of Chambéry, as we shall see in the course of this work.

· Two young postulants having, on one occasion, been sent by Mother St. John to inform a venerable priest, deeply interested in them, that they were about to receive the religious habit, he very kindly inquired if, under the strict rules of the house, sufficient food, at least, was given. "Oh, don't be at all uneasy about that, Father," they answered merrily ; " at dinner we always have *five* courses," which, however, they failed to specify. The courses were : soup, a dish of vegetables, a piece of cheese, bread, and water mingled with a little milk. The priest, satisfied that five courses were, at least, enough for the dinner of a religious, inquired no further. Coming in that day after the community meal was over, the two novices found, before the kitchen grate, their share of a plate of macaroni all covered with cinders which had fallen unperceived. Happy to imitate those Saints who had mixed ashes with their food in order to diminish its savor, they contented themselves with picking off the biggest cinders, and cheerfully ate the rest. " Another time," said they laughingly, " we shall be able to say truthfully that our dinner comprises *six* courses."

As sweetness is often the amiable companion of strength, so joy is always the complement of Christian mortification. Nothing is more admirable and, at the same time, more logical, than this joy of souls crucified by Divine love. " If there be joy in the world," says the author of the Imitation, " surely the man pure of heart possesseth it." Now purity and true liberty are the fruits of Christian mortification and renunciation. " The most terrible enemy of the soul," continues the same pious author, " is the body. Those who flatter it live in servitude. They are like prisoners loaded with fetters. [1] Christian mortification removes the stain, breaks asunder the chains of sin, and gives the freedom of the children of God, as has been admirably expressed by a holy religious in the following couplet :—

> " The body is enchained, the soul at liberty ;
> The iron of time becomes the gold of eternity."

It is not, then, surprising that from the interior of that

---

[1] Imit., Bk. II., 4; Bk. III., 13-21.

little Thebaid, which was the cradle of the second foundation of St. Joseph's Institute, there issued only songs of
gladness, hymns of praise and thanksgiving to God.

But that happiness attained its height when, on the 14th
of July, 1808, the fervent Community, laying aside the
secular dress so regretfully worn, were invested with the
habit of the former Congregation of the Sisters of St.
Joseph. Rev. M. Piron, an intrepid confessor of the
faith, addressing the new religious, said: " You are, indeed, but few, yet like a swarm of bees, you shall spread
yourselves everywhere. Your number shall be as the stars
of Heaven. But, while you thus increase, preserve always
that humility and simplicity which should characterize the
Daughters of St. Joseph."

On that memorable occasion, Mother St. John renewed
her youth like that of the eagle, and her spirit of activ-
ity gave a great impulse to the progress of the work.
God was with her, enlightening her understanding, clothing her with His strength, and communicating to her His
wisdom. Kind without weakness, firm without severity,
prudent yet large-hearted in her estimation of character,
she arranged all things with weight and measure. While
her great sanctity and amiable qualities drew souls to her,
her knowledge and experience won their confidence ; and
her admirable gift of discernment taught her how to dis-
tinguish the action of grace in the very midst of the miseries, weakness, and contradictions of nature. In everybody she could discern something good; so that it might
be said she was like the bee, which sucks honey from even
the bitterest plants. She knew how to weigh facts and
motives ; to judge, to understand, to love ; in a word, she
was, as our Lord says of the great Saint whose name she
bore : "A burning and shining lamp in the house of
God." Full well she understood that authority, in order to
be like that of God, which is its source, must ever unite

sweetness and goodness with strength ; and, led by the spirit of God, she endeavored to carry out the recommendation of St. Ambrose : Moderation in difficulties and business ; order in affairs ; seasonableness in time ; consideration in words.

CHAPTER II.

Mother St. John reopens the Asylum at Monistrol.—She restores the convent of St. Joseph and appoints a Superior.—The Government approves the Community of the Rue de la Bourse.—Opening of a House in Lyons.—The Community of Mi-Carême at Saint-Etienne.

HILE thus developing her work at Saint-Etienne, Mother St. John had not forgotten Monistrol to which her heart was so strongly attached, and, like St. Paul, she could have said to her spiritual daughters : " Our mouth is open to you ; our heart is enlarged. You are not straitened in us."

Time had brought her its lessons and experience ; and in the meanwhile, better days had dawned on that poor town, to which so much evil had been brought even by those whose office it was to do good. A holy and zealous pastor had replaced him who, to use the expression of Benedict XIV., had been "a wolf in the fold," *lupus in grege.* This good priest set himself zealously to repair the ravages of impiety ; and to assure his success, engaged as auxiliaries the Sisters of St. Joseph, who had formerly done so much for Monistrol. More fortunate than the Convent, the asylum, founded as we have seen by Mgr. de Gallard and Mme. de Chantemule, had not been sequestrated during the Revolution, and hence it was easy to restore it to its original charitable destination.

Mother St. John's faithful companion, Sister Martha, who had formerly been employed there, was still remembered as the mother of the orphans, and it was decided that she should resume her work. To the orphans and the poor her restoration was a kind of family festival; but when it became known that Mother St. John herself would accompany and reinstall her beloved daughter, the public joy was unbounded. Her entrance into the town was a triumph; the inhabitants flocked about her path; some wept for joy at again beholding her, while others uttered fervent prayers that Providence would restore her to a people who regarded her as a mother. But the holy Superior of the little Thebaid of Saint-Etienne belonged not to herself. Divine Providence had chosen her for a greater and more arduous work.

As to Sister Martha, she remained until death at Monistrol, devoting herself with ever-increasing charity to the solace of the unfortunate, whose servant she had become. She is still remembered at the scene of her labors as a humble, fervent, and charitable religious, whose highest eulogy is: "She proved herself the worthy daughter of Mother St. John."

The asylum thus re-established, God afforded Mother St. John the great consolation of being able, in conjunction with the worthy parish-priest, to purchase from its revolutionary proprietors her former convent, the cherished home of her early religious life. Nothing could have given her greater joy, and she hastened to recall her former daughters to their beloved home.

Who can describe the feelings of rapture and thanksgiving with which that little flock, so rudely separated, prepared to re-enter their blessed convent-fold? Who can tell with what delight the Mother looked for the spiritual children for whom her heart had so hungered? Revolution, the disturbance of the times, and death had, as might be expected, decreased their number, and hence Mother St. John took with her to Monistrol Sister Gonzaga and Sister Saint Louis, the latter of whom she intended to appoint Superior.

On re-entering that home of so many peaceful and happy memories, and while embracing, with all the ardor of maternal affection, her long-lost children, the Mother could not restrain her tears. "O my beloved children," she exclaimed, "what a sweet consolation to behold you once more assembled together in this dear home, the witness of our holy engagements, of our Christian and religious joys as well as of our sad and terrible trials! Blessed be God, who has restored you to my love and tenderness! You have been firm and unshaken under your trials; you will be no less fervent in your holy vocation.

"Remember, my beloved daughters, the holy and paternal exhortations made to us in this house by our saintly Bishop de Gallard. Oh, may his spirit live ever among you! From the height of Heaven, where God now recompenses his heroic virtues, he intercedes for us, he blesses us. I leave you here his portrait; it is his legacy; it will ever remind you of this great and venerable prelate and father.

"I leave you, moreover, a good and kind Superior. Love and obey her, follow her advice, and you will complete the joy of your former Mother, now grown old, who loves you so tenderly and truly in our Lord."

The good curé, after welcoming the Sisters in the most cordial manner, blessed the convent profaned during the Revolution, and promised his fatherly care, protection, and concurrence in all their works. His most ardent wish had been to provide for the religious education of the children, hoping thus to repair the evils brought on their fathers by the late unhappy strife : and this he saw could best be effected by the labors of the Sisters.

His parishioners, too, congratulated themselves on possessing again the nuns, whose dispersion had given them such poignant anguish ; many, even, of those who had shared in the late excesses, enlightened as to their true character, repented of their errors and joined in the general jubilation.

After Mother St. Louis's installation, Mother St. John remained a few days longer in the midst of her restored children, who seemed as though they could not see or hear enough of her. Her holy example, her pious exhortations, reanimated all hearts, and revived their courage, so that the community recommenced its labors and resumed its former mission with all the spirit and fervor of its early days, thus accomplishing literally this counsel of the Imitation : " Every day we ought to renew our purpose, and stir ourselves up to fervor, as if it were the first day of our conversion. And to say : Help me, O Lord God, in my holy purpose, and in Thy holy service, and grant that I may this day begin, indeed, since what I have hitherto done is nothing." [1]

Clothed with the mantle and spirit of her venerable Superior, Mother St. Louis continued to prosecute the works she had begun. Following her counsels and walking in her footsteps, she maintained in that house the spirit of fervor and regularity, so that its work was visibly blessed by God, and such numbers of pupils flocked to the establishment that it had soon to be enlarged.

When blessing His people God said by the mouth of His prophet : " Enlarge the place of thy tent, and stretch out the skins of thy tabernacles, spare not : lengthen thy cords and strengthen thy stakes. For thou shalt pass on to the right hand and to the left : and thy seed shall inherit the Gentiles." [2] This fruitful benediction was granted to the Sisters at Monistrol.

While carrying on, both in the convent and asylum, the work rendered necessary by this happy increase, the corner-stone formerly blessed by both Bishop de Gallard

---

[1] Imit., Bk. I., 19. [2] Isaias liv. 2, 3.

and Mother St. John was found. As we may well believe, it was removed, with great respect, to where it now rests, over the entrance to the Sisters' sacristy, which opens on the private grounds of the community. There, silently yet eloquently, it seems to repeat to the Daughters of St. Joseph this admonition of the Holy Spirit: "Remember your prelates who have spoken the word of God to you;" [1] remember those who have been your fathers and mothers in the faith; and, considering their conduct and the end of their lives, imitate their faith and their spirit of union.

After the completion of the new buildings, Mother St. John joyfully responded to the invitation to be present at their dedication, little dreaming of what her consent was to cost her. For the parish-priest, who had heard of Mgr. de Gallard's act under like circumstances, at the conclusion of the liturgical benediction insisted that Mother St. John should give her blessing to the new construction; and, great as was her confusion, she was again obliged to obey.

During her sojourn at Monistrol, Mother St. John let no day pass without visiting the Asylum, where she was accustomed to assemble her beloved poor around her, speaking to them individually, and, like an affectionate mother, inquiring into the trials, sorrows, and health of each. "Oh, how happy we used to be," the old men have often been heard exclaiming, "when the Rev. Mother came to see us! It was a struggle as to who should get nearest to her, speak to her, look at her, and receive that smile so sweet and so full of charity."

As the Asylum was in great need of a pharmacy, Mother St. John summoned from Lyons Sister St. Hilarion, a person well skilled in the requirements of such a charge, who established the same and presided over it

---

[1] Heb. xiii. 7.

until her death; around her name still lingers the perfume of her charity to the poor and distressed, and of her sanctity, as well as that of all those early daughters of Mother St. John who had passed through the fiery ordeal of persecution, the people of Monistrol long preserved the memory. The Rev. Mother, however, they venerated as a Saint, placing the greatest reliance on her prayers and assistance, as the following incident goes to prove.

A young lady of that town possessed a silver cross which her uncle, the curé of Bas, had received from Mother St. John. She preserved it reverently as a precious relic, keeping it on her person day and night, as a blessing and a preservative against possible danger. Having, on one occasion, when on a journey, been overtaken by a violent storm, at some distance from Monistrol, she was in great danger. When warned before her departure of the impending tempest, she had answered: " I shall not be uneasy, for I have Mother St. John's cross with me." When, then, she found herself in the depth of the woods, exposed to the fury of the elements, she fervently clasped her precious talisman, and interiorly invoked the venerable Mother St. John. " I was not at all terrified," said she afterwards, " for I knew our holy Mother would protect me." Nor was she disappointed; she passed safe and unhurt through the forest, and arrived home, to find her family overwhelmed with fear and dread on her account.

This firm and unshaken confidence in the sanctity and protection of Mother St. John was not confined to Monistrol alone, but was general in Saint-Etienne, Lyons, and other places where she was intimately known.

If the visits of the venerable Superior to Monistrol tended always to render the members of that community more holy and their works more fruitful, her constant residence at the Rue de la Bourse in Saint-Etienne, and the care which she devoted to the training and direction of that community, drew on it the special blessings of Heaven, blessings by which God was preparing that convent for marvellous and unlooked for development.

On the 10th of April, 1812, the establishment received the authorization of the government. Some time later, Father Cholleton, having been appointed Vicar-General of Lyons, summoned to that city some of his dear daughters of St. Joseph, and confided to them the direction of an establishment in the Rue St. Pierre-le-Vieux, near the Cathedral, founded for the relief of the poor of four parishes. Mother St. Paul was named Superior of that community, in which was afterwards received and trained to the religious life the celebrated Mother St. Joseph, whom grace adorned with such extraordinary supernatural gifts, and to whose zeal, rendered fruitful by the blessing of God, so many great works are due. Of these works we shall give a brief account later on.

In the city of Saint-Etienne there then existed, besides the convent in the Rue de la Bourse, another association of pious young ladies, under the government of Mlle. Benneyton, who were anxious to form themselves into a cloistered community. Their wish coincided with that of Rev. Father Piron, the curé of the parish; but by the advice of the Archbishop of Lyons, they, in 1808, applied to the Sisters of St. Joseph of the Rue de la Bourse to be received as novices into that Congregation.

On the 20th of April, 1809, they were clothed with the habit of St. Joseph, in the chapel lately constructed at Mi-Carême, and Mother St. Paul, recalled from Lyons, was appointed their Superior.

This, in the designs of Providence, was the House destined to carry on at Saint-Etienne the work of St. Joseph; for a short time afterwards, the Sisters of the Rue de la Bourse were dispersed on different missions. Several were sent to a house at Valbenoite; others accompanied Mother St.

John when she was called to Lyons to found the Mother House; while to others was intrusted the direction of the various Providences founded throughout Saint-Etienne by ladies of the city, under the title of Ladies of Mercy.[1]

In this same convent of Mi-Carême was to be received, clothed with the religious habit, and professed, some years later, Margaret Mary Virginia Tézénas du Montcel, known better as Rev. Mother Sacred Heart of Jesus, the successor of Rev. Mother St. John in the government of Lyons, she whom Mgr. Plantier, Bishop of Nismes, has called "the second foundress" of St. Joseph's Institute. At present, the establishment of Mi Carême, which numbers sixty religious, is, after the Mother House, the most important under the government of Lyons. None better than it preserves the primitive spirit of St. Joseph, imparted by Mother St. John in the Rue de la Bourse, renewed by Mother Sacred Heart, and continued successively by those daughters so worthy of her, Mother Euphrasia and the late Superior-General of the Congregation at Lyons, Mother Emilie.[2]

It was this spirit of humility, simplicity, renunciation, devotedness, and tender love for our Lord which led the

---

[1] Some Sisters of St. Joseph, designated by Mother St. John, established themselves in a little local institution, where they took care of the children. Sister St. Ambrose, former Mistress of Novices in the Rue de la Bourse, founded in the Rue de la Charité the first orphan asylum of that city. This was afterwards transferred to the Providence of Sainte Marie. The first President was Mme. Jovin des Hayes, but its life, its animating spirit, its visible Providence was Mlle. Balay, the intimate friend of Virginia Tézénas du Montcel (Mother Sacred Heart); her heart is still preserved in the Chapel of the Providence. In the records of all the charitable foundations of Saint-Etienne under the Sisters of St. Joseph, notably in the work *Du Pieux-Secours* and the *Refuge*, to which Mother Sacred Heart gave her private fortune, we find the names of noble benefactors, who vied with each other in charitable donations and munificent bequests.

It was of such Christians as these the Apostle formerly said: "They have generously assisted me and also our brethren the poor; they have labored much in Jesus Christ for the work of God and for the advancement of His kingdom in souls, and their names, blessed of God and man, are written in the Book of Life."

[2] Died March 18, 1886, at the Mother House of Lyons.

Sisters of Mi-Carême to call their chapel, their *salon*. In that convent religious simplicity was strictly preserved everywhere, save in that beloved spot where reposed the God of their hearts, the Spouse of their love. There, as doubtless Mary and Joseph had done in Nazareth, they denied themselves to consecrate to Jesus the best their poverty could afford.

In Nazareth, Mary, whose hands, according to St. Epiphanius, were as skilful as industrious in labor, wove for her beloved child that seamless robe for whose possession the soldiers quarrelled and cast lots on Calvary. Ah, well indeed does the care of that sanctuary which holds her Jesus suit the daughter of St. Joseph : it is the spirit of Nazareth!

At the head of the schools of Saint-Etienne, the numerous and zealous community of Mi-Carême to-day defend valiantly the cause of God, and strive to maintain the female sex in that dignity and nobility to which Jesus, the Son of Mary, has elevated it. And is it not eminently fitting that the Daughters of St. Joseph should co-operate in this work with Him who has deigned to claim the same father ? Happy, indeed, thrice happy those religious who thoroughly understand and faithfully fulfil their double mission : to love Jesus themselves, and to make Him better known and loved by others !

The cultivation of the mind and soul, says Père Lacordaire, was ever regarded as the most important business, the chosen work of the ancient sages, but since God Himself has deigned to become incarnate and dwell in our midst to cultivate them Himself, that office, so grand and glorious, has become a love surpassing all other loves, a paternity, a maternity which can find no rival.

And never has there been an age or an epoch that called more imperatively for the thoroughly Christian education of woman ; in this lies our only hope for social regeneration and salvation.

CHAPTER III.

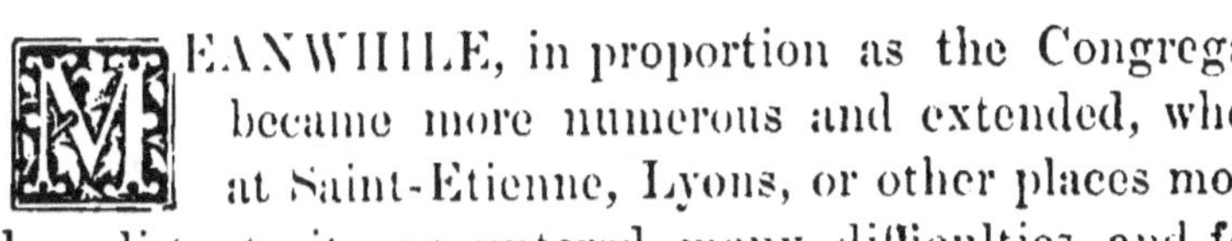

MEANWHILE, in proportion as the Congregation became more numerous and extended, whether at Saint-Etienne, Lyons, or other places more or less distant, it encountered many difficulties, and found itself in varied and untried circumstances. In 1812, the disturbances and exigencies of the times and the multiplication of Houses—some of which contained religious all too few for the requirements of community-life—made the Sisters feel the necessity of a new mode of government, and of a general novitiate which would assure a thorough and uniform training of their religious aspirants. In the absence of this uniformity, there were, necessarily, varieties of discipline, different lines of action, incomplete measures, and, at times, a kind of rivalry.

It has been by withdrawing from such isolation and erecting themselves into a Congregation under a Superior-General that many monasteries have taken, as it were, a new lease of life and gained an increase of holiness. In isolation we may find the monastery, but not the monastic Order. Such monasteries are like scattered members : they are not a grand and beautiful body animated by one spirit, and strong by unity against the inevitable relaxations of human frailty. The necessity, then, of forming these scattered convents into a strongly constituted body, through which authority might flow as the sap through the branches of a tree, or the blood through the arteries of the human frame—a body whose divers parts, without being changed, would become better fitted to attain their end—was speedily felt. There was but one way to effect this : to found a Mother House which should be at once the head, the centre, the bond of union, the source of discipline ; and for the same reason, it became necessary to choose a Mother or Superior-General. [1]

The choice of the latter was not difficult. She who had preserved in her heart the beautiful traditions of St. Joseph's Institute in the past, who had been the instrument of its happy restoration in later times, who had zealously watched over its early progress, and had, under God, given it new life and fecundity, was, assuredly, the most suitable person to direct its further development.

Lyons, too, seemed a most natural and fitting centre whence should radiate the various establishments of a great religious organization, such as the Congregation was to become. The Institute of St. Joseph, which had first sprung into existence in one of the most renowned strongholds of devotion to Mary,[2]—a city upon which, in our day, rests

---

[1] Up to their dispersion in 1793, the different houses of our Congregation had been, like those of the Visitandines, independent of one another. But when, after the restoration of peace, Napoleon permitted the Sisters to resume community-life, it was, as we learn from the letter of Mgr. Dampierre to the Superior of our Sisters of Clermont, dated Sept. 11th, 1811, with the proviso that there should be a central or Mother House, responsible for those affiliated to it. This mandate, coupled with the cogent reasons above given, led our communities, scattered throughout France. to form themselves into various diocesan Congregations, of which Lyons, Bourg, Chambéry, Le Puy, Clermont, Aux Vans, St. Gervaise-sur-Marc, and Annecy have become the most numerous and important. (Tr.)

[2] *Rocher Corneille,* which overlooks the city of Le Puy, is the spot concerning which we have the earliest record of an apparition of the Blessed Virgin : it occurred A. D. 46 or 47. Wonderful are the legends, traditions, and miracles related of the favored sanctuary of Mary built thereon. *Puy Notre Dame,* as it was called, has a special association with the history of the Crusades. There Urban II. spent the night of Aug. 15th, 1095, praying for the success of the expedition. There, too, Adhémar de Montheil, its glorious Bishop, before leaving his beloved city, prostrated himself before the blessed shrine ; and then, suddenly, as if inspired, rose and intoned that anthem, since so dear to every Catholic heart, the *Salve Regina,* which thence became known as the *Anthem of Puy.*

the protecting shadow of " Our Lady of France " [1]—had taken new birth in the Diocese of Lyons, and it was felt that the most proper place for its first Mother House was that " City of Mary," consecrated from time immemorial to Notre Dame de Fourvière. Thus it would seem that our Blessed Lady is desirous of keeping near her and guarding ever, under her own eyes, the chosen family of her holy Spouse ; it is a touching proof of her love, an assured pledge of her maternal affection.

Mother St. John was, accordingly, summoned by the Diocesan authority to Lyons, after nine years of labor and trials at Saint-Etienne. She arrived there on July 13th, 1816, with a party of fervent religious from the Rue de la Bourse, with whom were afterwards joined several Sisters from the House of Monistrol.

Sister Theresa remained at Bas, that, being near her aged parents, she might care for them in their feebleness and infirmities. Both had the consolation of dying in the arms of their religious daughters, for as soon as Mother St. John heard of their impending death, she hastened to assist them in their last moments. Before their departure they, like the ancient patriarchs, blessed their children : then, full of years and merits, they slept the sleep of the just, and went to receive the recompense of their faith and merits, leaving behind them a generation of Saints.

Mother St. John and her sister returned to Lyons, where, by the advice of Father Bochard, who had succeeded Father Cholleton after his death, in 1807, not only as Vicar-General but as Father-Superior of the Congregation, she took up her abode on the hill formerly sanctified by the Sons

---

[1] On the 12th of Dec., 1860, after the Crimean War, a colossal statue, representing Our Lady of France, was placed on the summit of Mont Corneille. This statue, which, with its pedestal, is 76 ft. in height, was cast from cannon captured during the War.

of St. Bruno, and in the very cloisters redolent of the virtues of departed generations of Saints.[1]

There the Sisters lived at first in extreme poverty. In addition to their school duties and the other employments of their vocation, they had to engage in the weaving of silk, the general industry at Lyons. A little milk, which took the place of wine, served also as the sole, the universal remedy in illness. The Sisters vied with one another in abnegation, mortification and Divine love, so that the little Thebaid of Saint-Etienne flourished again on the hill of St. Bruno, who delighted to behold in his holy cloisters such imitators of his departed religious. "I know how to be hungry and to suffer need : I can do all things in Him who strengtheneth me," were the words of St. Paul, re-echoed by this holy Superior and her worthy daughters.

"The higher a building is to be raised," says St. Augustin, "the deeper must its foundation be laid." "The highest rests upon the lowest," adds the author of the Imitation. Behold why humility, abnegation, and austerity were the foundation-stones of that edifice, destined, as it were, to be the dome of the Congregation, to serve as a Pharos to show to it the path of life. For a building of such an elevation, one destined to support such weighty burdens, extraordinary depth of foundation was a necessity. It is, then, the glory and solidity of the Mother House to rest on such basis ; and the respect of the Congregation was won by its being a model of regularity and true religious spirit, from the hour of its commencement. Seven years later, in 1823, Mother St. John purchased the neighboring Chateau of Yon, rich in traditions but greatly fallen into ruin. By dint of prudence and economy, she was enabled to make extensive repairs, and

---

[1] This hill, on the left bank of the Saone, opposite the Holy Mountain or Hill of Fourvière, is called the Hill of the Chartreux, because, formerly, on its summit, stood the Chartreux, the magnificent ruins of which are still to be seen.

even to construct additional buildings ; she, herself, with a wisdom and skill which won the admiration of the architect and workmen, overlooked all the details of the work, which, when completed, was blessed by the Father-Superior.

The Chateau of Yon is at present the *Pensionnat* of the Mother House ; the other building serves as the Normal School, the charge of which Lyons has, for many years, confided to the Sisters of St. Joseph.

But when God accepts a work, He impresses on it the sign of the Holy Cross ; and He permitted that after so many trials and difficulties, Mother St. John should meet her reward in this Divine acceptance. When Father Bochard had examined all the arrangements, he found the windows too large, in his opinion, for a religious house, and he blamed the Superior very severely. " You," said he to Mother St. John, " will, with the older religious, take up your abode in the new buildings. The novices and young Sisters shall remain in the cloisters, separated from you and under another Superior, exclusively charged with their direction."

Humbly, silently, and on her knees, Mother St. John received this harsh decision, which seemed to rend her heart by dividing her community ; which separated her young professed from their older Sisters, who were to be their models, and which tore her from that beloved novitiate to which she clung as the nursery, the hope, the life, the future, of her whole religious family.

Bitter, indeed, was the trial ; and despite the sorrow, tears, and incessant prayers of the whole community, it lasted for more than a year, until Mgr. de Pins arrived at Lyons. During all that time of trial, Mother St. John's humility and obedience were heroic. A true Christian, she knew that a bruising of the heart is good : it is a cross, —the cross is ever fruitful !

Resting on the Hill of the Chartreux, fronting on Fourvière, incessantly exposed to the vivifying looks of her who is called " Mother of Divine Grace," the Mother House of the Sisters of St. Joseph could not fail to become a home of benediction, a centre of life and spiritual fecundity. Hence it was soon decreed, by superior authority, that the local communities of St. Joseph should depend on and obey the House at the Chartreux as daughters of the same Mother. This important decision, given in 1828, made the Mother House a grand religious metropolis, on which depended a host of other houses, through which the rays of its sanctity and charity were to be diffused through the provinces of France. Thus, in former times, had shone Cluny, at the head of two thousand abbeys, the glory of their country, the ornaments of the Church. Advancing daily, by rapid strides, in the way of sanctity, and upheld by God, with whom her soul was constantly united by prayer, the venerable Superior kept pace with the requirements of her position. Potent in good herself, she had the rarer talent of winning others to its accomplishment. That God might be better known and loved was to her, as to the great Apostle, a consuming desire. How rejoiced, then, she was to find herself surrounded by fervent and zealous co-workers ! Among them, there was none more earnest, none who better seconded her designs than her worthy assistant, Mother St. Francis. She was an ardent, generous soul, whose zeal and self-devotion were unbounded. Strictly united with her Superior in views and intentions, she rivalled her in her efforts to maintain peace, humility, union with God, fidelity to prayer and labor, in a word, that union of the contemplative with the active life which is laid down in the Rule of the Sisters of St. Joseph. While thus sharing the burden and trials of her Mother, it was her endeavor to lighten them as far as possible, and often, under difficult and painful circumstances, to take upon herself the pain and embarrassment attendant thereon. When, for instance, alterations were being made in the Chateau Yon to render it fit for the Sisters' purposes, it was found necessary to open windows on the court-yard of the Missionaries of the Chartreux. The right, the necessity of doing so, were incontestable, no one denied it, yet it was a difficult matter to adjust, and one which called for great delicacy and address. Foreseeing this, the good Assistant took advantage of the fatigue from which her venerable Superior was then suffering to beg her to retire for a time to some convent, where she would be free from the incessant business of the Mother House, saying that she would have the repairs effected during her absence. Mother St. John yielded to her entreaties, and Mother St. Francis urged on the workmen and bore, herself, the annoyances and vexation inevitable under such circumstances. On her return, finding the work completed, Mother St. John understood and appreciated the ruse of filial love, and tenderly embracing her daughter, blessed God for the spirit she had shown. Ah, it is only those who love our good God above all things who know truly how to love and serve one another !

But God, whose designs, ever wise and adorable, are, at the same time, impenetrable, willed to deprive the Mother Superior of this beloved daughter, and at a time when her aid and counsel, amid the greatest difficulties, seemed more necessary than before. So sensibly did Mother St. John feel this loss, that, for a time, she thought it would be impossible to continue her work. But God, who wished, doubtless, to wean her heart more and more from every earthly affection, aided her by His grace: her faith triumphed, and with many tears, she made her sacrifice to God. "O my Lord," said she, "Thou didst give her to me to aid my insufficiency; Thou hast taken her from me; blessed be Thy Holy Name ! But deign, also, O Lord, to give us one whose virtues, mind, and qualities may replace her for whom we mourn." And He who strikes but to heal, heard the prayer of the sorrowing Mother, by giving her as assistant Sister St. Claire, a most fervent religious, who, imitating the devotedness of her predecessor, applied herself to perform all the duties of her position in the presence of God, with God, and for God.

Prayer was Mother St. Claire's attraction ; it was her delight, her solace, her stay. Every moment that could be snatched from her duties found her prostrate before the Blessed Sacrament, whence she drew from the Heart of Jesus the spirit which characterized her. Mother St. John was, under God, the soul of that fervor, the source of that Divine heat, for she applied herself zealously to cultivate, enlighten, console, sustain, and guide her Sisters to that perfection to which God called them. Hence it was that souls, enamored of the Divine love grouped themselves around her as satellites, receiving through her their light, and finding happiness in moving and acting with her and beside her in the exalted sphere of perfection and good works.

The first Mistress of the novitiate at Lyons was Mother Scholastica, a chosen soul, acting in all things under the inspiration of grace, and possessing, in an extraordinary degree, the gift of discerning vocations and spirits, and of leading hearts with most perfect tact. In the Christian life, over and above the precepts, there are counsels ; beyond mere duties lies perfection, a realm vast and undefined, wherein the religious may, wherein she must, advance daily until death. The power of leading souls step by step to the very heights of the perfect Christian life was a grace conferred by God on Mother Scholastica. Her gentle sweetness and amenity of disposition won for her the hearts of all her novices ; to lead them to God by the charms of holy love was the end and aim of her direction and instruction. "Let us do everything for the pure love of God," she used frequently to say. "Oh, let us, with all our heart, love the Spouse of our souls; then, indeed, every sacrifice will become easy to us." In truth, "love lighteneth all that is burdensome," says the Imitation. "It carrieth a burden without being burdened; it flieth, runneth, rejoiceth; it is free and cannot be restrained. Love lighteneth all that is burdensome, and maketh all that is bitter sweet and savory. . . . It performs and effects many things, where he that loveth not, fainteth and falleth prostrate." Led by this spirit so strong and yet so sweet, the novices learned to seek their happiness in self-immolation, while, with holy eagerness, they responded to their Mistress' efforts to form them to the solid virtues and true religious life of the early daughters of St. Joseph. The strength, light, love, and respect for souls necessary to the accomplishment of a ministry so sublime and difficult, the fervent Mistress found in continual union with God. To visit this dear novitiate, in which souls were learning to consecrate to the God of love all that love had given them, was Mother St. John's rest in fatigue and joy in trial, for she found it a nursery of true religious, souls worthy of love, souls necessary to the rising Congregation of St. Joseph. To the novices themselves the visits of their venerable Superior were occasions of rejoicing, and with avidity they drank in her instructions, so full of the spirit of God, so eloquent of His love. "Never," says a Sister trained in that novitiate, "never have I heard the vocation of a Sister of St. Joseph spoken of as by our Rev. Mother St. John. We novices hung on her lips, and treasured in our souls the words she uttered." Trained in the old-time school of religious perfection, the Rev. Mother not only had an experimental knowledge of all that the words suppose, but she had the power, God-given, to make others view it in the same true light. Our Blessed Lord Himself tells us that the path to Heaven is narrow, straight, and thorny ; that the Christian life is a life of labor, a workshop wherein are wrought out what shall give us a right to Heaven. That celestial kingdom is not to be a donation ; it is to be a reward : one cannot enter therein as to a public garden or promenade.

It is a fortress gloriously grand, magnificently, divinely beautiful, that must be fought for, that must be taken by assault. "Only the violent bear it away," says the Holy Scriptures. Virtue and perfection, then, must bear the sweat of toil upon their brow. To win the souls under their guidance to a love for such holy labor, such blessed fatigue, was the aim of both Superior and Mistress, an end which they attained rather by example than precept, for. as the Spouse of the Canticles says: "Draw me: we will run after thee to the odor of thy ointments." When there was question of her dear novitiate, Mother Scholastica counted difficulties, pain, and trouble as naught. Her zeal rose above fatigue, and to give holy religious to the Institute she would have cheerfully laid down her life. And such a sacrifice God deigned to accept. Immolated by labor on the altar of Divine love, she, day by day, wore herself away ; day by day her strength failed, her voice grew fainter, and at times inaudible; yet the flame of love increased its intensity in that holy soul, until, at last, consumed in its blessed fire, she died with her arms in her hand, laboring, until her last sigh, for the honor and service of the Divine Spouse, the Beloved of her soul. The extent, the bitterness of such a loss none knew so well as Mother St. John, yet she was obliged to crush and conceal her own feelings, in order to console, encourage, and support the community and especially the novitiate, inconsolable at such a deprivation. Happily, holy souls flourished and abounded in that Mother House under the impulse and influence of the

Superior-General. Mother St. Ignatius, who was called to continue Mother Scholastica's work, was a religious whose austerity towards herself was equalled only by her meekness and consideration for others. By her humility and love for the hidden life she was, as it were, a violet whose odor was diffused over the whole garden of St. Joseph. But this spirit of retirement concealed a virile soul, a character true and generous, capable of the most heroic sacrifices. Worthy of that Mother in whose soul the strength of martyrs was to be found wonderfully combined with the lovely simplicity of childhood, she suffered not the work of the novitiate to languish, and the *nursery* of the Congregation of St. Joseph continued to send forth numbers of souls trained to religious perfection, souls tried and true, who were destined to carry the Institute far and wide, and render it one of the greatest and most beautiful parterres of God's holy Church. Under Mother St. John's government, Mother Ignatius was succeeded by Mother Stephanie and Mother St. Xavier: the former died Superior of Givor; the latter, of Saint-Veran; both have left to the community a heritage of saintly memories. The good work was carried on by Mother Mary Dorothea, who, with angelic purity and virtue combined "the wisdom of the serpent and the gentleness of the dove," according to the admonition of the Lord. Appointed afterwards Visitor-general, she, like the dove of the ancient ark, bore from house to house the olive branch of peace. Communities vied with each other for her possession, but Heaven itself was desirous of her, and by an early death she entered into her eternal reward.

Nor were the class-mistresses less imbued with the spirit of their Mother, less one with her in heart and soul. Sister Delphine, the first, bent all her energy to the accomplishment of her Superior's lightest wish, regarding her will as the will of God. Her confidence in Mother St. John's judgment was absolute, and her filial affection so great, that what the Apostle had said of the Galatians[1] might well be applied to her, since she counted no thing a sacrifice that could aid her Superior. Sister Mary Antoinette, the Mother-General's faithful secretary, whose duties brought her into the closest and most intimate relations with her Superior, conceived the highest veneration for her virtues; and, beholding in her the worthy representative of our Lord, esteemed it her glory and honor to render those services for which her excellent disposition, cultivated mind, and rare talents so well fitted her. Of fatigue and privation she made no account, and when the day sufficed not for the accomplishment of her duties, she cheerfully sacrificed her rest. When unable longer to serve in the active life, she consummated, in the repose of the cloister, a life of devotion, disinterestedness, filial and Divine love.

We have not touched upon the labors and sacrifices of Sister Febronia, who aided her sister in the direction of the novices' classes; nor on those of Sister Teresa, who, although older than the Superior-General, her sister, was ever her most humble, obedient, and devoted child. All looked to their Mother with the confidence of veneration. United in her, united with one another, they drew from her direction the same impulse, the same religious spirit, the same love for our Lord, devotion to the Blessed Mother and St. Joseph, with which she herself was replenished. "It is only Saints who can lead others to be Saints." Near her, the weak became strong; the timid, courageous; the faint-hearted, bold and energetic; for under her engaging simplicity and good-nature, they recognized a heart that loved, a knowledge most enlightened, a wisdom inspired from above, a prudence that foresaw and prevented, a sanctity that communicated itself. "To speak worthily of our Mother," exclaims one of her venerable daughters, "one should hold the pen of genius."

---

[1] Gal. iv. 15.

One can well understand that so much good was not operated by Mother St. John without her having to encounter trials, contradiction, and the cross. We have already seen her severely reprimanded, humbled, nay, even put in penance, like a young novice, for an act which even those who condemned it were obliged to acknowledge later as praiseworthy, for the windows whose size had drawn upon her the censure of Father Bochard had to be still farther enlarged, to meet the requirements not only of modern taste, but even of the laws of health.

Rev. Father Charles Cholleton, nephew of the priest of that name before referred to, succeeded Father Bochard as Grand Vicar of Lyons and Superior of the Sisters of St. Joseph. He procured the admission to the Lyons novitiate of a young lady of exceptional talent and rare acquirements. Anxious to speedily utilize her varied attainments, he insisted that, whilst still a postulant, she should be employed as one of the teachers in the novitiate. Such an extraordinary mark of confidence did not fail to greatly increase the young lady's natural pride and self-sufficiency. Her actions, her conversation, her claims to preference, of which she spoke even to seculars in the parlor, her whole conduct, in a word, was so eccentric, so utterly at variance with the spirit of a religious, that Sister Delphine and Sister Febronia, the class-mistresses, could not, in conscience, despite their deference to Father Cholleton, vote in favor of his unworthy protégé, and she was rejected at the Chapter.

The Grand Vicar, being persuaded that their objections arose from mere prejudice, if not even from jealousy, insisted that the two religious should be sent away from the Mother House. This command fell like a thunderbolt on Mother St. John, for she foresaw that it could not but prove detrimental, nay, injurious, to the course of instruction organized in that dear novitiate, on which depended the future of the Congregation.

Thus banished from the Mother House, the two Sisters were, moreover, assigned to very difficult and painful positions, Sister Delphine to one that would inevitably have ruined her health. Mother St. John, who had promised the father that she would act as a mother towards his daughters, felt obliged to procure her removal to a place more favorable to one of her feeble and delicate constitution. But as to Sister Febronia, she, by wise and prudent advice, simply encouraged her to obey blindly and simply, without remark, observation, or delay.

As the local Superior to whom the latter was sent was unfavorably disposed towards Mother St. John, her position was one of great delicacy ; but so prudently and holily did this worthy niece act, that not only were the prejudices of the Superior dispelled, but they gave place to sentiments the most religious and most elevated. For, going to Mother St. John, she cast herself on her knees, and humbly begging her pardon, conjured her to forget the past, and not to withdraw her niece, whose conduct and virtues had so greatly edified all the Sisters, and so happily enlightened and undeceived herself.

Thus did God, who draws good out of evil, bless and recompense the sacrifice of the good Superior, whose profound humility, perfect obedience, and prudence, as well as those of her persecuted nieces, were soon clearly revealed. For, after their departure, that same postulant who had given rise to the suspicions regarding them had to be dismissed from the Congregation, all means tried for her improvement and perfection having failed.

Undeceived at last, Father Cholleton recognized his error, and failed not to render due tribute to the prudence and virtue displayed by the Superior and Sisters concerned in the matter; and, to the end of his life, he preserved the utmost esteem for Mother St. John, and the greatest confidence in her judgment.

CHAPTER IV.

THERE is no more saddening, nay, more terrifying, characteristic of modern society than the want of love that is revealed everywhere around us. The world, in this respect, has become almost a barren waste, a frozen desert. Consequently, it is with a sense of relief, a feeling of happiness, that one meets with souls elevated, generous, unselfish, devoted, as was that of Mother St. John.

"There is nothing truly great save goodness," says Bossuet. The heart rules the faculties; and, according to a great master of the spiritual life, "all beauty, whether physical or moral, is imperfect, unless it is good." Such was the character of Mother St. John's charity and tenderness to her daughters, that each believed herself the recipient of special marks of affection. In her heart there was no forgetfulness : no matter how far business carried her from home, no matter how anxious, occupied, or embarrassed by multiplicity of affairs, if she heard of or saw anything likely to be useful or pleasing to her children, she tried to procure it, and would carry it to them with all a mother's unselfish delight. When she went abroad on ordinary occasions, she would herself purchase little delica-

cies for those who needed them, for the teachers, especially, whose wearisome and often painful duties are so trying
to the health, courage, and patience.

An aged Superior, still living, is accustomed to tell that
during her novitiate she was allowed to have for her lunch
only a piece of dry bread; but that often on going
for it to the refectory, she would find some fruit or other
tasty morsel put with it in her drawer. For a long
time she was at a loss how to account for the indulgence,
but finally perceived that Mother St. John, to whom, at
meals, a little extra was sometimes given on account of her
great age, used to deprive herself of it in favor of her
delicate little novice. The Mother-General's charity and
goodness were not restricted to those whom she might, in
some sense, claim her own ; but their beneficent influence
was exerted on all with whom she came in contact ; and,
by the charm of her intercourse, many souls were drawn
to her family of St. Joseph.

Two young girls of the same family were anxious to
enter the religious life, for which they felt great attraction,
but the age and circumstances of their father presented a
seemingly insuperable obstacle to their wishes. Convinced
of the solidity of their vocation, and also of their possession of qualities likely to promote the glory of God, the
Mother came to their aid. On receiving the daughters into the novitiate she installed the father as gardener to the
convent. By her kind consideration, her careful provision
for all his wants, she filled, until his death, the place of
the children whom he had given to God, and thus assured
both his and their happiness for time and eternity.

Another young girl, whose mother was dependent on her
for support, felt an ardent longing to enter the Congregation. Having obtained the consent of her ecclesiastical
Superiors, Mother St. John gave the mother a room in the
convent, and charitably provided for all her necessities, to

the astonishment and gratitude of mother and child, who could not sufficiently bless and thank our Lord for having raised up for them such a benefactress. To be able to do good to others was Mother St. John's delight; and God, who knew that the dearest wish of her heart was the increase of that novitiate on which the future of the Congregation depended, was preparing, as the reward of her charity, a great and holy consolation.

Near the Mother House there lived a family esteemed and revered by all who had the honor of its acquaintance. It bore a name honored and blessed throughout the Church, —that of St. Bernard, the glorious Abbot of Clairvaux; but, better still, it reproduced his virtues and renewed the memory of his and his brothers' extraordinary vocations.

The parents were fervent and devout Christians, whose faith and courage had been put to the proof; their whole ambition was to make their children Saints, and God crowned their desires. Mother St. John fully appreciated the worth of the Bernards, who, on their part, loved and reverenced her as a Saint, as the following anecdote will prove. When, on one occasion, M. Bernard was giving instruction on the Christian Doctrine to his children, he told them that our Lord Jesus Christ had died to save man, and that through His precious death alone man had acquired a right to Heaven. On hearing this, the youngest child, who, in her simple veneration for Mother St. John, could not believe that she could have been included in the general reprobation, expressed herself to that effect. On being undeceived, she burst into tears at the very thought that she, whose rare virtue had made so deep an impression on her childish heart, could, under any circumstances, have been damned. Such veneration could not remain barren : the result was that not only this child, but all her sisters, felt irresistibly drawn to the Congregation of St. Joseph. As the eldest daughter had been educated by nuns of another Order, the father objected that, perhaps, gratitude would require a preference for her former religious home. "No, father," she replied; "my desire is to be the child of Mother St. John. Her virtues have won my heart. Give but your consent, and my happiness will be complete in having her for my mother." Her six sisters followed the like attraction, so that M. and Mme. Bernard gave seven daughters to God in the Congregation of St. Joseph. One son remained to them, but, he, like Samuel, consecrated himself to God, and entered the ecclesiastical state. Blessed and happy the family which produces such children! As St. Bernard's arrival at Citeaux with his numerous band of holy companions diffused joy thoughout that ancient abbey, so the entrance of these seven sisters into St. Joseph's Novitiate filled the heart of the Rev. Mother with supernatural joy, while, at the same time, it delighted, encouraged, and stimulated the fervor of her novices. All those young ladies were models of Christian virtue and the religious life; one still survives and is Superior of an important mission of the Congregation. Is it not grand and inspiring to see, in modern times as in those of St. Bernard, families of such generosity, such Christian enlightenment and wonderful sanctity?

"Charity seeketh not her own; charity never faileth," and in Mother St. John's heart there was pity, compassion, and generous help for every suffering or sorrowing member of Jesus Christ. The better to discover and assist those unfortunates, she organized a band of Sisters adapted to such work by nature, character, and grace. Well indeed and wisely had St. Francis de Sales and St. Vincent de Paul foreseen the wants and circumstances of our times, in which, to use the expression of St. Bernard, faith becomes acceptable only by her works of charity. Man, in proportion as he loses faith, becomes like the animal, sensible only of what flatters his body.

On this account, charity is become an apostolate, and virginity, through which it is exercised, a veritable priesthood, which cares for the body in order to reach the soul.

Prayer, mortification, and penance are no longer understood : men enamored of sensual pleasures esteem a thousand times more highly what is done for the body than any service that can be rendered the soul. The heart which fails to understand the cloistered and contemplative Orders understands, nevertheless,—when not wholly spoiled or influenced by sectarian hate,—the religious who dresses the sores of the poor, soothes their sorrows, dries their tears, and, becoming a mother without ceasing to be a virgin, harbors and nourishes their children. And this all the more, because epochs the most eager for material pleasure are, also, the most fruitful in catastrophes and misfortunes that call for bitter tears.

In thus, then, organizing her Sisters for works of charity, the Superior-General was but carrying out the inspiration of God. Under her wise regulations, the religious were to be found at the bedside of the dying, in the loneliest and most infected attics, carrying help to the unfortunate, giving medicine to the sick, food to the hungry, garments to the naked: mingling, with corporal alms and attentions, that spiritual assistance all the more necessary because unsought for.

The religious in such a ministry, says a philosopher, reminds one of a swan walking beside a stagnant marsh, with pure and stainless plumage ; or in the more expressive words of Benedict XII.: " She is the morning star, shining in the midst of a fog." "She is, as it were," says another grave author, " the beacon of innocence and purity shedding its Divine rays over the abyss of human depravity." From such angelic hearts an odor of grace, sanctity, and edification is exhaled over the world.

It was in view of this salutary influence that Mother

St. John, acting on the advice and entreaty of Rev. Father Cholleton, gave several of her religious to the Lyceum at Lyons, where they were to attend to household duties and care for the sick. But here below, in Christianity, above all, says a great Bishop, nothing can be done without contradiction, suffering, and the cross. Mgr. de Pins, who had for some time been absent, blamed, on his return, the concession made to the Lyceum, and severely reproached Mother St. John for having, in this case, been wanting in her usual prudence and tact. Strong in her humility, the Mother-General received the Bishop's reproaches with the most religious respect : she made no attempt to justify her conduct, and did not even speak of the wish, nay, the formal orders she had received from the Grand Vicar, in regard to the work.

God, who exalts the humble, rewarded her delicate charity and humility. Every undertaking must be blessed by God, says a holy prelate, otherwise it is good for nothing : now what so powerful as humility in drawing down the blessing of Heaven ! This Mother St. John was on this, as on many previous occasions, to experience. The virtue and prudence of her daughters, rendered the more forcible by the tender devices of their charity, operated wonders in the Lyceum. Example is more powerful than precept, for, as says the proverb, " Words move, but example draws." As the tree is judged by its fruits, so the Sisters, revealing, by their blessed works, the power and beauty of our Divine religion, led both masters and pupils to recognize, respect, and love it, while they admired the simplicity, modesty, and indefatigable charity which it inspired. The sick, especially, regarded the Sisters as tender mothers, and the care they lavished on the body often gave them entrance to the more diseased soul.

Among the pupils of the Lyceum at that time were two young Jews, one of whom was stricken with malignant small-pox. It is needless to say that his masters fled from him; his parents and the Jewish Rabbi refused to visit him, and the doctor himself gave his prescriptions at a distance. The Sisters of St. Joseph, alone, remained night and day by his bedside, tenderly watching over him, soothing his pain, until they led him back to life even from the shadows of the valley of death. The impressions thus produced on the mind of the patient were shared by his brother, one in heart and soul with him. In such heroic charity, practised in the name of Jesus Christ, they recognized the marks of the truth. Their conversion to Catholicity thus begun was happily perfected, and to-day, the two Fathers Lemann are priests, missionaries, and apostles of Him in whose name, and for whose love, the Daughters of St. Joseph took the place of their natural mother. Nature is inferior to grace; yet grace admits the concurrence of nature, since the gifts of God never contradict, they harmonize.

The charitable care of the sick and infirm has ever been a favorite work of the Catholic Church, the beloved employment of her Saints. Mother St. John earnestly recommended it to her Sisters, and it was obedience to her counsels and directions which won their success in the Lyons Lyceum.

But if charity diffuses its perfume abroad, it is prodigal of its Divine sweetness " to those who are of the household of the faith," and Mother St. John was now to have an opportunity of putting in practice the admonition of the great Apostle.[1]

An epidemic broke out in the Mother House, and many of the Sisters succumbed to its ravages. The Mother, ever attentive even to the slight indispositions of her children, was overwhelmed with grief. Prayers, visits, vigils, reme-

---

[1] Gal. vi. 10.

dies, the most celebrated doctors,—nothing was spared that was likely to avert the danger or lessen the virulence of the scourge. She caused an infirmary to be fitted up near her own room, so that she could watch over the administration of remedies, and hear the slightest moan of her dear invalids, to whose succor she would immediately run. The number soon became so great that, to relieve the infirmarians and assure continued attendance on the sick, she was obliged to call on the other Sisters. Fearless of danger, and undismayed at the prospect of death, so many eagerly pressed their services, that she had to moderate their zeal, and choose a favored few from among the crowd so desirous of self-immolation. But maternal care and tenderness proved unavailing where God exacted the sacrifice. Many of the Sisters died, and the sorrow of the afflicted Superior was so great as to draw tears from all who beheld her. Prayers and sacrifices were incessantly offered to procure the cessation of the scourge, and every moment left free from her ministrations to the sick, found the Mother prostrate at the feet of her crucifix or before the Divine Tabernacle, weeping and pleading with God for the pardon of her sins, which, she said, had drawn down the Divine vengeance on her house.

She implored prayers for this intention at Fourvière, La Trappe, and all the religious communities of Lyons, as well as from all holy souls whom she knew. Moved by so many fervent supplications, God permitted that a very distinguished physician should discover both the cause and remedy of the disease. The epidemic ceased, and sadness, grief, and desolation gave place to joy, gratitude, and thanksgiving. "To those who love God all things work together unto good;" joy and sorrow are alike susceptible of sanctification, and the rejoicing of that spiritual family was as edifying as had been its grief.

But besides maladies and accidental infirmities, people

have to bear with those that are the result of years and labor. Life wears us out ; every hour takes from us some portion of our strength and existence. Life is made up of our vanished hours, says St. Gregory Nazianzen, whose own existence was but a continual death. We shall become aged ; we shall wax old as a garment, says the Holy Spirit.

Labor is a law imposed alike on the good and the bad. Adam, even in his innocence, labored ; and he who disobeys the law, descends by rapid strides from idleness to weariness and disgust, thence into moral disorder ; hence the axiom, '' Idleness is the mother of vice.'' Labor, on the contrary, even while making time pass quickly, sanctifies and renders it fruitful ; but it also exhausts and enfeebles the bodily powers.

'' When, then,'' says Father Lacordaire, '' we have paid the debt of labor, and arrived at the term of old age, repose is befitting, and we can enjoy it, with the blessing of God. The rest of the laborer and the aged is a right, a dignity.'' Around a life of sanctified labor, above all, there glows an incomparable aureola. Nothing is more venerable, nothing more touching than the sight of an old and faithful worker in the school of Christ. Hence, the Holy Spirit, so sparing in praise, is prodigal in regard to the aged.

'' One great cause of regret for old age is,'' says Mme. Swetchine, '' that our Lord has not sanctified this period of life by passing through it Himself. It is the sole age to which He has not bequeathed His example.'' The Divine plan had other magnificent views, of which St. Paul gives us only a glimpse.[1] To Mary, His beautiful Mother,—Mary, whom, in His gentle sweetness, He has drawn nearer to our miseries,—to her He has left the mission of

---

[1] Eph. iv. 13.

being the model of Christian old age. Those who grow old shall meet their Mother in the retired pathways of life, hidden in a little house on Mount Sion, in the company of St. John, who there celebrates the Sacred Mysteries, and gives Holy Communion to his adoptive Mother. There, in that retreat, she prepares herself for her departure to Heaven.

To afford to her daughters, enfeebled by age and worn out by laborious service in the cause of God, religion, and mankind, such a place of retreat, such a home of precious and holy memories, was Mother St. John's ardent desire. While her eyes and heart were occupied in seeking, in the neighborhood of Lyons and Fourvière, a spot which, to her cherished invalids, should be what Mount Sion was to our Blessed Lady,—a place of repose, of prayer, of union with God and preparation for the great voyage from which they would never return,—her soul offered ardent prayers that our Lord would, in His Providence, provide the necessary means for its acquisition. Nor was He deaf to her entreaties. He enabled her to purchase at Vernaison, in the suburbs of Lyons, on the banks of the Rhone, a beautiful country-seat, endowed with every charm that salubrious atmosphere, delightful scenery, sparkling waters, and vivifying sunlight can impart.

She would not have thought a palace too good for those daughters, majestic by their age, labors, self-devotion, and virtue. But everything must have a beginning. Hers it was to lay the foundation : Mother Sacred Heart was, later, to continue and develop her work, whose enlargement has been necessitated by the extension of the Congregation, as well as by the greater enfeeblement of constitutions in our day.

Death follows, nay, often anticipates old age, but it had not the power to remove Mother St. John's loved ones beyond the sphere of her affection. Faithful to the requirements of her holy rule, she procured for the dying every help and consolation, spiritual or temporal, that could soothe their passage to eternity. Nothing could tear her from the bedside of the agonizing. There she persevered in incessant prayer, suggesting aspirations and encouraging the departing one to suffer holily, by holding up her crucified Jesus as her Model, and Heaven itself as her recompense. She was accustomed to assemble the Sisters around their dying companion, that while receiving in that solemn moment a lesson and a warning, they might, by their united suffrages, afford consoling help, and, like their Divine Master, "love their own even unto the end."

To those who love in God, absence brings not forgetfulness ; and faith, overleaping the bounds of time, gives aid and comfort even in eternity. Not content with the suffrages obligatory in the Congregation itself, Mother St. John would implore prayers and sacrifices in other religious communities. We have read hundreds of letters written by her under such circumstances, wherein she weeps and loves as did our Lord at the tomb of Lazarus. Under beautiful and varied forms she reminds her children of those great truths which the Holy Spirit recommends to the reflection of faithful souls : It is a holy and wholesome thought to pray for the dead. Think of your last end and you will ever be ready, for death comes like a thief in the night. Nothing defiled shall enter Heaven : in Heaven alone can the soul love perfectly :—hence the necessity of procuring release to those souls, so that they may enter Heaven, and become our intercessors with God.

For, as Mgr. Plantier beautifully says, "the Saints' concurrence to the works of God ceases not when they depart this earth ; it is transformed ; it is elevated : servants of God as they were upon earth, they become protectors in Heaven." In view of this double end,—to give help and consolation to her beloved dead, as well as to increase the number of protectors before God, Mother St. John procured many Masses in sanctuaries the most highly venerated and most richly privileged. The soul of that daughter latest called from life seemed to be her *chosen one*, because she looked on it as the most necessitous. "One hour in purgatory," says the Imitation, "shall be more terrible than a hundred years of most rigid penance upon earth."

What a contrast between religion and the world! "In the world," says the Imitation, "when one passes out of sight, quickly also is he out of mind;" which has made a wise man say: "Distrust the world; the absent stay not long in the heart."

Ah, the Church, our Mother, forgets not the absent, the dead! Her teaching in regard to the departed is not a dogma alone; it is the charm of life, the consolation of the bereaved heart. Nothing is so sweet, so beautiful, so thoroughly human as the Communion of Saints, which unites us, even after death, to those whom we have loved in life.

CHAPTER V.

IN the meantime, in the midst of all her holy undertakings, Mother St. John suffered a privation which nothing could lighten, a sense of loneliness ever on the increase. In the depth of her heart resounded ever these words which the author of the Imitation puts in the mouth of our Lord: "If thou wishest to be with Me, I wish to be with thee;" to which she responded: "Deign to dwell with me, O Lord; I ardently desire to be with Thee. All my desire is that my heart may be united with Thee."

This insatiable longing was to have our Lord under her roof, in the house, as a father in the midst of his children, for hitherto the Mother House had possessed no chapel, not even the Divine Tabernacle. For the Church offices and other devotions the Sisters were obliged to go to the parish-church, where, indeed, they continued their blessed apostolate, preaching by their faith and profound recollection to the edification of their fellow-worshippers. But their heart suffered from the absence of their Beloved; and, like the Spouse of the Canticle, they cried to Him with all their strength. Their loving invocation: "Come, Lord Jesus, come quickly," rose incessantly before the throne of grace.

To procure the necessary means for the realization of their hope, neither Mother nor daughters thought any economy or privation too great : love never counts the cost.

The veneration won for Mother St. John and her community by the odor of sanctity which pervaded it, led many charitable persons to contribute to the work ; and the blessing of Divine Providence multiplied the means in her hands, so that, as one of her Sisters expresses it, *she could do very much with very little.*

Soon that chapel, the object of so many earnest prayers and sighs, was erected. It consisted of a nave sufficiently spacious for the wants of the community, a graceful and beautiful sanctuary, two chapels dedicated to the Blessed Virgin and St. Joseph, and a place whence the sick could assist at the Church offices.

What the ancient tabernacle was to Moses, this chapel was to Mother St. John, and with the Prophet she could exclaim : "Lord God of my heart, I have cried before thee night and day." Thither she went to seek her Stay and her Light, her Teacher in the science of the Saints and her Director in doubts; there she plunged herself into the Heart of Jesus, the ocean of love, whence she came forth imbued with Its spirit of charity, zeal, and benignity. Nor were the daughters less eager than their Mother to pay court to Him who dwelt in their lowly Tabernacle; in His presence they inhaled, as it were, a breath, a breeze from Heaven, which their hearts again exhaled, laden with the odors of humility, sanctity, and piety which pervaded the whole convent.

"Godliness is profitable to all things, having promise of the life that now is, and of that which is to come," says the Apostle St. Paul,[2] which words were fulfilled in the Superior General, by her wise and prudent temporal administration.

We acknowledge that the Chateau Yon, the House of

---

[1] This structure has since been replaced by a beautiful church, magnificently frescoed and adorned, and large enough to accommodate the numbers of religious who flock to Lyons for their annual retreats.

[2] I. Tim. iv. 8.

Retreat at Vernaison, and the Chapel at the Mother House were not then what they are now. but human affairs are progressive; the beginning cannot be the end. Rome, to use a familiar expression, was not built in a day, and to realize what, under her government. was really effected, one must bring himself face to face with the ravages and destruction wrought by the Revolution, and the extreme poverty of the Congregation in her day.

Obedient to the Scriptural admonition, " Owe no man anything." she had an abhorrence of debt ; and her punctuality in paying the workmen, her care in looking after them and providing for their wants, made them revere her as a true mother. Providence, undoubtedly, generously aided her in her difficulties. for without Its aid what can be done? Yet, as says the Imitation, one must first do his part, and God will do the rest. In this case, one becomes associated with Divine Providence. By wise administration, love of labor, and holy poverty, Mother St. John and her Sisters merited to be the associates of Divine Providence ; and this explains how their undertakings, accomplished in the midst of distress, were so beautiful, so solid. and so fruitful.

But her Divine Associate was more clearly to reveal His co-operation at a time when, all her available resources having been exhausted in the purchase of Vernaison, she was called to save an important work of charity, the Providence de la Croix-Rousse, near the Mother House. The benefactors and sustainers of this institution having died, the heirs—not indeed inheritors of their charity— wished to annul the will which assured definitely the present and future existence of the work. To preserve it from destruction, Mother St. John undertook to pay for the house the sum of forty thousand francs. Here surely was reliance on Divine Providence, and a just reliance, since the community agreed to redouble their labors, privations, and economy; persuaded that, their part accomplished, Providence would do the rest. Who has hoped in God and been confounded? Their confidence was not deceived; and their obligations were fully and honorably discharged.

The great and important work of the re-organization and unification of the Congregation of Lyons under a Superior General was effected, almost without contradiction, by Mother St. John's spirit of prudent conciliation. Many convents which had at first raised opposition were won by the sight of the general contentment: the reputation, above all, the visits of the good Mother, soon dispelled their prejudices, and calmed their fears. A particular community, somewhat better off in regard to temporalities, held itself aloof, from a fear of the control which centralization would exercise over superfluities. Mother St. John, who was personally unknown to the Sisters, claimed their hospitality as a religious travelling from Lyons; at the same time she expressly forbade her companion to reveal her identity. They were received with most cordial and religious affection, and the Mother *incognita* charmed the whole community by her amiability, exquisite tact, and profoundly religious spirit. So far was she received into their esteem and confidence that they begged her to use her influence to obtain some concession in favor of *their particular circumstances;* which she promised in all simplicity, frankly and willingly.

All that they saw of her so increased their respect and veneration that, as she was about to depart, one of the Sisters exclaimed aloud: "I do believe she is Reverend Mother St. John herself." The smile which this sudden exclamation won from her travelling companion, attested its truth, and told the community the treasure they had in their possession. No one would hear of her departure: the Superior and Sisters entreated her to remain with them for some time. She consented, and the result was that she wholly gained their hearts, dispelled every fear, and won their complete adherence to the government of such a Mother. Her visits to particular houses were productive of immense good, infusing sentiments of charity, confidence, and peace. Soon they grouped themselves lovingly around Le Chartreux, and that Congregation has ever since been distinguished for its filial love for the Mother House and the Superior General.

In the meantime, the Sisters of St. Joseph at Le Puy could not but envy Lyons the possession of her who had been Superior at Monistrol, and the beloved daughter and friend of their Bishop. On the other hand, Mother St. John felt a natural attraction and legitimate affection to that community to which she had been bound by birth, education, early religious life, and later trials and sufferings. A wholly unforeseen circumstance led to mutual testimonies of affectionate regret.

Being, on one occasion, on a journey, the Mother General found that, much against her inclinations, she would have to stop at Le Puy. As the Constitutions oblige the Sisters to lodge at the houses of the Congregation, if there be any within reach, she sought hospitality from the Sisters, hoping that, as none knew her personally, she might pass unnoticed. Orders not to reveal her identity were given her companion, and they presented themselves merely as two religious from the House in Lyons. As might be expected under such circumstances, the conversation turned on the Mother Superior of Lyons, who had so long been a member of the Institute at Le Puy. None of the Sisters had ever seen her, but they were thoroughly acquainted with all her past history, her life, and her virtues, and congratulated their guests on the happiness of having such a Mother. Continuing to speak of her actions and of her profoundly religious spirit, they put Mother St. John in a most embarrassing position, from which she vainly tried to extricate herself by adroitly changing the subject.

Finding this ineffectual, she said that their praise was exaggerated; she herself knew Mother St. John to be a very ordinary person, that she had seen nothing wonderful in her manner of life. At this juncture, an aged Sister, who had been a member of the community previous to the Revolution, but whose infirmities had hitherto prevented her appearance, entered the room. On beholding her who had once been her Mother, she cast herself into her arms, shedding tears of joy, and blessing God for thus allowing her to see once again the object of her love and gratitude. This scene, so surprising to the beholders and withal so touching, was followed by another far more painful to the heart of the Superior General. Overwhelmed with joy at the thought of possessing her whose worth they so well knew, the Sisters formed the project of keeping her with them as a pearl which belonged to their community rather than to that of Lyons. In the midst of the family rejoicing, from which the good Mother could not withdraw herself, the religious of Le Puy hastened to the Bishop, to implore his power and mediation, both with Mother St. John and the ecclesiastical authorities of Lyons.

But all was unavailing. God, by the voice of His vice-gerents, had spoken, and revealed His will by the course of events at Lyons. Tearing herself from the arms that tried so lovingly to retain her, she returned to those beloved children whom God, as in the case of Job, had given to console her for those lost by means of the Revolution.

Thus we see the great work of the restoration and unification of the Congregation of the Sisters of St. Joseph at Lyons, conceived, decided, and decreed by the ecclesiastical Superiors, carried out and happily consummated by Mother St. John. As a diocesan Congregation, it claims as its head and first Superior and Father the Angel of the

Diocese, the Archbishop of Lyons, who delegates his authority to one of his Vicar-Generals, who bears the title of Superior General or Rev. Father of the whole Congregation of Lyons.

With the concurrence of these Spiritual Fathers, and under absolute dependence on the Archbishop, Mother St. John, as Superior General, directed the spiritual and temporal matters of the Congregation, aided by an Assistant General, and a council of her most prudent and experienced daughters.

Regular classes for the instruction of postulants or aspirants were opened, as also one general novitiate, wherein the novices were trained to the religious life. This was a most potent means of procuring desirable uniformity in discipline, and that unity of spirit which realizes, as far as is possible to human weakness, that wish of our Divine Master: "That they all may be one, as Thou, Father, in me, and I in thee, that they also may be one in us." [1]

Admirably situated in the City of Mary, and established on the ancient hill of Saint Bruno, on a level with and directly fronting the sacred hill of Fourvière, the Mother House and Novitiate of the Congregation of St. Joseph is continually exposed to the sweet and vivifying glances of our Blessed Lady. It would seem that Mary wished to have constantly under her maternal eyes the beloved family of her holy Spouse. And is it not, in some sort, the right of the Sisters of St. Joseph to occupy the blessed and happy position of their Father, who lived with Mary, and daily met the glance of her pure and holy eyes ?

Sharers, also, in a grander privilege, they, like St. Joseph, dwell under the same roof with Jesus ; possessing

---

[1] John xvii. 21.

in their midst, in the Sacrament of His love, Him who was the joy of the Holy House of Nazareth, who is the eternal delight of the heavenly court.

By the establishment of Vernaison for the aged and sick, and by other works of charity heretofore spoken of, Mother St. John fulfilled that second commandment which our Lord declares to be "like unto the first,"—the love and service of one's neighbor.

Spiritually, temporally, administratively, all was then wisely accomplished in the restoration of the Congregation; —yet all was done in poverty, austerity, and humility, without ostentation or noise; all in the spirit of St. Joseph, with which the Mother General was so truly replenished.

It remained but to preserve, perfect, continue, and develop it by the like means and in the same spirit.

The continuation of this Life will prove that Mother St. John was animated by Him who, as the Apostle St. Peter says : "begins, continues, perfects, and consolidates whatsoever He hath done."

Third Book.

Mother St. John's administration and direction.—Wonderful increase of the Congregation of Lyons.—Its numerous and glorious spiritual offspring.

CHAPTER I.

Mother St. John's labors for the consolidation of her work.— Her love of regularity.—Wise disposition of affairs.—Admirable extension of the Congregation.— Important services rendered to the Church by the Sisters.

IT has been well and justly said, that, while it is much to conquer, it is far more to know well how to use the victory, by organizing, consolidating, and developing the conquest. By dint of humility, labor, wisdom, and prudence, Mother St. John had met and overcome all those difficulties which rise in hosts to attack holy and Christian works.

To found and firmly establish the Mother House, to lead communities, hitherto isolated and independent, to affiliate themselves to it, was a reform, useful, nay, even necessary, as we have seen ; a reform on which depended the consolations of the present, the hopes of the future, yet one that could be brought about only by the simplicity of the dove combined with the prudence of the serpent.

For a new creation often costs less than the uniting and reconciling of particular works, which, although all tending to the same end, have yet, from time immemorial, attained it, each in its own way, in accordance with its aptitudes, conveniences, and tastes. It is, as it were, to form a body united, young and vigorous, out of aged and scattered members. Such, as we have seen, was the happy result of Mother St. John's labors ; it remained now but to perfect, develop, and extend them abroad. From that blessed summit of St. Bruno, from the cloisters of the Chartreux, as from the fountain-head, were to flow those streams which to-day irrigate and fertilize the provinces of Lyons, Touraine, Vendée, Provence, Aquitaine, Dauphiné, Corsica, Savoy, Piedmont, and America. The reputation of the saintly Superior of Lyons drew thither many chosen and beautiful souls, which, like grace-laden clouds, rested on that privileged hill, and fed with their pure waters that beneficent source.

To maintain the purity of that source, Mother St. John accounted pain and labor as gain. Her own life was a mirror of religious perfection ; age, labor, fatigue, infirmities, multiplicity of duties were excuses which she never suffered to interfere with her fidelity to the least points of her rule.

Accompanied by her assistant and counsellors, she would strive to be first at the general exercises; and thus, animating others by her example, she established the most perfect order and regularity in the community.

Her visits to local houses were productive of the same beneficent results: the fervor of the Sisters was reanimated, fidelity to employments, punctuality to the exercises, to the rule and to little things—those tissues of which life is composed, and to which God attaches such a value—were increased; wheresoever she went, the religious life rose, as it were, to its level, and its most beautiful flowers sprang up wherever she trod.

Exterior practices of the rule are, to piety, what the bark is to the tree. Remove the bark from a branch, and it will speedily become dry; strip it from the trunk itself, the tree will wither away. The bark apparently is but a rough and coarse envelope, yet by its agency the strength and vigor of the tree are preserved. In like manner, it is by external regulations which often seem harsh and annoying, that the vigor of the internal spirit is preserved.[1] Hence that maxim of the spiritual life: "To live holily and for God, one must live according to the holy rule."

Thoroughly penetrated with these sentiments, the Mother General insisted on regularity, of which she herself was the first to give the example. On this point she was immovable. It was this preaching of example that gave to her orders. nay, even to her slightest suggestion, an irresistible power. "When Mother St. John had spoken," writes one of her daughters, "all was said. We obeyed promptly and cheerfully. When she reproved, we felt, we recognized our errors, and had only one desire, that of making reparation."

One day, after having recommended to the Sisters the observance of little things, because all that is done in conformity with the Divine will and for the love of God is truly great, adding that those who failed therein ought to impose some penance on themselves, it happened that she went to the kitchen, entering which, she forgot to close the door. The Sister-cook, then busily engaged, felt the current of air, and, without raising her head, said : "Sisters who leave the door open have to kiss the floor." Mother St. John immediately knelt down and performed the penance. Looking up. the poor Sister beheld the Superior General prostrate on the ground. Overwhelmed with confusion, she offered a thousand excuses, but the

---

[1] Dupanloup, *De l'Education.*

Mother simply and pleasantly replied : "I had committed the fault ; it was but right I should perform the penance."

Authority is never so strong as when upheld by the humility and obedience of her who exercises it. "To command safely and well," says the Imitation, "one must know how to obey." This principle is the key to the ready obedience, the respect and deference accorded by the Sisters to Mother St. John's decisions. There is no part of the Superior General's charge more difficult or more delicate, none more exposed to the clashing of various interests, than the removal or assignment of Sisters to the different missions. To the performance of this duty Mother St. John brought such simplicity and uprightness, such purity of intention and unselfish goodness, as disposed every one to obedience ; and even those least favorably situated could not but recognize that human considerations had no share in her decisions.

Before making her allotment, she took all things into consideration : age, services rendered, proofs of zeal, devotedness, knowledge, and capacity either for teaching or the direction of a house, health, climate, character, all were duly weighed and harmonized as far as is possible to human weakness. Her correspondence, her letters conveying counsel and encouragement, helped to perfect these arrangements, for in them she went directly to the point ; she showed such a clear knowledge of difficulties, such foresight in arrangement, as left nothing to chance or arbitrary interpretation. "I beg, Rev. Mother," writes the curé of an important parish, "that you will answer my letter yourself. Two lines from your pen is more satisfactory than two pages from your good secretary."

If her correspondence was productive of such results, what may we not suppose was operated by her presence, her conversation, her intimate personal communications? "How happy we were," says one of her aged religious, "under the direction of our venerable Mother! There was a rivalry among us as to who should be most obedient, most humble, and most mortified. Her example was continually impelling us to good, even to perfection. To see her profound humility one would have thought her the least and the last among us. Such she really was in her own estimation; hence, the lower she abased herself, the deeper grew her children's veneration and loving respect. "When on meeting her we used to salute her," writes one of her first daughters, "we experienced something of the feeling one has in passing before the Blessed Sacrament."

Another tells us that when, during her novitiate, she used to behold her venerable Superior eating off the floor in the middle of the refectory with the humble simplicity of a little child, she was unable to restrain her tears. "I have often seen her," says another, "kneeling at the chapel door on Good Friday, with a rope around her neck, and kissing the feet of the Sisters."

What an admirable thing it was—the effect, as well as the privilege, of true sanctity—to find this respect and veneration intensified the closer one was brought by duty or office to this worthy Mother! With the votaries of the world, it is the reverse. The greatest geniuses, the grandest minds, sometimes lose prestige as one gets a closer view of them, on which account a great wit has said that a certain distance is a varnish necessary to set off human greatness. The idea is more commonly expressed by the saying, "No man is a hero to his *valet-de-chambre.*"

Virtue, on the contrary, like the aroma of a flower, is perceived but the more sensibly the closer we approach to it.

Among Mother St. John's children was to be found no faction, no coterie, no party; her heart was large enough to embrace all, and, like the Apostle of Nations, she, by becoming all to all, bound them in closest union, *cor unum.* Ah, blessed union! union of hearts! The sacrifices necessary to accomplish it! These were her continual theme, the lesson she strove, daily, to impart. For, such is humanity, that even among the elect on earth dissimilarities of character are to be found; and amid the thousand incidents of common life, there must, inevitably, be some jar to our feelings and susceptibilities. "However holily peopled, however happily regulated a monastery may be," says Mgr. Gay, "it is but a laborious school of perfection. It is not a dwelling inhabited by angels; it is not yet Heaven."

Eminently worthy as was the Mother General by her personal character of her Sisters' filial devotion, she won it, also, by her own deference to her Superiors. "To fill well the first place," says the Imitation, "one must know how to take the last." In relations with Superiors, no Sister was more humble, docile, or submissive than she. Their will, their decisions, their slightest wish, was to her the expression of the Divine will, of which she would not omit or alter one iota. Blame, severity, coldness on their part she considered less than she deserved; their praise or commendation she looked upon as the effect of their goodness, not of her deserts.

How she conducted herself under severe and unmerited censure, as in the case of Rev. Father Bochard and under a year's painful penance, we have had occasion to allude to heretofore.

Her silence and abnegation, yet more, her sentiments of self-accusation, were heroic; all had been, she said, the result of her self-sufficiency, her pride, her want of judgment.

It was this generous and profound humility which drew down the Divine benediction on her undertakings, for He who "putteth down the mighty from their seat," loveth also "to exalt the humble."

Her intimate and continual union with God was another source of heavenly blessings. She undertook nothing without consulting Him. "Like Moses before the tabernacle," say her daughters in America, "she had incessant recourse to God by prayer. Our Lord in the tabernacle was her Adviser, her Counsellor." It is not, then, surprising that her subjects recognized and loved in her will the will of God, before whom they saw she placed everything.

The interior life, intimate union with God, the hidden source of piety and wisdom, have been compared to those subterranean streams which reveal themselves by the coolness they diffuse, and by the brilliant verdure which clothes the soil under which they flow. Union with God, the interior life is the life of Mary ; the active exterior life is that of Martha. They are sisters, they should dwell together, one sustaining the other. The interior life is the soul, the strength, the light of the active.

With Mary, Mother St. John knew how to rest at her Saviour's feet and hear His words ; yet, at the same time, she could occupy herself actively, with Martha, in the divers cares imposed upon her. It was these combined forces which gave to her administration its grace, suavity, wisdom, and efficacy.

In her hours of prayer she loved, with St. Paul, to contemplate Jesus in His Passion, on the cross : *et hunc crucifixum.* We have already said that in Christianity there is nothing without the cross, without suffering. One would often wish to arrange things otherwise.

We make plans wherein everything succeeds to our desires ; everything is grand, magnificent. But God has not in such ways wrought out our salvation ; the crib and the cross were different things. "There must of necessity be sickness, contradictions, sometimes even false brethren and treason," says a holy bishop. . . . "The works of God are operated amidst such things."

The cross is, then, the practical lesson of life. Mother St. John had experienced the truth of these words of the Imitation : "In the Cross is salvation ; in the Cross is life ; in the Cross is protection from enemies ; in the Cross is infusion of heavenly sweetness ; in the Cross is strength of mind ; in the Cross is joy of spirit, the height of virtue and the perfection of sanctity." [1]

These sublime lessons of the Cross were the constant theme of her meditations, her great school of humility, patience, sweetness, sacrifice, and love.

In truth, nothing is so well calculated to render a soul generous, energetic, valiant in good, as devotion to Jesus Crucified. How could she dread pain or fly from it, when her heart habitually turned to that Jesus who had shed His blood for her sake ? "I judged not myself to know anything," writes the incomparable Apostle, "but Jesus Christ, and Him crucified." [2]

" O you, whoever you be, who have not, perhaps, the happiness of sharing our faith, if with us you will not adore the Cross, at least forbear to insult it !" cries out a holy Bishop. [3] " For, I ask you, where should we go, henceforth, to learn the secret of forgetting your injustices, where learn to pardon, to love you ? Where would the afflicted seek consolation, the enfeebled look for strength, penitents for mercy and pardon ? In pity for the hosts of unfortunates who people this valley of tears, in pity for the sick, the dying, for *the people,* of whom you are incessantly talking, in pity even for yourselves,—for there will come a day when, abandoned by all upon earth, you will find the Cross of Jesus your only resource in pity,—we implore you, then, no longer to insult it !"

After Jesus, Mother St. John sought refuge with His Blessed Mother Mary. Although she dwelt on the Hill

---

[1] Imit. Bk. 2, 12.　　　[2] I. Cor. ii. 2.　　　[3] Mgr. Dupanloup.

of Chartreux, one could see that her heart ever turned to Fourvière, to the privileged shrine of her Mother.[1] Pilgrimages to that sacred spot were the delight of her life, and even at the age of seventy, when her health was seriously impaired, it was her custom to steal out, long before dawn, from her convent, and fasting and barefoot, to climb, unperceived, the heights of Fourvière, where she would hear Mass, communicate, assist at a Mass of Thanksgiving and return in time to preside at the community exercises. The obligation of secrecy as to these pious excursions she used to implore on her companion, lest discovery should lead to her being debarred from a practice in which she found such holy delights. It is a principle of our holy religion that the Blessed Mother is the Dispensatrix of grace. Bossuet, in his time, thus spoke of this sweet truth, one of the consequences of the Divine maternity. " God," he says, " having once willed to give us Jesus Christ by Mary, will not change this order, because the gifts of God are without repentance. It is, and it ever will be true, that, having received by her the universal Principle of grace, we shall receive, through her agency, its divers applications in the different states and situations of Christian life. Her charity having so greatly contributed to our salvation in the mystery of the Incarnation, which is the universal principle of grace, she will contribute to it eternally in all those operations dependent upon it." Hence we see that, as God is the principle, the primary source of all grace, Mary is its instrument, its channel.

---

[1] Rev. Dr. Northcote, in his work on *The Celebrated Shrines of the Madonna,* relates that, in 1834, while the sanctuary of *Fourvière* was in the hands of a sacrilegious mob, the Superioress of the Sisters of St. Joseph (who, at that time, was Mother St. John) had the inestimable privilege of being able, under God, to save the Blessed Sacrament from profanation, and the sacred treasures of the sanctuary itself from the rapacious hands of the insurgents. Her success, which, under the circumstances, was little less than miraculous, was due, undoubtedly, to Our Lady's protection of her courageous client.—Translator.

God is its Author, Mary its Dispensatrix. Actuated by the like sentiments, Mother St. John, even from the break of day, had recourse to Mary. hoping for the accomplishment of her promise in the Book of Wisdom: "I love them that love me, and they that in the morning early watch for me shall find me."[1]

"Let him that is just," says St. John in the Apocalypse, "be justified still ; and he that is holy, let him be sanctified still." In this respect the Saints are very dissimilar. Some, like St. Mary Magdalen, St. Jerome. and St. Augustine, have been converted to God after years of sin and error. Others, like St. Teresa, having begun well, have for a time relaxed their efforts. Both these classes have, according to the prophet, hastened their march towards Heaven, to redeem the time lost. Many, on the contrary. like St. Francis de Sales, and St. Jane de Chantal, consecrated to God from their birth, have continually advanced in virtue without delay or relaxation. To this latter class did Mother St. John belong.

Childhood, girlhood, womanhood, and old age were all but stages of her spiritual life. She had placed, as it were, a mystic ladder in her heart, which she ceased not to ascend step by step, even to its very summit.

Thus did she prove herself a worthy daughter of him whose name signifies increase : *Filius accrescens Joseph ;* and by her continual, undeviating progress in perfection, she merited that the like advancement should attend her undertakings ; for as the Holy Scripture says, the Lord punishes oft in those things wherein man has sinned, so, also, does He act according to the same just law in recompensing merit.

St. Jane de Chantal, whose entire life was an ascension to the heights of sublime sanctity, was granted to behold,

---

[1] Prov. viii. 17.

in her own life-time, a prodigious increase of her monasteries of the Visitation, of which she left eighty-six at her death.

St. Teresa, at the close of her mortal career, could count sixteen monasteries of Barefooted Carmelite nuns, and fourteen of friars, either founded or reformed by her.

The humble Superior of Lyons had the happiness of founding two hundred religious houses of the Congregation, without counting the numerous colonies which went forth from the same source, as we shall see later on, to edify and sanctify distant lands.

Lyons, Mary's own city, has always loved and sought after the Daughters of St. Joseph. We have seen how, previous to the Revolution of '93, she had entrusted to them nearly all her charitable institutions. To these, after the rehabilitation of the Congregation, she added others by placing them as adoptive mothers in her Lyceum, and appointing them teachers and directresses of her normal school for girls. Thus she has constituted them, in a great measure, the guardians of her happiness, of her future well-being. Would that other cities would profit by this salutary example, and thus save France from the evils about to be entailed on her through the domination of infidel and irreligious partisans!

Their aim—no longer concealed—is to substitute laics for religious : to banish the latter from the school, the orphan asylum, the hospital. Now religious, having neither husband, children, nor relations around them, have more leisure for study and class-preparation.

Their minds, free and disengaged from family cares, have more energy, more spirit and aptitude for intellectual and scholastic pursuits.

Again, their pure and virgin hearts are given wholly to their duties and their pupils. The latter are their family, the beneficiaries of those zealous and affectionate cares of which the lay instructor is, justly, most prodigal to his own private circle.

Let us, for the moment, consider the different phases of the lay instructress' life : as a young girl, expecting marriage ; as a bride ; as a wife and mother ;—do such conditions appear favorable to the self-sacrifice, the study necessary to a successful teacher ? Do they not rather convey ideas of preoccupation, of cares and solicitudes incompatible with a teacher's obligations ?

There are, no doubt, exceptions, but exceptions serve but to prove the rule. It is on this account that, in many places of the United States, married women are ineligible to positions in the public schools.

The religious virgin, on the contrary, has no interests that militate against those of her class. The school-room is to her a sanctuary, wherein, even more than the ancient vestal, she is bound to feed and increase the sacred flame of virtue and knowledge. Free from the trammels of social life, she can devote to school, asylum, or hospital, every hour of her life; she is ready to undertake the greatest sacrifices, even unto complete self-immolation, which is not to be expected from a wife or mother, save in the case of her own family. This consideration has drawn from M. Waddington, a Protestant, and Minister of Public Instruction in France, the significant avowal: " Among the Congregationists, self-devotion is the rule; with seculars, the exception."

So thoroughly did the comprehensive mind of the First Napoleon grasp this principle, that he incorporated it in the constitution of his lay university, as will be seen from Article 101 of the Decree of 1808: " In future, masters and censors of lyceums, principals and regents of colleges, the teachers also in such colleges, shall be bound to celibacy and the common life."

But such a parody could not long exist. True religious, virgins not in name but in reality, are the offspring of faith and the grace of God imparted by the sacraments. Such peerless jewels gleam only on the brow of Christ's immortal Spouse, the Church.

It was these exceptional advantages of the religious state which made the convents and monasteries of by-gone days shine out as beacon-lights in the darkest and most critical periods of European history, as both Balmes and Guizot, two of our most celebrated modern philosophers, declare. " To deny this," says Father Monsabre, " is to invite the counter-blows of history, and to suppose that men are so insensate or so indolent as to swallow, unquestioning, the errors and slanderous misrepresentations of our revolutionary adversaries, as though there were no historical documents to disprove them."

Yes ; notwithstanding base calumnies to the contrary, the Church has ever labored for the enfranchisement, the enlightenment of the people; whereas the infidel, the free-thinker, by the pen of his acknowledged patriarch, Voltaire, declares that " the people are not made for instruction, for reason .... that no one has ever pretended to enlighten servants or shoemakers ..... that is the part of apostles ; and that the portion of the laborer or artisan is *the goad, the yoke, and a little hay.*"

Of all Catholic creations none has been more glorious, more fruitful, and more beneficent than the various Congregations of Brothers and Sisters devoted to the education and care of youth.[1] Religion says to them: " I wish you to become laborers in the cause of popular education. That you

---

[1] Since everything pleads so powerfully in favor of schools directed by religious, why are our rulers so eager to secularize the schools ? Ah, it is not hard to reach the concealed motive ! To banish God and the idea of religion is their ultimate aim, to attain which they see but one way,—to dechristianize the education of youth. Religious teachers defeat their satanic scheme ; they must then give place to seculars, among whom the most irreligious are often the most sought after and applauded. Whence it follows, says M. Chesnelong, that laicization means the dechristianizing, the demoralizing of the school.

may be wholly consecrated to this work, you shall bind yourselves to God by the three grand acts of religious renunciation. You shall possess neither family joys nor priestly
honors. Your lives shall be spent in poverty and obscurity,
in labors continuous, wearisome, unrecognized, and unap-
preciated. But your work shall be noble, your recompense,
glorious; and you shall be sustained in all dangers, under
every difficulty, by two grand motives, the love of God
and the love of man."

Under the influence of such sublime lessons, Mother St.
John and her daughters entered on the educational and
charitable works which the Department of the Rhone—
then less occupied with politics and more wisely attentive
to its best interests—eagerly and gratefully confided to
them.

In the Department of the Loire, the venerable Mother
had the consolation of founding one hundred and fifteen
houses of St. Joseph. Falling on good ground, the labors
of the Sisters have brought forth fruit in the numbers of
young persons eager to embrace the life and emulate the
virtues of their instructresses. Families have glorified
God for the religious vocations of their members, and
gladly made the sacrifice of the brightest ornaments of
their home and hearth.

After a pastoral visitation of his diocese, comprising the
above-mentioned departments, Mgr. de Pins, astonished
and delighted at the good effected by the Sisters, hastened
to the Chartreux to congratulate and thank Mother St.
John and the Congregation. But she, referring all glory
to God, blessed Him for having deigned to employ such
unworthy instruments for the good of the Church and the
salvation of souls.

The Departments of the Rhone and Loire were not the
only places fertilized by the prayers and toil of her Sisters.
Corsica, Hérault, La Vendée, Poitou, Aude, the Lower

Alps, Creuse, Saône-et-Loire, Isère, Côte-d'or, and Allier soon became harvest-fields for the Daughters of St. Joseph.

Thus does God bless humble souls ; thus have the virtues and humility of the Superior drawn down the Divine benedictions on the poor labors of her subjects, who attribute their success only to "Him who giveth the increase."

CHAPTER II.

THUS, like a tree that flourishes in rich and fertile
soil, the Mother House at Lyons continued,
every year, to strike its roots more deeply, while
it developed new and vigorous branches, whose delightful
shade and delicious fragrance attracted numbers of souls
enamored of the beauty of the Divine Spouse, and eager
to contract their spiritual nuptials under the protection of
the glorious Patriarch St. Joseph.

In the words of Ecclesiasticus, it might have said: " I
have stretched out my branches as the turpentine-tree,
and my branches are of honor and grace." For as
formerly the glorious Abbey of Citeaux employed its
superabundance of spiritual riches in establishing colonies
whose glory it was to be the Daughters of Citeaux, so from
the parent-hive of the Chartreux of Lyons began to go forth
swarms of zealous workers, bearing not only the name but
the spirit of St. Joseph on every side.

From 1823 to 1840 were successively founded three important colonies of St. Joseph, those of Belley, Gap, and
Bordeaux, under Mother St. Joseph Chanay, born at
Villefranche, January 12, 1795. Endowed from her earliest
youth with extraordinary gifts and graces, Mother St.
Joseph received the habit of St. Joseph and was trained to
the religious life in the community of St. Pierre-le-Vieux, as
we have before remarked. Having made her profession in

1817 at Chazay-sur-Ain, she was appointed directress of the boarding-school. Her virtue and zeal, which even then gave promise of apostolic vigor, operated marvels of grace and effected unhoped-for good in that locality, so deeply imbued with the irreligious spirit of the Revolution, as, even then, to expose priests and religious to daily insult.

Thoroughly convinced of her abilities, Rev. Father Bochard, in 1819, sent her to found a House at Belley, then a part of the diocese of Lyons. In giving her her obedience, he added: "You must, my good Sister, expect to encounter many contradictions, for no one in Belley wants the Sisters of St. Joseph." This was too true, as even the curé of the cathedral, M. Guillemot, and Father Bochard's own family, who resided at Belley, were most decided in their opposition to the Sisters. This was but poor encouragement for the heavy and delicate task which obedience obliged Sister St. Joseph, then only twenty-four years of age, to assume. Weeping and trembling, diffident of self, but confiding in God, she assumed the charge imposed by the Divine Will, and He whose ears are open to the prayers of the humble, blessed her undertaking in an extraordinary manner. Opposition vanished as if by enchantment, and Rev. Father Guillemot became the zealous friend, tender father, and devoted protector of the convent of St. Joseph. During the ten remaining years of his life, says the author of the Life of Rev. Mother St. Joseph, he never ceased thanking God for the "treasure He had given him *in spite of himself.*"[1] His confidence in Mother St. Joseph was unbounded; he took her advice on all matters, and there never arose between them even the shadow of a disagreement.

In 1823, the ancient see of Belley was re-established, and

---

[1] Life of Rev. Mother St. Joseph.

Mgr. Devie, Vicar-General of Valence, was appointed its Bishop. This holy and learned prelate, one of the greatest of modern times, recognized, at his first interview, Mother St. Joseph's rare merit, and the amount of good that could be operated through her, and he resolved to support her with the whole weight of his episcopal authority. It was his wish, however, that the Sisters in Belley should form themselves into a diocesan Congregation, independent of the Mother House of Lyons, and under the government of Mother St. Joseph. The first part of his plan was soon carried out: to succeed in the second was a more difficult matter.

Claimed, at once, by the Superiors at Lyons as a professed religious of that diocese, and by Mgr. Devie as necessary to the work he had inaugurated, Mother St. Joseph's heart instinctively turned to Lyons. But Providence having, by some extraordinary circumstances, manifested Its will, the authorities at Lyons yielded, and the youthful religious was installed as Superior General of Belley, where a novitiate had been previously opened by order of Rev. Father Bochard. This novitiate having been afterwards transferred to Bourg, the community has become generally known as the Sisters of St. Joseph of Bourg.

The zeal and devotedness of the new Superior rose in proportion to the obligations of her office, and so wonderful was the progress of the work, that at a retreat given at Belley, July, 1824, the religious numbered one hundred and twenty-seven. [1] At the close of this retreat Mother St. Joseph, through humility, resigned her office of Superior General, but was immediately appointed Assistant. A short time afterwards she was sent to Ferney to found a House of the Congregation. To prepare her for this ar-

---

(1) The Congregation of Belley now numbers 1625 religious, who direct 223 schools and numerous works of charity.

duous mission, Mgr. Devie had given her a course of special reading and instructions, directed mainly against the errors of Protestantism, with which the inhabitants were deeply imbued, and also against the impious ideas of the free-thinkers, who, in homage to Voltaire's memory, flocked thither from all parts of Europe. Those very people who laugh us to scorn for reverencing relics or performing pilgrimages to the shrines of our Blessed Lady and the Saints, see nothing ridiculous in their veneration of Luther, or their pilgrimages to the dwelling-place of a man as devoid of purity as of probity; as averse to faith and loyalty as to mercy and humanity.

Led by obedience and humility, Mother St. Joseph took up her abode in the little fortress of Voltairianism; and, armed with faith and ineffable charity for the miseries of the poor, she triumphed over all obstacles, and effected the good so much desired by the Bishop of Belley.

But the demon, enraged at the loss his cause thus sustained, endeavored to make even the charity of his implacable enemy redound to her confusion. From the arrival of the religious, the Protestants had regarded them with great ill-feeling, but their exasperation reached its height on beholding the ascendancy which Mother St. Joseph was daily acquiring among the people.

To destroy this influence they devised the following plan: On a certain day, they assembled together their most astute ministers and the principal inhabitants of the town; and then sent a message to the zealous and charitable Mother that a Protestant, at the point of death, wished to see her about his conversion. Accompanied by one of her religious, she hastened to the designated spot, only to find what a snare had been laid for her. Recommending herself interiorly to God and placing all her confidence in Him, she remained calm and tranquil, merely expressing her satisfaction at finding so many men thoroughly alive, where she had expected to meet only one in the agony of death.

Although this sally turned, for a moment, the laugh on her side, her opponents opened the attack by a running fire of calumnies against the Catholic religion, and objections to the religious state.

God, according to His promise, put into the mouth of his faithful servant such solid and unanswerable arguments, couched in the very language of Holy Writ, that her adversaries withdrew, silenced and abashed, from a contest in which they had hoped to be victorious.

Thus did God, who by the foolish things of this world loves to confound the strong, make use of a humble religious woman to bring to naught the stratagems of those haughty and over-confident sectaries.

When about to take her departure, Mother St. Joseph, turning unexpectedly to one of the gentlemen who had been most virulent in his attacks, said: "In you God will some day consummate His work, for you will become a Catholic, and will die the death of a Saint."

Laughing scornfully at such an unlikely prophecy, the party dispersed, inveighing loudly against "the indomitable fanaticism of that nun." But her words were literally accomplished; the gentleman himself came afterwards to Mother St. Joseph to declare the fact of his conversion; and, in 1851, he died a most holy death.

Many such special lights for the conversion of sinners were bestowed on Mother St. Joseph, but the details of these and other extraordinary graces are recorded in her Life.

In 1837, Mgr. de la Croix, Vicar-General of Belley, who, as Superior of the Sisters of St. Joseph, had co-operated in the undertakings of Mother St. Joseph, was appointed Bishop of Gap. Before taking possession of his see, he begged Mgr. Devie to allow her to found in Gap a novitiate, which should become the source of future establishments of the Sisters of St. Joseph. Great as was this sacrifice, the Bishop of Belley resigned himself to it in favor of his late Vicar-General, with the proviso, however, that, after five years' residence in Gap, Mother St. Joseph should return to Belley.

The Institute of St. Joseph had been established in Gap in 1671, twenty years after its foundation in Puy ; and, at the time of the Revolution, that diocese had possessed several communities. After almost half a century of interruption, Mother St. Joseph was called to link the present with the past, by the re-establishment of her Order in that part of Dauphiné. The early days of her foundation were days of difficulty, trial, and extraordinary privation, not only of food and common necessaries, but almost of a place of shelter. The sharp air of the Alpine region proved, also, very injurious to the already enfeebled frame of the Foundress. But God, who is the God of obedience, supported her ; and Divine Providence, on which she relied to an extent which seems audacious to human prudence, failed her not. Destitute as she was of both funds and provisions, she opened in poverty the novitiate of Gap, which, at the end of that year, contained thirty novices and postulants. She opened, also, a boarding-school and classes for day-pupils, which were numerously attended.

At the close of the annual retreat, Mgr. Devie, then on a visit to Gap, gave the religious habit to a large number of postulants, and received the vows of several novices. The holy prelate was affected even to tears, and rejoiced exceedingly at finding, amid the Alps, so vigorous and fruitful an offshoot from his beloved Congregation of St. Joseph.

At the expiration of her first three years' term of office, the state of Mother St. Joseph's health obliged her to return to Belley, but the Mother House and novitiate of

Gap were then solidly established, and affiliated convents had been opened.

At Aix, whither Mother St. Joseph was sent for the benefit of the baths, she had the inexpressible consolation of meeting Rev. Mother St. John of Lyons. To see, to consult, to listen to her whom Mother St. Joseph's biographer calls "the living tradition of the spirit and rules of the Order," was, as it were, to rest like a child in the arms of her Mother, and pour out her heart to one who could understand its sorrows. Mother St. Joseph had labored hard, had suffered much. In the future lay concealed a heavier task and more bitter sorrows, for, here below, all that is for good must be signed with the cross, the emblem of salvation. Was it not a sweet and loving act of Divine Providence, thus to bring together the aged Restorer of the Congregation and the young Superior, destined so greatly to augment its posterity? Who more proper to reanimate the courage of the latter than she who had had the strength to confess Christ and cling to her vows, in spite of trial, dungeon, chains, and threatened death?

Accustomed to recognize the hand of Providence in all the events of life, Mother St. Joseph profited by the occasion thus presented, of studying, as from the very fountain-head, the traditions and regulations of the Congregation; and, desirous of having the Sisters' habit conform in every particular to that of Mother St. John, she copied its every detail. The *guimpe* she at that time made, has ever since served as pattern to the Sisters of Bordeaux, which community was founded a little later by Mother St. Joseph.

Wonderful are the workings of Divine Providence! This woman, truly extraordinary, who had already accomplished so many works which revealed the impress of faith and charity, was, at that time, says the writer of her Life, regarded by her Superiors as a worn-out servant, a broken instrument, no longer fit, either physically or mentally, for the works of God. In the depth of her humility such also was her own opinion.

And yet, from the depth of this abasement, Heaven was about to call her to a most important undertaking, to the crowning work of her life !

Mgr. Donnet, Archbishop of Bordeaux, who, as Curé of Villefranche, had intimately known and greatly admired Mother St. Joseph, had been inspired by God to found, in his diocese, a novitiate of the Congregation of St. Joseph. To Mgr. Devie he looked for the help necessary to the work, and after much negotiation, he finally wrote : " Send to us, I beg, as soon as possible, that good Sister St. Joseph whom I have known for so long a time. If you can spare her a little colony of two or three Sisters, we shall be so much the better pleased."

Encouraged to assume the burden, Mother St. Joseph set out for Bordeaux, taking Lyons, however, in her way, that thus she might revisit the cradle of her religious life, and recommend herself, her Sisters, and her work to Our Lady of Fourvière, prostrate at whose feet she spent nearly an entire day. A Divine peace took possession of her soul ; God, by the hands of His Blessed Mother, seemed to bless the work, and to show her, in the future, a host of virgin laborers, who should devote themselves to the instruction of youth and the sanctification of souls.

On the 10th of December, 1840, Mother St. Joseph, with two companions, arrived at Bordeaux, where the third Sister joined them somewhat later. At the profession of one of these religious held in the chapel of the Ladies of the Sacred Heart, on the 23d of the same month, Mgr. Donnet said : " Look at these pious ladies, who have traversed France in answer to our appeal. I foresee that this day I plant in your midst the roots of a great tree. It is the mustard-seed of the Gospel. I drop it into earth, but

God will give it increase, so that one day you shall behold it overshadowing my whole diocese."

His previsions have been realized. The Institute of St. Joseph in the diocese of Bordeaux numbers, at present, three hundred and sixty religious, who have charge of three orphanages, seven boarding-schools, and about forty-four day-schools, including those under State control.

We pass over in silence the details of the work, remarking only, that in Bordeaux, as in Gap and Belley, its solid basis was the profound humility of the Superior, a virtue in which she had been most sedulously exercised by her directors, the Bishop of Belley especially.

A man of lively faith as well as a profound theologian, this prelate was far from rejecting her extraordinary supernatural gifts, but he feared the danger of illusion, to assure her against which he caused her to tread the path of constant humiliation. Thus did he prove her as gold is tried in the crucible, and strengthen in her soul that root of humility, from whose hidden sweetness the other virtues derive their heavenly odor. Her confidence in Providence seemed to others sometimes a tempting of God; but it was a filial boldness, to which His Divine Majesty so marvellously condescended, that Mgr. Devie was compelled to exclaim : "It is really wonderful ! Her course through life has been one continued miracle."

Of poverty she, like the Patriarch of Assisi, was an ardent lover. When, at the opening of Bordeaux, the Sisters' trunks formed the whole furniture of the convent, serving now as chairs, again as tables, and at night as beds, she was supremely happy ; and at Gap she rejoiced at the fact that she had not enough money to redeem a letter.

"Great order, rigid economy, many labors, many privations are," she used to say, "the strongest foundations of a religious house: and it is by these means we are enabled to assist the poor."

Speaking of St. Teresa's foundations, M. Boudon represents her as *in the midst of a forest of crosses.* The same may be said of the works undertaken by Mother St. Joseph. Long and painful illnesses, trials within and without, desolation and a sense of abandonment by God, threats of death,—all beset her path. On one occasion she gave vent to her feelings in the following words : " When I remember the inconstancy and injustice of men, even of Saints, I pray God not to let me live to make further proof of it. However, I will what He wills, and pardon everybody with my whole heart."

Worn out by the sorrows and trials attendant on three diocesan foundations, she died in 1853, in the odor of sanctity. A friend, unaware of her death, having asked M. Vianney, the saintly Curé of Ars, to say Mass for her restoration to health, he smilingly replied : " She is dead. She is no longer in need of it ; " and he refused to say the Mass. This proves that the holy Curè must have received special revelation of the death and eternal salvation of this predestined soul. Long and painfully had she labored in the harvest-field ; may we not believe that, when presented before the Father of the family, the Lord of the harvest, she heard the consoling words : " Well done, good and faithful servant ! Enter into the joy of thy Lord "?

" Going they went and wept, casting their seeds," says the Royal Prophet. " But coming, they shall come with joyfulness, carrying their sheaves."

We shall conclude this sketch of Mother St. Joseph's life by the testimony of the great Cardinal Donnet himself.

" Mother St. Joseph," he says, " was ever to her community a perfect model of the religious spirit. Her wise administration was visibly seconded by Heaven. To the world she has given an admirable example of piety and charity ; and to souls desirous of acquiring perfection, we may hold up her life as a realization of its most beautiful precepts."

CHAPTER III.

Mother St. John Marcoux founds the Congregation of St. Joseph in Oulias and Chambéry.—Development of that Congregation under Mother Félicité Veyrat.—Establishments in Denmark, Scandinavia, Russia and South America.—Foundations of Rome, Annecy, India, and England.—The Foundations of Ajaccio and other places in Corsica.—Mme. de la Rochejacquelin provides for establishments in La Vendée and Touraine.—The Sisters are asked for America.

IN August, 1812, Cardinal Fesch, who had accompanied the Empress Josephine and her court to Aix-les-Bains, was led to notice how deficient in religious instruction were the young girls of that town. After a consultation with Mgr. de Solles, Bishop of Mont Blanc, it was decided that a colony of the Sisters of St. Joseph from the Mother House at Lyons should be established there ; and at the Cardinal's special request, Sister St. John Marcoux, of whose rare educational talents he had had proof, was appointed Superior.

This young religious, born at Andance in Ardèche in 1785, was adorned with precious gifts of nature and of grace. Formed in the sweet school of the Cross, in the midst of that austere Community of the Rue de la Bourse, and under the direction of Mother St. John, she there imbibed those lessons of solid virtue which, in the designs of God, she was afterwards to impart to others. She it was whom we have heard proclaiming the joy and delights drawn in that blessed house from the bitterness of interior and exterior mortification.

In 1814, she was called to Chambéry, but on her return to Lyons in the summer of 1817, for the annual retreat, she was appointed to another mission which called for special virtue and talents. Her children in Savoy had recourse in their distress to the sanctuary of Our Lady of Myans, and she whose mediation has never been sought in vain, granted their petition. Providence permitted that obstacles should prevent the accomplishment of the proposed work, and Mother St. John was restored to Savoy.

In 1824, however, the Cardinal having resolved to found in Rome a house of St. Joseph under her direction, she was a second time recalled to Lyons, to prepare for her important mission. His project again, however, failed; and as Mgr. de Pins, Administrator of Lyons, then wished to establish the Sisters at Oulias in the Diocese of Albi, Mother St. John, with the thirteen religious originally named for Rome, was ordered to go thither. A true daughter of obedience, despite the attraction that drew her to her foundations in Savoy, despite the sorrow and desolation of her subjects there, she, without a word of objection, entered on her new charge. "It is necessary for my advancement in virtue," said she, "that I should renounce all that tends to my satisfaction in life."

At Saint Pons, a parish in the diocese of Montpellier, whose curé was a friend of Mgr. de Pins, several Sisters were left to open a house; the remainder continued their journey to Oulias. As an instance of that wonderful increase with which God has ever blessed the Institute, we may here mention that that colony to-day numbers three hundred religious, whose houses extend over the six Departments of the South, wherein they operate great good.

Mother St. John, however, remained but a short time at Oulias. God had destined her for a great work in Savoy, to which she was providentially restored in 1824. Mgr. Bigex, Archbishop of Chambéry, entered into an agreement with the Superiors at Lyons, whereby Chambéry became a separate diocesan Congregation, of which he appointed Mother St. John first Superior General. Establishments had already been made at Motte-Servolex, Turin, and Saint-Jean-de-Maurienne; others were now asked for at Pignerol, Moutiers, Montmelian, Saint-Pierre-d'Albigny, and divers other places.

The extraordinary virtue and charmingly simple manners of the new Superior, while proving her the true child of her spiritual Mother, gave her a wonderful and mysterious power of attracting souls to God. We have seen in what esteem she was held by Cardinal Fesch and all her ecclesiastical Superiors. Queen Hortense, the Cardinal's niece, who had become acquainted at Aix with the Sisters of St. Joseph, desired, ever after, to keep up a correspondence with their Superior. In the " Memoirs of Queen Hortense of Holland," by Mlle. Cochelet, we read: " The Queen was anxious to see and converse with the Sisters who had watched and prayed by the remains of her friend, the Baroness de Brol, after the sad accident that had deprived her of life. . . . Among those Sisters was one called Sister St. John, the Superior, who appeared to be truly an angel on earth. The Queen met her frequently and became greatly attached to her. 'Behold,' she would say, 'there, indeed, is true virtue on earth! And we, proud creatures that we are, are nothing in presence of such angelic abnegation. . . . . We must go sometimes to visit those worthy religious. From them we shall receive lessons of practical virtue, from Sister St. John especially; and it seems to us, we shall return improved.'"

If her success as Superior proved her admirable administrative talents, the closing years of her life, as a simple religious, revealed, more strikingly, the solid virtues and sublime self-annihilation of this true daughter of the Saint of Nazareth.

Resigning into the hands of the Archbishop of Chambéry, in 1843, her office of General Superior, she, by earnest entreaty, obtained permission to retire as a simple religious to the Community of La Bauche, where, for ten years, she edified the whole Congregation by her spirit of mortification, prayer, and obedience. Her favorite devotion, strengthened by the example and instructions of her early Mistress and Mother, was the adorable Passion of our Lord. " Oh, how she loved, in her last illness," write the Sisters of Chambéry, " to clasp to her heart the image of her crucified Redeemer! How eagerly she pressed it to her lips ! It was from the Crucifix she drew that patience and resignation which so greatly edified all the Sisters who waited on her. She never spoke of her sufferings, so that we were able to judge of them only by their outward effects." On the 10th of May, 1855, this true daughter of St. Joseph, this faithful lover of the humility and abnegation of the Cross, entered into her eternal reward.

Our sketch of the Congregation of Chambéry would be incomplete, did we fail to mention Mother M. Félicité, who, succeeding Mother St. John Marcoux, thoroughly organized the community, and brought it to that state of development which renders it, at the present time, so potent for good. This admirable religious, known in the world as Josephine Veyrat, [1] seems to have received in baptism not only the name but a supernatural attraction to devotion to St. Joseph. Educated in the *Pensionnat* of the Sisters of St. Joseph at Chambéry, she petitioned to be re-

---

[1] She was sister to the poet Veyrat, who, in his immortal Ode, *A ma Sœur*, in his most celebrated work, *La Coupe de l'Exil*, expresses his sentiments at her entrance into religion. To her exertions he was indebted for his recall from exile by the king, and for the still greater grace of restoration to the arms of his Mother the Church, in whose service he employed the later years of his brief life. (See *Un Poète Savoisien, Jean-Pierre Veyrat*, by A. Weiss, Geneva, 1884.)—**Translator.**

ceived into that community, which she entered in 1830, at the age of fifteen. Mother St. John was not slow to perceive her great natural and mental abilities, and extraordinary virtue, and she was appointed successively Mistress of Novices and Assistant. After Mother St. John's resignation, she, at the age of twenty-nine, was unanimously elected Superior, a choice which was confirmed by succeeding elections for forty-two years. Her Life, written by the Abbé Bouchage—from the second edition of which these details have principally been taken—presents a wonderful picture of her laborious and holy career, but we shall content ourselves with giving proof here of that extraordinary development to which we have alluded.

In 1854, she founded the Province of Moulins ; in 1856, that of Denmark ; in 1858, that of Brazil, South America ; in 1862, that comprising the houses in Norway, Sweden, and Russia, and in 1876, by annexation, that of Rome, which had been founded in 1839, as we shall see. These, with the Province of Chambéry, comprising in all ninety-two houses, and over eight hundred religious, she organized into a Provincial Congregation under the headship of the Mother House at Chambéry, for which she obtained the final approbation of the Holy See in a Brief of Pius IX., dated July 30th, 1875. During the terrible scourge of cholera, which in 1854 and 1867 desolated her country, this valiant Superior and her heroic Sisters offered themselves as public nurses ; seeking by preference the poorest and most desperate cases ; and in documents issued at that time by the different municipal authorities, we find ample and grateful testimony to the Sisters' self-devotion and efficiency.

In the disastrous war of 1870–71, Mother Félicité transformed the asylums into hospitals, installed the Sisters as nurses, and organized, under the presidency of the Countess de Beauregard, the Society of the Ladies of Mercy, to attend the sick and wounded.

"The privilege of a Superior," says Père Olivaint, "is to be a victim; he is constituted Superior in Jesus Christ for that end." In virtue of this law Mother Félicité's existence had been for years a series of infirmities, but the last sixteen months of her life were wholly spent upon the cross. During the Holy Week of 1885, she shared, even beyond what seemed the limit of human endurance, in the chalice of her suffering Lord. At last, fortified with all the spiritual graces of Holy Church, even the Benediction of our Holy Father, Leo XIII., which was telegraphed to her by His Eminence Cardinal Howard, the Protector of the Congregation of Chambéry, she entered into her reward on Easter Monday, April 6th, 1885, in the seventy-first year of her age, and the fifty-sixth of her religious life. Previous to her death, holding in her hand the blessed Sign of our Redemption, she blessed the Sisters individually, and her last words were: "O my daughters, let us be Saints: all is comprised in that."

Among the first foundations made from Chambéry, those of Turin, Saint-Jean-de-Maurienne, Tarentaise, Moutiers, Aösta and Pignerol, in the Sardinian States, have become independent communities, having their Mother Houses at the places above named.

The foundation in Rome, which Cardinal Fesch had failed to make in 1824, was brought about in 1839, under the following circumstances :

The pious Countess Luzof, the Austrian Ambassadress, having noticed that Rome, otherwise so richly endowed with societies and religious Orders, was still in want of some of the more recently founded Congregations, devoted to external works and the general service of humanity, was anxious to secure for the Eternal City this great advantage. To compass her object she employed the mediation of the Marchioness de Berol, who prevailed with the Superiors of the Sisters of St. Joseph [1] to send some religious to Rome. The first work undertaken was the instruction of poor children, whose numbers increased so rapidly that, in a short time, the building provided could no longer contain them. In her perplexity, the good Ambassadress had recourse to the munificence of Gregory XVI., to whose paternal goodness the Sisters are indebted for their house in the Via Maurino, near the Roman Forum.[2] They have, moreover, a *Pensionnat* and day-school at St. Mary Major, and three other schools in the city, besides the direction of the *Œuvres des Petits Artisans;* schools at Albano, Veroli, and Ceccano, with school and hospital at Ceprano. In 1876, the Roman Province, as before mentioned, became, by annexation, a part of the Chambéry Congregation.

The opening of the first House of St. Joseph in Annecy is due to that noble benefactress of the Congregation, the Countess de la Rochejacquelin, daughter of the Duchess de Duras, who, having been married to the Prince de Talmont, was left a widow at the age of eighteen. Made a sharer in the fortunes of the Bourbons by her marriage with Count de la Rochejacquelin, she was compelled to leave France after the Revolution of 1830. During her sojourn at Annecy, she grieved to find among the children, those of the lower classes, especially, an almost absolute want of religious education. The Bishop, while acknowledging the fact, deplored his inability to remedy the evil, destitute as he was of funds wherewith to provide schools and teachers. Great was Mgr. Rey's joy and surprise when the Countess offered to defray the expenses herself; and with grateful tears he blessed God for having sent him so generous a benefactress.

By a providential coincidence, the first house of the Visitation, called *La Galerie,* sequestrated during the

---

[1] Most probably at Turin.   [2] Mother House of the Roman Province.

Revolution, was then offered for sale by the family in possession.[1]

The Bishop rejoiced at being able to withdraw from secular hands that "parterre of religion," wherein St. Francis de Sales had watered "his lowly plants," and cared for "his dear doves," as he was accustomed to call his first Daughters of the Visitation.

Sharing in the Bishop's sentiments, the Countess hastened to make the desired purchase, and set on foot the repairs necessary to make the monastery habitable. As both Mgr. Rey and his noble coadjutrix were anxious to confide the good work to the Religious of St. Joseph, the former summoned from Pignerol, of which diocese he was the Administrator, several Sisters of the Congregation, whom, on their arrival, he received with truly paternal kindness, and lodged in his episcopal palace until their future home was ready for their reception. Schools for the poor were at once opened, and the visitation of the sick and other duties of the Institute undertaken.

The religious of the Visitation, however, who, returning to Annecy, after the storm of the Revolution had spent its fury, had taken up their abode in larger and more commodious quarters, were desirous of recovering the cradle of their Institute. To them it was a precious treasure, a relic whose acquisition they could not but ardently crave. "Here it was that we were born," said St. Jane Frances de Chantal; "it is our source, the origin of our life." The Bishop, to whom they addressed themselves, understood all this, and referred the delicate question to Rome.

---

[1] The Abbé Rivaux seems here to have confounded the purchase of the Visitation Monastery (the second of the Order, I believe) with that of *La Galerie*, hallowed by the presence of St. Francis de Sales, St. Jane F. de Chantal, and her first heroic daughters.

The Monastery, *alone*, was acquired by Mgr. Rey and Mme. de la Rochejacquelin in 1833; *La Galerie*, which is within the enclosure, was, as we learn from our Sisters in Annecy, purchased only in 1855.—Translator.

A Jesuit Father, charged to examine into the affair, declared that the Sisters of St. Joseph, according to the design of their holy founder, and in accordance with the end laid down in their Constitutions, were carrying out in reality the *first idea* of St. Francis de Sales, when he founded in *La Galerie* his Order of Visitandines. That, consequently, the providential circumstances which had given the Saint's first House into the hands of the Sisters of St. Joseph, whose mission is the realization of his primitive plan, should be regarded as *an expression of the Divine will and destination.*

His decision thus explained, impressed every one with the historical truths it recorded; it was confirmed, and the Sisters of St. Joseph have ever since retained possession of the treasure given them by Divine Providence.

Thus was established and reaffirmed, in a solemn manner, that close and direct affiliation of the Congregation of St. Joseph with the mind and heart of the gentle Saint of Sales. The above decision, unanimously accepted, indicates that the little house in the Faubourg de la Perrière, in Annecy, called *La Galerie*, ought to be regarded as the cradle of the Institute of St. Joseph, also, since the blessed Daughters of the Visitation, by their first mode of life, brought it forth and inaugurated it, so to speak, before they entered on that to which their holy founder was led by a will other than his own.

Dear to the hearts of St. Joseph's children is this close and blessed affinity with the angelic Order of the Visitation, for which they are bound by their Rule to entertain sincere affection and veneration.

As soon of the Sisters had become settled at Annecy, the novitiate at Evian, on the Lake of Geneva—which had been founded October 15, 1822, by Sisters sent from Lyons by Mother St. John Fontbonne, at the urgent entreaty of the Abbé Picollet—was transferred thither, and the ancient monastery became, thenceforth, the Mother House of the Sisters of St. Joseph of Annecy. That Congregation numbers at present three hundred and sixty-three religious, who have charge of thirty-seven establishments, including *pensionnats*, day-schools, *Salles d'Asile*, hospitals, orphanages, and other works recommended by their Rule. This Congregation has, also, many dependencies in England and India, of which we shall now speak in detail.

In 1844, the Rev. Father Superior of the Missionaries of St. Francis de Sales of Annecy, having begged the Holy Father, Gregory XVI., to confide to that Congregation some mission in infidel countries, the Holy See assigned it the missions of Vizagapatam, then included in the Vicariate-Apostolic of Madras ; and, in 1846, six missionaries entered on that field of arduous labor.

In 1847, they received a powerful auxiliary in Rev. Father Neyrat, a priest whose ardent piety and zeal for the glory of God and the salvation of souls had caused him to be particularly remarked at Rome ; and, shortly after his arrival in India, he was consecrated Bishop of Olene *in partibus*, and appointed Vicar-Apostolic of the new Vicariate of Vizagapatam.

In the visitation of his flock, the zealous prelate learned the good dispositions of the natives, and the absolute spiritual destitution which reigned in many localities. Ignorance and the most revolting immorality held undisputed sway ; and he saw the imperative necessity of opening schools under the direction of religious, wherein the young, at least, might be rescued from the degrading influences that surrounded them.

Having, for fourteen years, been Chaplain to the Sisters of St. Joseph at Evian, he was thoroughly conversant with the rules, spirit, and work of that Congregation, and judged it admirably adapted to the wants of his flock. He, accordingly, earnestly entreated the Superiors at Annecy to send him some religious, and his request was complied with. In 1849, four Sisters, accompanied by two missionaries, arrived at Bordeaux, whence they were to embark for India.

They were received with open arms by Rev. Mother St. Joseph, Superior of the Congregation of Bordeaux, of whom it is mentioned, in her Life, that she had made a conditional vow to devote herself to the Indian missions. Unable to obtain permission for its fulfilment, she wished to become co-operatrix in the Sisters' labors, by providing them with the sacred vessels, church ornaments, and many other things calculated to be useful to them. Seeing the Sisters surprised at her generosity, she said : " You must not wonder at all I do for you, for some time ago I had a dream which made a vivid impression upon me ; and that dream is now realized. It seemed to me that St. Joseph and St. Francis de Sales appeared to me, and showed me a colony of their children setting out for a far distant mission ; they bade me receive them most cordially and do them all the good I could."

Towards the end of July the little band set sail, and arrived in February, 1849, at Yanaon, the inhabitants of which place constrained the Sisters to remain there instead of going to Vizagapatam, where they were anxiously expected. A second appeal was responded to by Annecy and Chambéry ; and, in 1852, Mother St. John Boissat, Superior General of the latter community, inflamed with apostolic zeal, resigned her charge, and, accompanied by six religious, embarked at Marseilles for Vizagapatam. After ten years of devoted labor, during which she bore the title and fulfilled the duties of Superior General of the Sisters of St. Joseph in India, she was called to her eternal rest, on the 6th of February, 1862. In the *Notice on the Missions of Vizagapatam,* published at Annecy in 1866, we read : " A true type of the valiant woman, Mother St. John Boissat was above the weakness of discouragement. In the midst of difficulties of every kind which she had to encounter, she placed all her confidence in her whom she used tenderly to call, ' *My sweet Mother in Heaven,*' and then went on calmly and fearlessly, compassing her end with incredible prudence of action. This was the secret of her success. She who, in life, was held in the highest esteem by persons of every class, native and foreign, is now regarded with a species of veneration, and her name and assistance are often invoked by the distressed. It would seem that Divine Providence could not have chosen a religious more capable of founding the educational establishments of the Mission." There are, at present, ten Houses [1] and seventy-eight Sisters of the Congregation in the Vicariate ; but the natives are so anxious to have their women elevated from their condition of abjection and ignorance, so full of admiration for what the Sisters have already effected, that they are continually urging the Superiors to send them more religious.

While exercising, in conformity with their Rule, all the corporal and spiritual works of mercy, the Sisters are obliged to adapt themselves to the peculiar social circumstances of the strange country in which they reside. Hence their schools have to be multiplied, not, indeed, as among us, on account of the number of pupils, but because of the strict limitations of caste. It is well known that were Indians of one caste to hold communication with those of another, they would immediately lose caste—the most serious calamity that can befall a Hindoo. On this account, the Sisters must maintain schools for each,

---

[1] The Convents of Kamptee, Tubbulpore, and Nagpore depend on St. Jean-de-Maurienne ; Vizagapatam (the Novitiate and principal House having supervision of all the others), Vizianagram, Cuttack, Cocanada, Yanaon, Sooradha, and Granapuram on Annecy. The total number of pupils is 1212 ; of orphans, about 100.

which adds, not a little, to their difficulties. Many interesting details of these institutions might be given, did not the limits of this work prevent ; but from the Report of the Government Inspector of the school of the Sisters of St. Joseph at Vizianagram, south of Calcutta, we extract the following : " This school is unique of its kind, and is one of the most useful and best managed of all the institutions of the Maha-rajah of V. It is pleasant to inspect a school where the instructresses seem to have so completely gained the confidence of their pupils, and where order and discipline are so admirably preserved."

This school was given in charge of the Sisters by the native pagan Governor, and there are in it more than a hundred pupils, all high-caste pagan Brahmins. Their families, no doubt, seek but the refining influence of the education imparted by the Sisters, but who shall tell the moral effect, who number the conversions brought about by the prayers and life and works of those instructresses ? Only when the women of India become christianized, and when the sweet influence of Mary, the Virgin Mother of God, begins to bear fruit, may we hope for great and permanent extension of the Gospel in that land.

The fact that the women, or rather girls of India marry at a ridiculously early age, [1] and that under no circumstances is a widow allowed to engage in a second marriage, exposes numbers of them to terrible dangers. On this account, asylums or refuges have been opened for their especial benefit, which are also under the charge of the Sisters.

Dispensaries for the gratuitous distribution of medicines, etc., have been established ; foundling asylums and orphanages, also, wherein the poor infants of both sexes, ruthlessly

---

[1] Often at the age of five or six years.

abandoned by their parents, are gathered. When grown up, these children are married, and thus villages of Christian families are formed.

In view of such blessed works wrought amidst that pagan people, not only by the Sisters of St. Joseph but by other religious, may we not hope for abundant fruit, especially when we consider that army of holy innocents, to whom, by those apostolic laborers and the associates of the Holy Childhood, have been opened, through the precious waters of Baptism, an entrance to eternal life, and who, our faith assures, interest themselves in favor of their benighted compatriots?

*   *   *   *

Up to 1864, England, so dear to every true child of the Church for its Catholic memories and traditions, possessed no house of the Congregation; but, in that year, St. Joseph began to assert his rightful claim to a share in "Our Lady's Dowry," and brought about, in a providential manner, the establishment on her soil of the only community in England which, so far as we can ascertain, bears this name of Joseph, name so sweet on Mary's lips, so dear to Mary's heart. The foundation is due to the zeal and enlightened patriotism of Captain Dewell, a Wiltshire gentleman of family and fortune, who, having been sent with his regiment to India, became convinced of the truth of the Catholic faith under the following circumstances.

Being in the habit of taking his Catholic soldiers to Mass, he was profoundly impressed with the solemnity of the Adorable Mysteries, and was led to inquire farther into a religion which he had previously understood to be but a tissue of superstition and idolatry.[1] The reward of his fidelity to grace was the gift of faith, never denied

---

[1] In *Terra Incognita* Count Murphy assigns this as the cause of his conversion. — Translator.

to the earnest inquirer; and, on the 2d of July, 1858, he made his abjuration, and was received into the Catholic Church in the Eternal City.

Returning to India, he remained some time with his regiment; but, moved by a lively sentiment of gratitude to God for the inestimable favor he had received, and desiring to make his fellow-countrymen sharers therein, he determined to devote part of his fortune to establishing in England the Missionary Fathers of St. Francis de Sales and the Sisters of St. Joseph, the beneficent results of whose labors he had seen fully proved in India. Negotiations were opened with the Superiors of those Communities at Annecy, and it was agreed that some of the Fathers and Sisters on the Indian mission should be recalled for the new foundation. Mr. Dewell, having sold his commission at a great sacrifice, sailed for England in company with Rev. Father Larive, his director, to make the final arrangements for the projected convents; and on Saturday, the 3d of August, 1864, three Sisters under Rev. Mother Athanasia, late of India, arrived at Devizes in Wiltshire and opened their first house under the invocation of St. Joseph.

God, who is never to be outdone in generosity, granted to Capt. Dewell himself the priceless grace of the apostolic vocation, and, a short time later, he entered the Society of Jesus.

The novitiate for England was opened at Devizes, but it was soon found that it did not afford sufficient opportunities for the general work of the Congregation, nor were the revenues or surroundings what were needed for a central house. It was, accordingly, decided, in 1873, to transfer the novitiate to Newport in Monmouthshire. There are now four houses in England, viz., Newport. Devizes, Westbury-on-Trym and Malmesbury, in all which places the Sisters have charge of Government schools, besides private boarding and day-schools ; at Westbury, they have also an orphan-asylum. Besides their school duties, the Sisters are much engaged in the instruction and preparation of converts, and in the visitation of the poor and sick. They have been asked for in many other places in England, but, owing to want of subjects, the petitions have, with regret, to be refused. Great, indeed, is the harvest, and new fields are daily thrown open to the Church and her religious in that land consecrated by the blood of martyrs ; but the laborers are few. Would that the Lord of the harvest would send laborers into His harvest by multiplying vocations to the apostolate of religious education, of which He is Himself the Model, the Co-worker and the Reward !

* * * *

While endeavoring to make our readers even slightly familiar with the affiliations of the Congregations of Chambéry and Annecy, we find we have gone far beyond the date of the early colonies sent from Lyons, and that, to return to our subject, we must give a backward sweep to the hand of time, now that we desire to speak of Corsica.

Having failed in his project of opening a house in Rome, Cardinal Fesch, in 1824, decided to send the Sisters to Ajaccio in Corsica, his native city. As might be supposed, the Sisters previously named for Rome were assigned to the new foundation, with the exception of Mother St. John, who, as we have seen, was restored to Savoy. On the 17th of September six religious set out for Corsica, and Sister St. Regis, one of the number, appointed at first to attend the pharmacy, was destined by God to be the chief Superior, the soul of that important work ; and, in the words of Father Crozet, her biographer, " to cover the whole of Corsica with monuments of her zeal and charity."

After experiencing its full share of those trials and sorrows which must attend every Christian work, since on the cross alone can such work be securely based, the little colony was, in 1830, visited by the Abbé Barret, Missionary of the Chartreux and Chaplain of the Mother House in Lyons, a man of extraordinary enlightenment and wholly devoted to the duties of his charge.

There were at that time only two houses in Ajaccio in charge of the Sisters, the House of Schools, and the Foundling Asylum. Assembling the Sisters in Chapter, the Abbé Barret proceeded to hold an election. The scrutiny revealed that Sister St. Regis was chosen Superior of the Schools, and Sister St. Calixtus, her sister by blood as well as by vocation, Superior of the Asylum. Both were confirmed by the Visitor; and the former, whom the fires of tribulation had well proved, was named Provincial or chief Superior of the Houses of Corsica, which office she discharged for seventeen years, up to the time of her death in 1847. "Never was a soul more firmly grounded in faith and confidence in God," says Father Crozet; "never was one more filled with a desire of virtue, more ardent in its practice, more pure in intention, more just in action, or more constantly faithful and devoted to the religious life. Her admirable intelligence, her beneficent charity, have filled Corsica with good works, and marvellously developed the Congregation of which she was Superior." It at present numbers about two hundred religious, who direct fifteen important establishments, the chief of which are those of Ajaccio, Bastia, Corte, Calvi, Bonifacio, and Sartina, all founded by Mother St. Regis.

She was succeeded by Mother St. Calixtus, who, following in her sister's footsteps, fostered the true religious spirit of the community, and preserved the beautiful customs and simple traditions by which the colony of Corsica has become renowned as one of the brightest glories, one of the purest gems in the crown of the Institute.

Father Barret was succeeded as Visitor by Fathers Valois and Crozet, to whose indefatigable zeal and unwearied vigilance is mainly to be attributed the perfection of the Corsican community. The latter, in particular, devoted thirty years of his life to the work.

*   *   *   *

Catholic Vendée could not but desire to have the daughters of that great Saint, whose simple and patriarchal life was the prototype of their own. That grand race, that *people of giants*, as Napoleon called them, that " nation of martyrs," to use the more appropriate term of Rohrbacher, had made no alliance with vanity, luxury, frivolity, and modern vices.

We cannot, then, wonder that their hearts and sympathies were given to the Daughters of St. Joseph.

The Countess de la Rochejacquelin was the instrument in the hands of God for introducing and establishing them on that soil, sanctified and watered by the blood of her ancestors, whom faith and heroism have gloriously immortalized. Eagerly did Mother St. John respond to her invitation. Between her who asked and her who gave, there was perfect conformity of views and sentiments; both had that intuition of the wants of the age which has led a great bishop to say : " If men will no longer save the world, we have still our women and children. Yes; we may hope to revivify the world through religious who pray, and children who are brought up to be strong and valiant women."

Blessed by God and protected by this noble Christian lady, the little colony of Sisters struck root deeply in the west of France, and spread throughout Vendée and Touraine, in Saint-Aubin, la Roche-de-Brand Huismes, Curzay, Monlévrier, la Gaubretiere and other places. Despite difficulties and obstacles, it continues bravely its work of educating, of forming true Vendeans, women who degenerate not from the virtues of their Catholic forefathers.

" In our time more than ever before," said the Venerable Mother Barat, " the hope of salvation rests with the weaker sex. The men of this generation are become women; women, then, transformed by faith, must become men."

"When everything else is debased, O woman, do you at least remain great," exclaimed Victor Hugo. And it is only by the power of her virtue, by the influence of her Christian principles, that woman can maintain her moral empire, can uphold her greatness and her dignity.

"Virtue," says St. Mary Magdalen de Pazzi, "is feminine only in name, in all else it is virile."

Blessed, then, forever blessed be those who labor to train up true *Vendeans*, true women of any nationality! In the midst of general debasement of character, amidst modern error and perversion of mental faculties, what more potent agent for good can there be, than the humble religious who labors quietly, incessantly, unostentatiously, to inspire woman, both by word and example, with a just sense of the truth, the grandeur, the sublimity, of Christian virtue? In this lies the salvation of society in general ; in this only can woman find her true dignity,—that which associates her name with the names of Jesus and Mary.

If our modern atheists and materialists still show a certain respect for their wives, their mothers or sisters, it is because, all unconsciously to themselves, they are under the domination of ideas which Christianity has imparted to civilization.

"Family life, dignity, purity of morals, reciprocal rights and duties within the home circle, respect for human life, charity towards the weak and suffering, honesty in business, reasonable equality, rights of property, freedom from tyranny, honored labor, universal justice,—all these things," says Mgr. Dupanloup, "may apparently flourish of themselves. But such is not the case; so little are they the effect of human means, that at least one-half of the human race is absolutely deprived of them. Look abroad over the world!" And after forcibly depicting the state of Oriental paganism, he continues: "O charity! O Gospel! O Church of Jesus Christ! Falling on our knees, we humbly kiss your hands, which have drawn us from the depth of that terrestrial hell! O Divine Gospel! sun which has purified so many pestilential marshes, which has brought forth so many and such precious blossoms on our earth, we do not adequately bless and glorify you among ourselves, nor, let me add, do we strive as we should to make you known and loved by those outside of us."

But the Congregation of St. Joseph, not content with applying itself to the diffusion of this blessed knowledge among the nations of Europe, has, as we have seen, gladly accepted the invitation of the sons of St. Francis de Sales to aid in extending it on the far distant shores of Asia. Nay, even benighted Africa, that land once hallowed by the footsteps of the Earthly Trinity, is, in our day, blessed with the ministrations of the children of St. Joseph.

Nor have their labors been confined to the Old World alone. By a particular providence of God, the glorious name of St. Vincent, so closely linked with that of the Founder of the Congregation, is inseparably connected with the entrance of his children into the New World. In 1834, Rt. Rev. Joseph Rosati, Bishop of St. Louis, that worthy son of the grand Apostle of Charity, being on a visit to France to obtain co-laborers in his vast missionary field, stopped at the Mother House of the Sisters of St. Joseph of Lyons, and earnestly entreated Mother St. John to send to America a colony of her devoted daughters.

What such an invitation meant of trial, difficulty, and privation, fifty years ago, we, under present circumstances, cannot conceive; but self-sacrifice and apostolic zeal have ever been the characteristics of the religious of France, and Mother St. John, eagerly accepting the new field thus opened to her daughters, began immediately the preparations necessary to assure its success.

Unwilling to impose on any of her children an exile so complete, a sacrifice so heroic, and a mission so full of peril, the Superior contented herself with making an appeal to their zeal and good-will, recommending them to weigh the matter well, consult their director, and be led only by the Divine inspiration; that thus, like the Apostles, they might be endued with strength from on high, without which one is powerless, especially on such missions as that proposed. She implored God to be with her daughters, that His powerful and fatherly hand might guide them safe over the vast ocean to the boundless prairies of the West.

At the close of her appeal, many of the Sisters offered themselves; but what a trial to her heart to behold, foremost among them, Sister Febronia and Sister Delphine, her two beloved nieces! It seemed as though, like the Father of the faithful, she was called to immolate her own child. Mother St. John was at that time very old, and much weakened by infirmities. She had counted on her nieces to be the consolation and support of her declining years. She had even hoped to be able to resign the heavy burden of authority, and retire to the privacy of a little mission where one of them was Superior, there to close the door on earthly affairs and say with St. Gregory Nazianzen: " I love this cherished solitude, which is the place of my repose: I shall exchange it only for the Church of the first-born who have inscribed their names in Heaven, under the portico of the eternal palace."

In view of their mutual affliction, the aunt and her nieces faltered for a moment; but, accustomed to listen to the voice of grace alone, they soon made it quell the risings of nature. Worthy of each other, they generously ascended together the mount of sacrifice. Great was the emotion and edification of the whole community at the sight; and when, in touching allusion to the scene, the novices, some days previous to the Sisters' departure, represented the sacrifice of Abraham, the Mother and her spiritual family could not restrain their tears.

The little band of missionaries comprised Sisters Febronia and Delphine Fontbonne; Sister Febronia Chapellon; Sister St. Protais; Sister Marguerite (called thenceforward Sister Félicité, after the Countess de la Rochejacquelin, who wished one of the Sisters to bear her name); and Sister Philomene.

Sister Febronia Fontbonne was appointed Superior by Rev. Father Cholleton, Mother St. John's delicacy and fear of natural influence restraining her from taking any part in the choice. After her appointment, however, she signed the letter of obedience for the new Superior, and prepared her for her office by wise advice and instruction.

As the Bishop of St. Louis had begged for priests, also, for his diocese, Rev. Father Fontbonne, brother of the two Sisters mentioned above, with two seminarians, joined the little colony, of which he was appointed director and spiritual father. Thus was accomplished the prediction made at his birth that he would one day become a missionary. But what a grief it must have been to the heart of Mother St. John to see herself deprived, at one blow, of all those children to whom, from the hour of their birth, she had been so intimately bound! But God so willed it: it was for His glory and the salvation of souls. Seeking in the Divine will her happiness, the Sisters of America tell us she seemed not only resigned but even joyous, with a joy not of earth, while, with affectionate solicitude, she made all the necessary preparations for their departure.

At last the eve of the day of sacrifice arrived. The community assembled in the refectory to bid their last adieux to the little band of missionaries, whom they could expect to meet again only in eternity. Only they who have experienced the strength and sweetness of the bonds that unite Sisters of the same community, can understand the sorrow of such a parting. Casting themselves at the feet of their Sisters, the six missionaries implored their pardon for all that in the past might have been disedifying, and begged the prayers and blessing of all. Emotion choked their utterance; sobs burst forth from the whole community, and tears supplied the place of words. But their venerable Mother, silencing her own grief, and, like the Mother of the Machabees, rising above nature, tried to console her children, encouraged the missionaries, and invited her whole spiritual family to adore and bless the holy will of God.

What a ravishing spectacle! More blessed than St. Jane Frances, this holy religious, after consecrating herself to God, has been privileged, also, to devote to His service her whole family, and when, to further His glory, she is called to sacrifice them anew to Him, it is she who is brave enough to dry the tears and console the sorrows of those around her. With the author of the Imitation well may we exclaim: "Whosoever knoweth not how to suffer all and sacrifice everything to the will of the Beloved, knows not what it is to love!"

CHAPTER IV.

THE morning of January 4, 1836, having arrived, the brave and zealous band of Sisters bade adieu to their religious home, and began to descend the Hill of the Chartreux : then, at a little distance, at the last turn which afforded them a view of their dear Mother House, "we stood," writes one of the Sisters, "to take a last look at our cherished convent-home, to engrave, as it were, its every feature in the depths of our hearts."

Anxious to consecrate themselves and their future to Our Lady of Fourvière, and to beg her blessing on their work, they ascended the sacred height and entered the sanctuary of Mary. There they found their venerable Superior prostrate before the altar, imploring the Virgin Mother to take under her powerful protection the children she was sending to a foreign land, and to be to them on their voyage the true Star of the Sea.

At the altar of Our Lady of Fourvière, Rev. Father Fontbonne offered up the Adorable Sacrifice, in union with which Mother St. John and her children made that personal oblation which God required of them. Their devotions ended, they withdrew to the house of the Sisters attached to the Dispensary of the Rue Tupin, where they were to breakfast.

Mother Josephine Cessier, foreseeing the anguish the

final parting would inflict on the heart of the Mother
General, begged her to grant a few moments' interview
to a priest who wished to see her. Taking advantage of
this temporary absence, she urged the Sisters to set out
immediately to where they were to take the diligence for
Havre. Then Mother Josephine, presenting herself to the
Superior alone, gave her to understand that the hour of
separation had gone by; and Mother St. John, appreciat-
ing the tender delicacy of her filial affection, poured out
her sorrow on the heart of this beloved child, who, meanwhile, consoled her by speaking of all the good that would
be wrought, of all the souls that would be saved by that little band of missionaries. From that time, Mother St. John's
visits to Fourvière became more frequent, as if from the
spot where they had last prayed together, she could more
effectually bless her absent children.

The latter were, meanwhile, detained at Havre for
eleven days, the vessel in which they were to sail not being
in readiness. During that time they lodged at the house
of Mme. Dodard, a pious and wealthy lady, who had devoted her fortune to the receiving and harboring of priests
and religious destined for the foreign missions. The
Countess de la Rochejacquelin, whose name has occurred
so often in these pages and so much oftener in the angelic
records associated with the works of the Sisters of St.
Joseph, had taken especial interest in the American Mission, and had carried her zeal and charity so far as to sacrifice her personal jewels to defray the expenses of the
voyage, and provide articles necessary for the undertaking.
Borne thus on the wings of faith and charity, the Sisters,
trusting in the protection of the Blessed Virgin and her
Spouse, set sail from Havre, January 17, 1836.

The voyage was long and perilous, and all the party suffered much from sea-sickness. After forty-nine days' sail-
ing, they came in sight of New Orleans, only to encounter,

almost in the harbor itself, a violent tempest, which threatened them with shipwreck and death. Encouraged by Rev. Father Fontbonne, the Sisters remained calm and tranquil amid every danger; and by their angelic modesty as well as by the charity exercised in favor of their fellow-passengers, they won the esteem and respect of all on board.

What was the happiness of the Sisters when, on landing, they were met by the good Bishop of St. Louis, who, with Father Timon, afterwards Bishop of Buffalo, had travelled for eight days, to meet with a welcome and a blessing, in the very harbor itself, the new family which Providence had sent him! The Ursulines of New Orleans received with cordial sisterly affection the wearied voyagers, who, after some days' rest, were able to proceed on their journey.

Accompanied by the Bishop and Father Timon, they ascended the Mississippi, and, after eleven days, arrived at St. Louis on the 25th of March, 1836, where they were hospitably received by the Sisters of Charity. How soothing to the lonely, and, we may well believe, somewhat home-sick strangers, must have been the welcome given them in a foreign land by the Daughters of St. Angela and St. Vincent! Never has it been forgotten, and to this day the thought of those who sheltered their first Mothers is dear to the American Sisters of St. Joseph.

Father Douterligne, pastor of Cahokia, a village three miles from St. Louis, composed in great part of Canadians, was anxious to put his children in care of the Sisters. For two years this heroic priest had eaten only corn-bread, and had often gone without food, to be able to found this establishment, which would provide assistants for his work. Touched by such zeal, Bishop Rosati decided that Mother Febronia, Sister Febronia Chapellon, and Sister St. Protais should go to Cahokia, and that Sisters Delphene, Félicité, and Philomene should remain in St. Louis to learn English. The Bishop would himself conduct the Sisters to Cahokia, where their first visit was to the church to adore the Most Blessed Sacrament. The inhabitants, whose dialect of Canadian French the Sisters could understand much better than English, welcomed them with the greatest joy; and there was a pleasant rivalry as to who should be most attentive, or who first provide for their pressing wants.

One wealthy lady caused a pretty little chapel to be erected beside their house, and this the Sisters adorned the best they could with the ornaments they had brought from France. The schools were opened at once, and so many children, both boarders and day-pupils, entered, that it soon became necessary to enlarge the establishment.

Dear to the hearts of those brave Canadians was that little French convent! The sound of its chapel-bell floating out over the waters of the Mississippi, or reverberating in the depths of the surrounding primeval forests, had for them an indescribable charm. The Sisters they venerated as Saints, as charitable Mothers who had left their homes in France, their loved *Mère-patrie*, to tend their sick and poor, to teach and care for their children.

One day in winter Mother Delphine came from St. Louis to visit her sister, Mother Febronia. On her return, the latter accompanied her some distance through the forest, but when she attempted to retrace her steps, she became confused and lost her way. When night came on, freezing and bitter cold, and brought no tidings of the Superior, the grief and dread of the Sisters became extreme, nor were the people less excited.

Ringing the alarm-bell to assemble the villagers, one of the principal men thus addressed them: "My friends, our good French Sisters are in great affliction. Their Superior is lost in the great forest of La Pointe: at any cost, we must find her. Provide yourselves with torches that you may be able to see your way, and take your guns, so as to defend yourselves if you encounter any danger. Separate into parties of ten or twelve, and scour the woods in every direction. From time to time cry aloud : 'Mother of Cahokia, don't be afraid. Your children are seeking you.'" These arrangements were carried out to the letter, and the searchers penetrated into the deepest recesses of the forest.

Mother Febronia, who, in the meantime, had followed a hundred little by-paths in her endeavor to reach the convent, had, at last, exhausted by hunger and fatigue, taken refuge in the hollow of an old tree : hope failed with her strength, and recommending herself to God, she resigned herself to death. Fortunately her feeble moans were heard by one of the bands ; they ran to the spot, and found her in a ravine. Joyously they sounded the horn to give the signal of success, and the men quickly gathered from all quarters. Constructing a litter of branches they would fain have borne the Mother thereon, but one of the old men, remarking that she was almost frozen with cold, said it was necessary, at any cost, to make her walk, thus to restore circulation to her stiffened limbs, and throw off the torpor even then settling on her. The rescuers yielded to his reasons, adding : "We will support her, and, if necessary, even carry her in our arms."

Thus, in the midst of a triumphal cortège, as it were, she was restored to her spiritual family, whose gratitude to their kind neighbors was second only to the thanksgivings they rendered to Almighty God.

Informed by letter of all that had occurred, Mother St. John blessed God for the affectionate consideration shown her children by the people among whom they labored, and rendered fervent thanks to Our Lady of Fourvière for what she considered a most signal mark of her protection.

But a time of severer trial soon came to the missionaries. In 1844, a terrible inundation of the Mississippi submerged the entire village, and the waters rose to the second story of the houses. All the residents that could, fled to places of safety, taking, where time afforded the opportunity, their live-stock and most valuable effects. The Sisters were in great peril, but Mother Celestine, then Superior in St. Louis, and Rev. Father Fontbonne, having chartered a boat, hastened to their assistance. The Sisters were rescued from the porch on the second story, whence they stepped into the boat. The waters retired but slowly, and fevers broke out which made great havoc among the inhabitants. Returning to the field of their labors, the Sisters suffered much from sickness, and they were, a second and a third time, driven away by the flood.

Mother Febronia had contracted a disease which caused her excruciating suffering ; and Sister Febronia Chapellon, her health shattered by hardship and unfavorable climate, was reduced to a state of great exhaustion. The physicians advised their return to France, and they were both recalled by their Superiors, after having, for ten years, labored indefatigably in the field allotted to them.

Shortly after the establishment of the Cahokia mission, Bishop Rosati decided to open a convent at Carondelet, about six miles from St. Louis, under the direction of Mother Delphine. Sisters Félicité, Philomene and St. Protais were assigned to the new foundation, but the latter was prevented from leaving Cahokia by an attack of fever.

In 1837, the little community had the inexpressible consolation of welcoming two additional Sisters from Lyons, Sister Celestine, afterwards Superior of Carondelet, and Sister St. John, the foundress, some years later, of the Congregation of Philadelphia. These two religious, who, in 1836, had been sent to Saint-Etienne to prepare themselves for the instruction of deaf-mutes on the American mission, had been long and anxiously expected. The Bishop was informed of their departure from Brest on the 17th of April, 1837 ; but as months rolled by bringing no tidings of the travellers, both he and the Sisters gave them up as lost. The vessel, meanwhile, had put in at the West Indies ; and it was only in September that the two Sisters, having reached St. Louis by way of New Orleans, presented themselves to the Bishop. He, however, would not, at first, believe they were the Sisters of whose coming he had despaired ; and to assure himself of their identity, he bade them converse before him in the sign-language. Whether or not they had their letter of obedience the Annals do not say ; if they had, probably the Bishop feared its authenticity. This reception, serious though it was, had its ludicrous aspect, and the tired and, it would seem, hungry travellers, were somewhat at a loss for a subject on which to converse. But there was no alternative. Prove themselves to be the deaf-mute teachers they must, so Sister Celestine, turning to Sister St. John, asked in signs, " What are you thinking of, Sister ?" to which the latter, in all the simplicity of truth, replied : " I am thinking of the bread we ate in France." So unexpected and evidently so candid an acknowledgment overset Sister Celestine's gravity, and she could not restrain a laugh. The Bishop insisted on knowing what had been said, and whether or not hunger was a sufficient proof of their being the expected travellers, it would appear they had to undergo no further examination. Going to a closet in the room, the Bishop took therefrom a piece of brown bread, which he gave to Sister St. John with the injunction to eat it.

This pleasant little episode put an end to all embarrassment, and at the close of the interview the prelate gave them his letter of obedience to the Superior at Carondelet. We can better imagine than describe what must have been

the feelings of Mother Delphine and her Sisters, when just as
they had assembled for recreation on the 4th of September,
the two French Sisters, unannounced and unexpected, appeared in their midst. Had they been angels from Heaven
they could not have been more rapturously welcomed.
The *Te Deum* and *Magnificat*, chanted from the depths of
happy hearts, were all that could be heard for some time in
that poor, lowly cabin, into which had swept, as it
were, a breath of their native air, a glimpse of their native land ; for the dear travellers brought to the exiles for
Christ's sake, news from home and friends, messages from
the cherished Sisters whom absence made but the dearer,
tender counsel and blessing from the Mother, whose
heart, under the twofold influence of nature and grace, was
full of love for her expatriated children. The virtues and
zeal of the newcomers, the encouragement and assistance,
spiritual and temporal, which they brought from Lyons,
infused new life and vigor into the little convent, if such
indeed it might be called.

Carondelet, although far superior to Cahokia in climate
and situation, was, at the time of the Sisters' arrival, a
mere collection of log-cabins, inhabited by Creoles or poor
wood-mongers, who earned a scanty livelihood by selling
at St. Louis the timber cut from the surrounding forests.
After clearing away the trees, they used to make little
gardens or plantations ; it was all hard work, misery, and
poverty, with but little of earthly comfort to be looked
for.

For their convent and school the Sisters had two small
log-cabins, given up to them by Rev. Father Saulnier,
first pastor of Carondelet, who lived himself in a log-
cabin contiguous to one somewhat larger, which served as
a church. The Sisters' dwelling had but one room,
which was known by different appellations at various hours
of the day ; at one time the kitchen or refectory, it was

anon elevated to the dignity of parlor or oratory, only later in the day to be rechristened the dormitory. Whatever else was wanting, there was always a superabundance of fresh air; and it was no unusual thing for the Sisters, on awaking in the morning, to find themselves provided by Nature with extra coverlets of snow, which had fallen through the many sky-lights in the roof, or entered through openings left by the logs' refusal to enter into partnership. From St. Louis they had brought some coverlets and sheets, and two sacks, which, when filled with straw, served as beds for the community.

By the exercise of that mathematical ingenuity which convent-life so often has the power to develop, what would, in ordinary circumstances, have sufficed for two, was made to do duty for six; while the Rule requiring that each Sister should have a separate cell, was, for the time being, dispensed with, in view of the fact that were one to keep it, the rest would be homeless. Joy and light-heartedness are ever the companions of privations undergone for God, and happier days than those spent by the first Sisters of Carondelet, have hardly been the portion of any of their Sisters. The shifts they were called on to make, by appealing to their keen sense of the ridiculous, converted into a source of recreation what to more gloomy temperaments might have seemed cause for tears; and we cannot wonder if, being obliged to take turns, during meals, to hold an umbrella over those who were making the best of what, more than once, had been procured by begging, the Sisters should rejoice at the fact that of water, at least, there was "full and plenty."

Under such circumstances did the Sisters spend the early days of the Carondelet mission, amidst a population not only poor and rude, but destitute of any taste for either religion or education. But rich in their poverty—the pearl without price—and hopeful for the future, they struggled on.

Rev. Father Fontbonne, who had been stationed at the Cathedral in St. Louis, visited his sister and her spiritual family from time to time, and, finding them in want of the necessaries of life, sold for their benefit some church ornaments which he had brought from France.

Owing to the bad state of the roads, which, in winter, were impassable to foot-travellers, Bishop Rosati, to his great regret, was prevented from visiting the poor Sisters as often as he could have wished, to console them amid their privations, for his poverty was such he could not afford a horse. But his expressions of sympathy and the little attentions he was able to show, proved to the Sisters that he was not only their Superior but their Father. One instance of his delicate consideration goes far to prove that he bore not in vain the title of " Son of St. Vincent."

Noticing that the habit of the Sisters of St. Joseph, as worn in France, did not afford sufficient protection against the inclemency of our northern winters, he had cloaks made for them, like those worn by the Sisters of Charity. Carrying them himself to Carondelet, he presented them to the Sisters, saying : " See what I have for you. These will be very comfortable, especially when you have to go to the Church, which is so very cold." Then he made the Sisters try them on in his presence, that he might be sure they answered his purpose.

Rev. Father Saulnier, the missionary pastor of Carondelet, a fervent and zealous priest, often denied himself bread to give it to the Sisters ; and when, some time later, by the exercise of the most rigid economy, he had saved enough to purchase a cow, it was the Community of St. Joseph which profited most by the produce of his not very extensive dairy.

Deeply grateful for the kindnesses received, the Sisters were not, meanwhile, regardless of the Apostle's injunction to labor assiduously; and to the onerous duties of their profession, they added the employment of seamstresses. Application for work was made to stores and industrial establishments, and for some time during the Mexican War they were engaged on shot-bags at a cent apiece, for a firm on the Mississippi River. As may well be conceived, this did not bring them much income: but He who multiplied the loaves in the desert in favor of men who hungered for His heavenly doctrine, failed not to support those who had abandoned home and friends and native land, to plant in Western wilds the knowledge of His love and His law. Work which is to be a continuation of His Divine apostolate must ever bear the marks that characterized His own, poverty, humility and privation. "They who sow in tears shall reap in joy," and ere long God crowned the Sisters' faith and patience by giving the first fruits of the coming harvest.

In the month of October, 1837, Miss Anna Eliza Dillon, the first American daughter of St. Joseph, entered the novitiate at Carondelet, which, to one reared like her in the lap of luxury, must have seemed a reproduction of the stable of Bethlehem. The only daughter of a prominent merchant of St. Louis, she, having lost her mother, had been educated at the Convent of the Sacred Heart. Feeling herself called by God to join the Daughters of St. Joseph, she asked her father's permission to do so; but of Carondelet he would not hear, because of the Sisters' extreme poverty. That poverty, however, was the ointment whose exquisite odor drew that precious soul to her Divine Spouse, and casting aside and forever the world and its glittering allurements, she, at the age of eighteen, entered the novitiate. As she was naturally of delicate constitution, the Sisters were very solicitous about her health; but her fervent piety, spirit of abnegation, and natural energy of character, made her forget everything to labor earnestly for the advancement of God's greater glory. To the poor, struggling Sisterhood, she was, veritably, a God-send. The inability of most of the Sisters to teach English had been, previously, an obstacle to the general reception of pupils, but as Miss Dillon was thoroughly conversant with both English and French, she was able, by conversation and instruction, to perfect the Sisters in the English tongue. On the 3d of January, 1838, she was admitted to the religious habit by Rt. Rev. Bishop Rosati, who gave her the name of Sister Frances Joseph, name admirably suited to one who had been drawn to the children of Joseph mainly by her love for that poverty which had such charms for the Seraph of Assisi.

Endowed with rare natural attractions, her well-cultured mind, affable manners, sweet and gentle disposition, rendered her virtue amiable even in the eyes of externs; and the skill and tact she displayed in teaching inspired her Superiors with bright hopes of her future usefulness. But, fair and fragile as the emblem of her Blessed Father, this Lily of St. Joseph was, at an early hour, transplanted by the Heavenly Gardener to more congenial soil, for, to the great grief of her community, she died in 1842. The will which she made in favor of the religious family to which she belonged was not recognized by her father; but the dearer and richer legacy of her virtues and example is the inalienable right of the American Sisterhood of St. Joseph. As the early spring-flowers have a charm and sweetness all their own, so this young Sister, the first to bloom, the first to fade, holds a place in the annals and traditions of the American Congregation which none else can ever fill.

Meanwhile, the number of boarders and day-pupils at Carondelet began to increase, so that the Sisters were obliged to enlarge their house: this they were enabled to do by succors brought from France by Sisters Celestine and St. John.

Influenced by the grace of God, and encouraged, no doubt, by Miss Dillon's example, several young ladies had entered on their novitiate with the zeal of the truly fervent; and, as a life of poverty is, necessarily, a life of sacrifice, their progress to perfection was steady and unfaltering. Under the power of grace, privation became joy ; and self-forgetfulness, mortification, and abnegation had for them no terrors. As the grain cast into the ground, when it dies brings forth abundant harvest, so the community of Carondelet, planted in the most absolute want, began " to sink root downwards and bear fruit upwards."

In 1839, Mother Delphine, at the expiration of her first term of office, was succeeded by Mother Celestine Pomeril, of whom we shall have occasion to speak later on.

In 1840, Bishop Rosati, before his departure for the Fourth Provincial Council of Baltimore, took leave of his flock, who little dreamed the farewell was to be final. At the conclusion of the Council, he set out for Rome for the transaction of important business connected with his see. Gregory XVI., who then occupied the Chair of Peter, entrusted him with a delicate mission to the Republic of Hayti, in which he was fully successful, though at the cost of his life ; for through the exposure attendant on it, he contracted a disease of the lungs of which he died at Rome, September 25, 1843, deeply mourned by his flock, but by none more than by the Sisters of St. Joseph.

Under the zealous supervision and fatherly care of his successor, Bishop Kenrick, the Sisters began to work in new and hitherto untried fields. In 1844, they opened in St. Louis a school for colored children under Mother St. John Fournier, who, in 1846, was transferred thence to the male orphan asylum of that city. Several parish-schools were next put under the Sisters' direction, and as the community began to increase in proportion as it extended its sphere of usefulness, it became necessary to settle definitely certain matters relative to its government.

Finding that the Sisters could the better adapt themselves to the rapidly increasing demands of this country, if freed from dependance on the Mother House of Lyons, it was decided, by the advice and direction of their Bishops, that the communities of St. Joseph in the United States should retain their diocesan character, as had been done by many of the French and Italian foundations, as before noted. But this separation, made under authority and by mutual agreement, was not detrimental to the affectionate and sisterly relations that had subsisted between them, and the communications which the various Mother Houses hold with one another have been a source of consolation to the Daughters of St. Joseph on both sides of the Atlantic.

In 1836, the Sisters established at Carondelet, on an elevation commanding a magnificent view of the mighty Mississippi, an academy and day school for young ladies, which was incorporated in 1853. Under efficient management, it has become one of the best educational establishment, not only of the West, but of the Union.

The Sisters of the St. Louis Congregation teach over one hundred parochial and select schools, extending over a wide range of territory, all of which are carried on under a uniform graded system of instruction, the outcome of varied experience of the educational wants of this country, and thoroughly enlightened views as to what constitutes a solid and Christian education.

The work of instructing and evangelizing the Indians, which the Sisters began among the Sioux and Winnebagoes at Long Prairie in 1850, under the direction of the pioneer Bishop Cretin, has, up to the present, been continued with unabated zeal, and they have schools at Baraga, Yuma, Keshina, and other places.

So extended became, in a few years, the affiliations of the Mother House of Carondelet, that the Superiors, convinced of the benefits that would accrue from centralization, decided, in 1863, to organize it into a General Congregation of four Provinces, subject to the Mother House of St. Louis.[1] The approbation of the Holy See was solicited, and fully and finally granted by Pius IX., in 1877.

The Province of St. Louis comprises the dioceses of St. Louis, Chicago, Peoria, Alton, Marquette, Green Bay, Denver, Mobile, New Orleans, Kansas City and St. Joseph ; that of St. Paul, the diocese of St. Paul ; that of Tucson, Arizona, San Francisco and Los Angeles. From the table of statistics added to this work, it will be seen that the Congregation of St. Louis is in a most flourishing condition and contains more than one-third of the religious of St. Joseph in the United States.

---

[1] By the wish and advice of their respective Bishops, the communities of Philadelphia, Wheeling, Buffalo, Erie, Brooklyn, and Toronto preserved their autonomy.

CHAPTER V.

Foundations at Philadelphia.—The Novitiate at McSherrystown.—
Its removal later to Chestnut Hill.—Establishment of the Congregation of St. Joseph at Wheeling, Buffalo, Rochester,
Brooklyn, and other Eastern cities.—Convents of St. Joseph in
the South.—Foundations of Canada.

EARNING from his brother, the Archbishop of
St. Louis, the good that had been effected by the
Congregation of St. Joseph, Rt. Rev. Francis P.
Kenrick, the glory of the American Church, then Bishop of Philadelphia, and, later, Archbishop of Baltimore,
asked for a colony of Sisters to take charge of St. John's
Male Orphan Asylum, then on Chestnut St., contiguous
to St. John's Church. Mother St. John Fournier was appointed Superior ; and with two other Sisters she arrived
in Philadelphia and took charge of the Asylum, May 6th,
1847, just three years from that sadly memorable day on
which had been inaugurated the " Native American " riots.
During that unhappy period the Sisters of Charity, then
in charge of the asylum, had been grossly insulted, and it
had been found necessary to scatter the children to different places of safety.

And although, in 1847, the external ravages of the tempest had been repaired, the churches rebuilt, and Catholics, in general, accorded the rights and privileges of their
fellow-citizens, the fire of religious hatred but smouldered
in many breasts, ready, in individual cases, to flame forth
at sight or sound suggestive of Catholicity.

Wishing, therefore, to render the Sisters less conspicu-
ous and thereby spare them the petty insults and persecu-

tions of which they were sometimes the object, the Bishop decided that, on going abroad, they should add to the ordinary habit of the Institute a black bonnet and cloak, afterwards superseded by a shawl, which addition to the costume is still retained by the Sisters in several of the Eastern dioceses, although the feeling which was the cause of its adoption has long since died away. The disguise was not, on the whole, an effective one, and when the Sisters appeared abroad they had many annoyances to endure, and were frequently saluted with epithets more expressive than flattering, which in later years have become traditional matter for amusement.

The Sisters had, in the meantime, been called to direct the schools attached to St. Patrick's Church, Pottsville; St. Joseph's and St. Philip's, Philadelphia, the latter in a district from which the turbulent mobs of 1844 had been largely recruited. Nothing daunted by the terrible scenes through which he had passed, and from which he had barely escaped with his life, Rev. N. Cantwell, the heroic pastor of St. Philip's, hastened to re-open his parochial school; but for some time it was found necessary to have gentlemen protect the children in going to and from the church. When, however, there was question of the Sisters' assuming the charge, the Rev. Felix J. Barbelin, S. J., of dear and blessed memory, who, from the Sisters' coming to the diocese until his death, ever showed the greatest interest in them, advised them to trust more to the people's good will, dispense with the escort, and go calmly on their way, as if no interference was expected.

The event proved that he was right; neither teachers nor children were from that time molested on such occasions; prejudice began to be dissipated, and " the nuns " were suffered to undergo in peace " the horrors of conventual life," since it was clear they did not intend to force them upon others.

In 1850, Mother St. John Fournier was recalled to St. Louis, and sent thence to found missions in St. Paul, Minn. She was succeeded as Superior of the Philadelphia convents, first by Mother Delphine, and later by Mother Agnes Spencer. But in response to urgent and reiterated entreaties, and through the kind mediation of Rt. Rev. Bishop Neumann, Mother St. John was restored to Philadelphia, in May, 1853.

As, owing to want of means, the community was unable to have a regular Mother House, applicants had up to this period been received at St. John's Orphan Asylum, which, for many reasons, was not suitable for a novitiate. Mother St. John's first endeavor on her return was to provide a suitable place for the training of the young Sisters; and, by the kind co-operation of the Bishop and Rev. Fr. Enders, S. J., the Academy of McSherrystown, lately vacated by the Ladies of the Sacred Heart, was secured, and opened May 4, 1854, under the invocation of St. Joseph. Among the advantages which this convent afforded, one of the most precious was that of the community's being under the spiritual direction of the Sons of St. Ignatius. Not content with spiritual benefits only, the good Fathers aided the Sisters by every means in their power, even so far as to become their professors in those secular sciences and accomplishments necessary to their success as teachers.

Graphic and amusing details of the early days of "dear McSherrystown," and the ever-to-be-remembered names of its kindly and truly Catholic residents, have been recorded for the benefit of succeeding generations of the community, but the trials and make-shifts of a new religious foundation is an "oft-told tale," with which we shall not now delay our readers.

Religious vocation is a flower that has ever flourished in the congenial soil of the Conewago Valley, hallowed by the truly Catholic lives and traditions of the early settlers from the German Fatherland; and many have been the daughters of McSherrystown and surrounding places who have found in conventual life "that peace which the world cannot give": not a few of them have embraced the humble and laborious life of the Sisters of St. Joseph.

The field of labor opened to the Sisters continued, meanwhile, to grow more extensive; and as McSherrystown was too distant to admit of Mother St. John's readily visiting and supervising the Houses in Philadelphia, the Mother House and Novitiate were transferred to Chestnut Hill, a suburb of that city, and one of the most beautiful locations in the State, on the 16th of August, 1858. On the 21st of the same month, the saintly Bishop Neumann offered up the Holy Sacrifice for the first time in the house that had been purchased, blessed it, and delivered a most touching and fatherly discourse to the assembled Sisters.

Rt. Rev. Dr. Wood, Coadjutor of Bishop Neumann, accompanied by many priests, visited the new establishment on the 24th of August, named it "Mount St. Joseph," and presented a large sum of money to help the Sisters to meet the debt they had incurred. Thus, on that day, did he inaugurate a series of benefactions and favors to St. Joseph's Sisterhood, continued throughout his long episcopate, even to that hour when the hand of death stilled his noble and magnanimous heart, and the silence of the grave fell on those lips whence had proceeded so many fatherly counsels, admonitions, and blessings.

In the October of 1858, the Sisters opened their academy, and the house—an ordinary dwelling—was found wholly inadequate to the requirements of the community. The Sisters were soon compelled to use the cellar as their refectory, from which they were wont to emerge, bearing evidence, on face and linen, that contiguity to a coal-bin does not greatly enhance one's personal appearance. Yet, unlike Emerson's lady, to whom the "sense of being perfectly well-dressed imparted a peace and tranquillity religion was powerless to bestow," the Sisters' recreation was never merrier than on such occasions.

It happened, however, that on a certain day, Rev. T. Kyle, in company with Rev. H. McLaughlin, visited the convent, and met the Sisters coming up from what he could never have imagined to be the dining-room ; and his warm, generous, Irish heart found more pathetic than amusing the sight of "the Spouses of our Lord coming like rabbits out of a burrow," as he himself expressed it. Sympathy with him was no barren feeling ; it bore the fruit of immediate action, and, carrying out Father McLaughlin's suggestion, from church to church, from parish to parish he went during the following three months, describing what he had seen ; appealing, not in vain, to Catholic generosity, and acting as collector himself until he obtained sufficient funds to erect an addition to the convent, in which the "Sisters could see, at least, what kind of food was before them." This, the first addition to the original building, was blessed by Bishop Wood on St. Joseph's Day, 1860. Several additions have since been made, and new buildings erected, but with none other shall be associated the thoughts of noble charity, of generous devotedness that are an integral part of "Father Kyle's building; " and while a stone remains upon a stone, successive generations of St. Joseph's children will deem it a sacred duty to remember, before the throne of God, him who, they confidently hope, has already heard from the lips of his Judge and Redeemer: "Inasmuch as you did it unto these my least brethren, you did it unto Me."

When, in 1862, war, with its attendant horrors, was desolating the land, Mother St. John, at the request of Surgeon-General Smith, sent Sisters to take charge of the Church Hospital of Harrisburg and that improvised at

Camp Curtin, outside the city, where they remained in devoted attendance on the sick soldiers until their regiments were called to the front, and the camp broken up. Later on we find the Sisters of St. Joseph from Philadelphia in charge of the floating hospitals which received the wounded from the battle-fields of Virginia.

The cause of Catholic education had, meanwhile, made great progress, and schools began to multiply on every side, far more rapidly, indeed, than religious teachers could be provided. At the request of the lamented Archbishop Bayley, several houses were opened in the dioceses of Newark and Baltimore, which, by the wish of the ecclesiastical Superiors, still remain subject to St. Joseph's Convent, Chestnut Hill.

The communities of Toronto, Brocklyn, and McSherrytown have been founded from the same diocese ; and petitions for Sisters from the West Indies, South America, and Australia have had to be regretfully refused for lack of religious to meet the demand.

At the solicitation of the late Archbishop of Philadelphia, the Sisters, in 1881, undertook the spiritual instruction of the female Catholic deaf-mutes, for which no provision had been previously made, and many of those afflicted ones have since learned that knowledge of God and His Church, which to them, otherwise, had been unattainable.

It may not be amiss to make some brief mention here of the other diocesan foundations of the Institute in the United States, all of which, except those of Georgia and Florida, owe their origin either to the first Sisters sent from France by Mother St. John Fontbonne, or to Houses founded by them.

*   *   *   *

The first House of the Congregation in the diocese of Wheeling was founded by Mother Celestine of St. Louis, in the April of 1853, at the request of Rt. Rev. Bishop

Whelan. Six Sisters were appointed to the mission, of which Mother Agnes Spencer, recalled from Philadelphia for that purpose, was appointed Superior, Mother Celestine herself, however, remaining for six weeks, that, by her wise counsels and assistance, she might help the new community over its first difficulties, and establish it on a solid basis, that of most exact regularity.

At present the Sisters have charge of the Hospital, Orphan Asylum, and all the parochial schools of Wheeling and its vicinity.

*   *   *   *

Rev. John Timon, Visitor of the Lazarist Congregation in the United States, was, as we have seen, one of the first to welcome and bless the little French colony of Sisters of St. Joseph when they landed in New Orleans, in 1836. Having, in 1847, been consecrated first Bishop of Buffalo, he, like another St. Vincent, set himself to provide comfort and consolation for every species of human woe and misery. While seeking co-operators in his works of charity and beneficence, he was not unmindful of the children of St. Joseph, a Saint to whom he had special devotion, and whose praises, as Father Faber remarks in his work, "The Blessed Sacrament," Bishop Timon took such delight in hearing.

In response to his invitation, a colony of Sisters was sent from St. Louis to Canandaigua, a village most beautifully and picturesquely situated at the head of Lake Canandaigua, and then included in the Diocese of Buffalo. Arriving there on the 8th of December, 1854, that day forever glorious in the annals of the Church ; that day on which, to use Bishop Timon's own expressions, " the Christian world crowned its Mother," they placed under the glorious invocation of Mary Immaculate the Academy for young ladies which they then opened. " Besides teaching the youth," writes Mr. Deuther in his " Life of Bishop Timon," "they undertook other works of mercy, such as providing a house for poor girls of good character, whose only alternative, previously, had been the poor-house or shame."

In the same year, A. P. Le Couteulx, Esq., a distinguished benefactor of the Church in Buffalo, donated to the Bishop a lot which should be the site of an Institute for the Instruction of Deaf-Mutes. The funds necessary for such a building were not, however, obtainable; but, in 1856, the Bishop having purchased three small frame houses in the neighborhood, had them removed to the above-mentioned lot.

Knowing that the Congregation of St. Joseph was, in several parts of France, engaged in teaching this class of the afflicted, he made application to St. Louis for the Sisters, and three who had studied the methods employed in the Institution of Caen, France, were, in 1857, sent to take charge of the projected school. But although the Bishop contributed, as far as he could, to the furnishing of the house, and sometimes donated to its support funds of which he was in need himself, the means of subsistence were very precarious, and the work made but slow progress; indeed, had it not been for the benevolence and indomitable zeal of the prelate, its continuation would have been abandoned. In November, 1862,—the Bishop having, in the meantime, sent one of the Sisters to the Pennsylvania State Institute at Philadelphia, that she might become thoroughly conversant with the methods most in vogue in the United States,—the classes were reorganized in the new building, which he had caused to be erected. The novitiate was transferred from Canandaigua to Buffalo; and, under the Superiorship of Mother M. Magdalen Weaver,—a most saintly religious, and one of Mother St. John Fournier's first companions in Philadelphia,—the community and its works seemed, thenceforth, to be included in that promise which the lamented Archbishop Spalding has applied to Bishop Timon's undertakings : *Et omnia quæ-cunque faciet, prosperabuntur.*

In 1865, the Sisters addressed a Memorial to the New York Legislature, praying that Le Couteulx Institute might be included among those to which the State annually made appropriations for the education of deaf-mutes ; and a bill to that effect was passed, April 28, 1875. From that day, the prosperity of the Institute was assured, and the Sisters have indefatigably labored to keep it in the foremost rank among institutions of its kind. From the Annual Report of 1885 we learn that its pupils of both sexes numbered one hundred and fifty-two, who, in addition to the ordinary branches of instruction, are taught various trades, so that, in after-life, they may be self-supporting. Most competent judges of different denominations, as well as the State and County Supervisors, have testified to the thorough and practical education there imparted; and as its pupils hail from all parts of the Union, the sphere of its usefulness is widely extended.

We have written somewhat at length of this Institute, not only because it is one of the largest in the United States under Catholic control, but also because, as has been beautifully remarked by a Catholic poetess, [1] its work is one " that finds its appropriate place under the patronage of St. Joseph, the silent Saint of the Church ; the greatest Saint the world has ever known, the Saint of whom no spoken word has ever been recorded."

The Sisters have not, however, restricted their labors to one field : they have charge of St. Joseph's Boys' Orphan Asylum at West Seneca ; teach the classes and attend to the domestic affairs of the Catholic Protectory at the same place ; have the administration of St. Mary's Orphan Asylum at Dunkirk, and teach in fifteen of the parochial schools of Buffalo and its vicinity.

---

[1] Miss E. C. Donnelly.

Among the sad results of the late Civil War, there was none that appealed more eloquently to sympathetic hearts than the number of children whom it left fatherless and often homeless. To the Catholic Church, whose Divine characteristic it is to "have the poor always with her," the majority of those desolate children belonged. and she was not slow in asserting and exercising her maternal rights, gathering them into homes already open to them, or providing such where none had previously existed.

In the autumn of 1864, at the instance of Rev. J. M. Early, V. G., Bishop Timon sent three Sisters of St. Joseph from Buffalo, to open, in Rochester, an asylum for soldiers' orphans. On the Feast of All-Saints they took possession of a small house on South Street, and immediately began their work. placing it under the patronage of Mary, the true Mother of orphans. Three years later, the number of children having increased to one hundred and thirty, the asylum was transferred to more commodious quarters : here new buildings have recently been erected, and the institution can now accommodate three hundred boys.

In the meantime, the vast diocese of Buffalo had been divided, the See of Rochester created, and on the 12th of July, 1868, Rt. Rev. Bernard McQuade, founder, and, for many years, President of Seton Hall College, New Jersey, was consecrated first Bishop of Rochester.

This zealous prelate, whose name and fame as one of the ablest champions of Catholic education, have spread not only through our country but even to Europe, set himself, at once, to that work which the Church deems second to none. Voice and pen he supplemented by most energetic action : and verbal protest against irreligious education he eloquently emphasized by sacrificing means, leisure, even necessary rest, to the building up of a school-system wherein religion should be mistress and science her handmaid.

With this end in view he determined to make choice of some religious community of women, whom he could employ as teachers in the parochial schools. After having examined the Rules and Constitutions of the Congregation of St. Joseph and consulted with the Superiors, he came to the conclusion that it would meet his requirements and carry out his views. A diocesan organization then became necessary; the Sisters at Canandaigua and Rochester were freed from dependance on the Mother House of Buffalo, and St. Mary's Asylum, Rochester, was chosen to be, temporarily, the Central House and Novitiate of the Congregation of St. Joseph of Rochester.

On the 11th of November, 1870, St. Patrick's Girls' Orphan Asylum was placed under their care; and on the Feast of the Assumption, 1871, the Sisters took possession of the handsome and spacious building which their Rt. Rev. Superior had purchased for them, and which he destined to be the Mother House and Novitiate for his Diocese. This convent received the beautiful and appropriate name of "Nazareth," in the hope that the Earthly Guardian of the Blessed Home of Nazareth would, in a special manner, protect the Sisters who bore his name, and the children to whose welfare they had devoted themselves. An academy and boarding-school were soon opened in an addition built for that purpose, in which, at present, there are more than one hundred pupils.

The parochial schools attached to the Cathedral and Church of the Immaculate Conception were opened in September, 1871, under the charge of the Sisters of St. Joseph, and each succeeding year has widened their field of labor, as the different parishes have become able to make provision for the Christian instruction of their children. The Sisters attend to seventeen parochial schools, either German, French, or English, and have also opened on Lake Avenue, Rochester, a preparatory boarding and day-school for boys under twelve years of age, and an orphan asylum at Canandaigua.

The Rochester Home of Industry was founded in 1873, to supplement the work of St. Mary's Asylum, by affording boys of a suitable age every facility for acquiring a practical knowledge of farming, gardening, or useful trade.

A similar institution for girls was opened a few months later ; and here, under the supervision of the Sisters, every branch of needlework is carried on, and employment afforded working-girls of good character temporarily in need of a home.

Such, up to the present, have been the works confided to the Congregation of Rochester ; and if, to use the words of their Rt. Rev. Bishop, " the success attending the work of years gone by, since the Sisters of St. Joseph began their educational labors in this diocese, be any guarantee for the future, then, surely, the years to come must produce wonderful fruit in the portion of the vineyard committed to their care." May God perfect the work He hath Himself begun ! and may *his* " name be held in everlasting remembrance," who " has planted and watered " while imploring God " to give the increase."

* * * *

While the Congregation was thus permanently establishing itself in Western New York, another branch had taken root in the congenial soil of " The Isle of the Apostles," [1] under the fostering care of Rt. Rev. John Loughlin, first Bishop of Brooklyn. His request for a colony of Sisters, presented to Mother St. John of Philadelphia in January, 1856, could not be complied with until August of the same year, owing to the scarcity of Sisters.

In the latter month, two Sisters, under the direction of Mother M. Austin, arrived in Brooklyn, where they were

---

[1] Insula Apostolorum, the name given to Long Island by the early Catholic explorers.

most cordially received by the Bishop; and, under his kind patronage, they, on the 8th of September, opened St. Mary's Academy for Young Ladies. One year later, they took charge of their first parochial school, that attached to SS. Peter and Paul's Church, whose pastor, the venerable and zealous Father Malone, has ever since continued a true and faithful friend to the community. A novitiate had, in the meantime, been opened at St. Mary's; and there were the Sisters wont to gather for several years, week after week, to listen to the conferences on the duties and privileges of their State, given by their zealous Bishop to the community, in imitation of St. Francis de Sales. Like his blessed prototype, the prelate knew he could most effectually advance the Sisters' work among the children and the poor by thoroughly grounding them in the spirit of their Congregation, and by increasing and extending in them that knowledge of God and His truths which it is their primary duty to inculcate to others.

Applicants began to seek admission to the community, and it was not long before St. Mary's was found to be wholly inadequate to its requirements. Acting on the suggestion of Rev. Father O'Bierne, pastor of the beautiful village of Flushing, within easy access of Brooklyn, the Sisters purchased in that place a large frame building, know as St. Thomas's Hall, which had, up to that time, been used as a Seminary under the presidency of Rev. Dr. Hawkes, an Episcopalian clergyman.

Thither the novitiate and academy were transferred; a boarding-school was opened, new and extensive buildings erected, and to-day, St. Joseph's Academy, Flushing, holds its well-earned place in the foremost rank of the educational establishments of the State of New York. The chapel, Romanesque in style, is a perfect gem of art; and, on beholding its altars, ornaments, and statuary, all in such perfect keeping, one feels rise, involuntarily, to his lips the words of the Royal Psalmist : They " have loved, O Lord, the beauty of Thy House ; and the place where Thy glory dwelleth." [1]

In 1868, St. John's Male Orphan Asylum, one of the greatest of Brooklyn's Catholic charities, in which boys, sometimes to the number of eight hundred, find a home, was given into the care of the Sisters of St. Joseph; St. Malachy's Home for orphans and destitute children has also since been intrusted to them. Their principal employment, however, has been the teaching of parochial schools, an all-important work which is rapidly assuming its rightful place, *the foremost* in every scheme of Christian education.

To the self-sacrificing zeal of the Congregation of Flushing four other foundations are due, viz., those of Ebensburg, Pa.; Rutland, Vermont ; Boston, and Springfield, Mass.

*   *   *   *

The Novitiate of Ebensburg, opened in 1869, perpetuates, under the name of Mount Gallitzin, the memory of that princely priest [2] whose feet so often pressed, in his weary missionary wanderings, the soil whereon it stands. This community has three affiliations in the diocese of Columbus, Ohio.

In response to the appeal of Most Rev. Archbishop Williams and Rev. Thos. Maginnis, of Boston, six Sisters were sent to take charge of St. Thomas's Schools, Jamaica Plains. The community rapidly increased in numbers ; other places in the diocese sought for their services, and schools were opened in South Boston, Amesbury, Stoughton, and Cambridge. To the latter place, in 1884, was removed the novitiate previously established at Jamaica Plains.

*   *   *   *

---

[1] Psalm xxvi. 8.

[2] Rev. Demetrius Augustine Gallitzin, a Russian prince, who was the pioneer priest of western Pennsylvania.

Mount St. Joseph's Convent, East Rutland, the novitiate of the diocese of Burlington, was founded in 1876, under the patronage of Rt. Rev. L. De Goesbriand and Rev. T. Boylan. The Sisters have charge of one boarding-school and the parochial schools of East Rutland, Brattleboro, and East Bennington.

The establishment of the Congregation in Springfield is due to the energy and kind persistence of Rt. Rev. Bishop O'Reilly, who, having had previous knowledge of the Sisters' work in several small missions of his diocese, applied to Flushing for Sisters to teach the Cathedral schools, and, in the convent attached thereto, to open a diocesan novitiate. The Sisters were accordingly sent to Springfield in September, 1880. Four parochial schools, also, are under the Sisters' direction, and their educational labors have been attended with extraordinary success.

The first convent of St. Joseph's Sisterhood in the diocese of Erie, Pa., was opened at Corsica, in 1862, by Mother Agnes Spencer and two companions ; another at Frenchtown was founded shortly afterwards, and in both places the Sisters were put in charge of the parochial schools. At the request of Rt. Rev. Bishop Young, a hospital and orphan asylum were established in Erie ; another hospital has been opened at Meadville, and a home for the aged in Erie, in addition to which the Sisters direct four academies and eight parochial schools.

* * * *

It has been noted heretofore that the Philadelphia novitiate formerly located at McSherrystown was transferred to Chestnut Hill in 1858.

An academy and boarding-school continued, nevertheless, to be maintained at McSherrystown ; and when, in 1868, the see of Harrisburg was created, its late lamented Bishop, Rt. Rev. J. F. Shanahan, appointed it as the diocesan novitiate. Mother Magdalen Weaver, recalled by Mother St. John from Buffalo, was named Superior. which office she held until her blessed death, August 21, 1876. Besides the academy above mentioned, the Sisters maintain a home for orphans at the novitiate and at Lebanon; they also teach the parochial schools of McSherrystown, Hanover, Oxford, Rock Hill, and Leb anon.

To the ordinary works of the Congregation they have added the instruction of the blind, for whose benefit a school has been opened under the superintendence of one of the religious, a graduate and former teacher of the Philadelphia Institute for the Blind. A number of the novices also are being continually trained to carry on this charitable work, hitherto so much neglected.

The course includes reading and writing with pin-type, New York point and Braille system, and the other ornamental and industrial branches usually taught in such institutions; and the apparatus and school appliances are all that modern progress has been able to devise for facilitating such instruction.

* * * *

In 1866, shortly after the close of the late Civil War, Rt. Rev. Augustin Verot, D. D., Vicar Apostolic of Florida, seeing the sadly demoralized condition of the but newly emancipated slaves, the majority of whom were in profound ignorance of the truths of religion, undertook with great zeal the work of their evangelization. Finding that he had neither priests nor religious sufficiently numerous to cope with the difficulty, he resolved to seek the necessary aid in his native France, where apostolic zeal seems to be a constituent element of the Christian life. A native himself of Le Puy, the birth-place of the Sisters of St. Joseph, he was well acquainted with the scope and organization of the Congregation, and judged it to be admirably adapted to the pressing wants of his Vicariate. To the Superiors of

Le Puy[1] he accordingly applied; his request was made known to the community, and sixty of the religious offered themselves for the mission, only eight of whom, however, were accepted. On the 6th of August, 1866, the Sisters embarked at Havre, but it was not until the 2d of September that they reached Pilatka, Florida. Thence they immediately proceeded to St. Augustine, where they were charitably and hospitably received by the Sisters of Mercy.

In January, 1867, they opened schools for the colored children, in St. Augustine, and on the 22d of April, the same work was undertaken in Savannah, Ga.

Those of our readers who know the sad state of affairs that prevailed in the South at that epoch will readily understand that the poor missionaries had much to endure from poverty and trials of various kinds, but they were not disheartened, knowing that " comfort and luxury and home and ease are not for those who wish to follow Christ."

At St. Augustine a regular novitiate was opened in 1880, under the auspices of Rt. Rev. Bishop Moore, who succeeded Bishop Verot after the holy death of the latter

---

[1] A few details here concerning the reorganization of the Sisters of St. Joseph at Le Puy, after the Revolution, will, we think, prove interesting.

Owing to the Sisters' labors among the lower classes, the Asylum of Montferrand, the cradle of the Institute, was, for a few months after the outbreak of the Revolution, saved from the fate of the surrounding Houses. But its turn came; and it was only with great difficulty that the relations and friends of the religious were enabled to save the greater number from the scaffold. Some were imprisoned, and three, as we have already seen, gave their lives for their vocation.

When Religion began again to raise her head on the blood-soaked soil of France, the remaining Sisters presented a petition to the Prefect of Haute Loire for the restoration of their former home, but it was rejected. It was only on the 14th of January, 1815, that they were again put in possession of that convent endeared to them by the lives and deaths of generations of holy religious. The Act of Restoration is a very interesting document, but on account of its length, we cannot reproduce it here. It sets forth that the Sisters have been invited to return and have returned to the convent, save some, who on account of their age and infirmities, were not able to bear the excessive cold of that day. Also that the Mayor has installed the Sisters and given them the keys of the buildings, which are in a very ruinous condition; that the chapel has been desecrated and partly destroyed, the Sisters' choir torn down, the altar, windows and wood-work broken, etc., etc.

But sad as such a sight must have been to the reunited religious, and painful

in 1876. The Sisters have now charge of two boarding and six select schools, eight schools under the control of the State, and six for colored children.[1] Under the guidance of the Sisters, several quite prosperous associations have been formed among the Catholic colored females, such as St. Monica's Society for the care of the sick, St. Frances' for married women, and St. Cecilia's for young girls.

When, in 1877, the yellow fever began its ravages in Fernandina and other places of Florida, the Sisters, who were then engaged in the exercises of their annual retreat, waited not for its close, but leaving God in prayer to find Him in the service of His suffering children, they hastened to the scene of death, and immediately began their loving ministrations to the fever-stricken patients. Seven of the Sisters themselves were attacked by the dread malady, but only two were privileged to render up their lives as pure holocausts on the altar of Charity.

* * * *

As has been already noted, the first foundation of the Sisters of St. Joseph in the diocese of Savannah was made April 23, 1867, when four Sisters were sent from St. Augustine to take charge of the school for colored children. Some time later, the Bishop put the male orphanage also under their care ; this establishment was afterwards transferred by Rt. Rev. Bishop Gross to Washington, Ga.,

---

as must have been the memories it evoked, the joy of finding themselves once more within the convent-walls made them almost forget the sufferings they had still to endure. With a zeal all the more ardent because of long repression, they set themselves to re-create, develop and reorganize their former undertakings, and success crowned their efforts. Sister St. Augustin Robert, the last of those heroic confessors, died in Le Puy in 1830.

Like the Sisters of St. Joseph in others parts of France, the Congregation of Le Puy found a centralized government better adapted to the exigencies of the times: and in 1842 a generalate was definitely established. Seventy-five establishments are under the obedience of its Mother House, and its seven hundred and forty-five members are employed in seventy-one schools, eight pharmacies and four asylums. —Translator.

[1] The schools for colored children are at St. Augustine, Jacksonville, Mandarin, Fernandina, Pilatka and Moccasin Branch.

where the Sisters opened under his patronage a boarding-school and academy for young ladies, establishing, at the same time, a novitiate and separate diocesan government. In addition to the works above mentioned, the Sisters teach two parochial schools for white children, and one for the colored ; and have also opened a boarding-school for little boys at Sharon, Ga.

*   *   *   *

The foundations of Canada—of which, although anterior to most of those above alluded to, we have, for obvious reasons, deferred speaking until now—were begun by Mgr. de Charbonnel, Bishop of Toronto, in 1851.

This zealous prelate, whose father had aided Rev. Mother St. John Fontbonne in her efforts to restore the Congregation of the Sisters of St. Joseph of Lyons,[1] shared in the esteem which all his family felt for that venerable religious.

Returning from a visit to Rome, Bishop de Charbonnel, in 1851, stopped at Philadelphia to visit Mother Delphine and her brother, Father Fontbonne, and being highly pleased with what he there saw of the Congregation, entreated Rt. Rev. Dr. Kenrick to send Mother Delphine, with some of her religious, to make a foundation in his episcopal city, and his request was granted.

On receiving her obedience from the Bishop, this good religious cheerfully severed the new ties she had contracted, and with three companions, set out for her field of labor. The Sisters arrived in Toronto on the 7th of October, 1851, and were at once installed in the Orphan Asylum on Nelson Street, in which, after a short time, a novitiate was opened.

The parochial schools of the city were placed under the direction of the community, and, notwithstanding the oppo-

---

[1] The record from which these details are drawn is, on this point, somewhat obscure, and our rendering may not be absolutely correct.—Translator.

sition raised by bigotry, then rampant in Toronto, and the wretched accommodations to which the poverty of the Catholic population restricted them, they were numerously attended. The fruits of the Sisters' arduous labors ere long became apparent, and won grateful recognition. "The orphans were well provided for; the children prepared for the worthy reception of the sacraments without detriment to their progress in secular learning; sinners were reclaimed; prisoners visited and instructed; the sick and dying consoled;" in a word, the works of charity entrusted to the Sisters in Toronto gave them opportunity to fulfil literally the words of their Rule, which urges them to consecrate themselves to the service of their neighbor by exercising *all* the works of mercy, both spiritual and corporal.

In 1857, the House of Providence—a building erected by the charitable public under the auspices of Bishop de Charbonnel for the reception of the aged, the infirm, and the destitute of every religious denomination—was opened under the direction of the Sisters of St. Joseph; several additions have since been made to this institution, which has been most appropriately named, not only because, like the Adorable Providence of God, it is open to every human creature in distress, but because on this Divine Providence it relies for its support from day to day, there being no fixed revenue or regular income for its maintenance. At present it harbors 260 orphans and 240 adults, either blind, aged, crippled, or incurable. A branch of this institution has been opened at Sunnyside, Brockton, where the orphans are kept during their infancy; the inmates are about fifty in number.

The "St. Nicholas's Institute," a home for working boys founded in a central part of the city by Most Rev. Abp. Lynch, and by him placed in charge of the Sisters, has, under the blessing of God, been able to afford the comforts and safeguards of a home to many children at a most critical period in life.

"Notre Dame des Anges," an industrial school and boarding-house for young girls pursuing different occupations, although not a charitable institution according to the general acceptance of the word, has, nevertheless, for years done much good in a field, the importance of which is being, lately, more fully recognized.

The small house erected for a novitiate having been found wholly unfit for its purpose, the Sisters, unprovided themselves with the necessary resources, turned with confidence to Him for whose sake they had stripped themselves of all. A novena of Adoration of the Most Blessed Sacrament was offered for their intention; and the Prisoner of Love was not slow in responding to the prayer of those who visited Him so assiduously. In February, 1862, the Honorable Capt. Elmsley donated to the community two acres of the Clover Hill estate, one of the most eligible sites in the city, and a convent and academy were built thereon, of which the Sisters took possession August 15, 1863. The boarding-school there opened has succeeded beyond their most sanguine expectations, and with the various additions which circumstances have since rendered necessary, "St. Joseph's Convent and Novitiate" has become one of the most imposing structures in Toronto. Fifteen of the separate[1] schools are taught by the Sisters, and in the diocese of Peterborough—the convents of which are still subject to the Mother House of Toronto—they have four schools—one for Indians—an orphan asylum and a hospital.

To Toronto, moreover, the dioceses of Hamilton and London have been indebted for their first colonies of the Sisters of St. Joseph. In the former, the Sisters direct ten

---

[1] Canada, more just in this matter than the United States, allows the Catholics a *pro rata* share in the school funds, out of which the teachers are paid, and the schools maintained.

separate schools, a training-school for teachers, the orphan asylum of Hamilton, a hospital and two Houses of Providence. In London, from the Mother House called Mt. Hope, the Sisters go daily to teach the parochial schools of the city; and at Goderich, St. Thomas, and Sandwich, they have both select and free schools. At the novitiate there is an asylum for orphans and a home for the aged poor.

Thus have we endeavored, by the above compilation of details from varied and authentic sources, to give an outline of the foundations and undertakings of the Congregation of St. Joseph in North America during the half a century that has elapsed since Mother St. John first sent to our shores her heroic children. Crude and defective as it necessarily is, it will not, we are confident, be devoid of interest to those who have succeeded them or reaped the fruit of their labors. Glorious, indeed, has been that fruit springing from "the root of wisdom that never faileth." Well may the Daughters of St. Joseph, to whom they have left the blessed heritage of saintly lessons and example, exclaim in the words of Wisdom: "Oh, how beautiful is the chaste generation with glory: for the memory thereof is immortal: because it is known both with God, and with men. When it is present, they imitate it: and they desire it when it hath withdrawn itself, and it triumpheth crowned for ever, winning the reward of undefiled conflicts."

CHAPTER VI.

IN our desire to give even a brief sketch of the labors of the Sisters in North America, we have gone far beyond the term of Mother St. John's life ; it is, then, necessary to resume the thread of our narrative at the foot of the Hill of Fourvière, where the Mother and children held their last earthly reunion. Pilgrimages to that sacred shrine had ever been the consolation of her heart, but thenceforth they became more frequent, more fervent ; and at the feet of Mary she united herself, heart and mind, to the Sisters' painful struggles and arduous toil. Prayers for the absent were ever on her lips or in her heart ; and "it is those prayers," write the Sisters, "which like a gentle and beneficent dew have fallen on the seed of our humble labors, rendering them fruitful for the glory of God ; while her example, her virtues, and her blessed instructions have been as a pillar of fire going before us to lead us to the perfection of our Rule and the religious life."

But her maternal sympathy sought vent not in prayer alone ; the news of the Sisters' extreme destitution excited her to constant efforts in their behalf. Glad to become a beggar for the poor of Jesus Christ, she solicited material aid of every available kind. Money, clothing, articles of devotion, and church ornaments were gratefully accepted and transmitted with all speed to the settlements on the Mississippi.

Little articles of personal adornment, pretty dress materials, ribbons, etc., she, with provident forethought, sent for the children ; with the injunction that the Sisters should teach the pupils themselves to convert them into wearing apparel, and thus train them to habits of neatness and industry. For this true daughter of St. Joseph was a great lover of manual labor, and regarded instruction in the feminine art of the needle as one of the most indispensable elements of womanly culture, one of the most effective means of remedying the indolence to which many children are naturally prone, and which, alas, for but too many, is the first step towards destruction. In this, as in other duties of a woman's life, she would have the example of Mary held up as a spur and an encouragement. " Oh, how sweet it is, how useful," exclaims Fénélon, " to represent to ourselves the august Queen of Heaven, attending, like other Jewish women, to the sewing of the family, mending the garments of St. Joseph or weaving that seamless robe of her Divine Son, for the possession of which the soldiers strove on Calvary. Sometimes we see her drawing the water for household necessities, again preparing the frugal repast, at which she seats herself with her holy Spouse and her Divine Son."

But " O spectacle admirable above all others ! " cries out Bossuet : "Jesus, the Son of God, consubstantial with the Eternal Father, follows the trade of an artisan. and, after St. Joseph's death, labors with His own Divine hands for the support of His widowed Mother ! "

It was this spirit of sublime reverence for labor which led Mother St. John to call it, in the words of the ancient monastic Constitutions, " the holy labor of the hands," and to desire that her daughters and those under their care should be deserving of the commendation of the Holy Ghost:

"She hath sought wool and flax, and hath wrought by the counsel of her hands."

Her spirit of profound faith taught her to regard as doubly blessed, work that contributed to the adornment of God's holy altars ; and she took delight in placing within the sacred walls evidences of loving remembrance, mute yet eloquent witnesses to a love that fed on sacrifices for the Beloved. The first Stations of the Cross used by the Sisters in Cahokia were her gift, to which she added from time to time flowers, candelabra, everything she could beg or procure to adorn the tabernacle of her God in the wilderness. One of her gifts was a clock for the chapel : acknowledging which the Sisters say : "Oh, how suitable a gift! Whenever it strikes it will remind us of the voice of our beloved Rev. Mother; we shall imagine that she is calling us and recommending regularity ; and, as in the good old times, we shall hasten to put in practice her wise and maternal advice." Under present circumstances those gifts may seem little and unworthy of record, but in the time of which we write they were priceless to the receivers, not only as evidences of maternal love and thoughtfulness, but as treasures otherwise wholly unprocurable. *Little* acts of kindness have a delicacy all their own ; and it has been well and truly said that no one attends better to little things than the really great in mind and soul. In this they resemble God, who concerns Himself with the infinitely great and the infinitely small : *Ima summis.*

It is a matter of the greatest regret that, of the correspondence maintained between Mother St. John and the founders of the American mission, only two letters have reached us. On the 6th of January, 1843, she writes :

"MY DEAR DAUGHTERS AND BELOVED NIECES :

"For three or four months I have been expecting Mgr. Rosati, Bishop of St. Louis, to come to Lyons : hence I have deferred writing, but I can wait no longer; my heart is hungry to write to you. It seems an age since I received news of my beloved children, and I know not how you are. My affection for you makes me impatient, for distance does not separate us ; far from diminishing our love, it but renders it more tender and active. Everything here, moreover, reminds me of my absent ones, and I seem to meet you again in all those places in which I have so often seen you."

"Friends," says St. John Chrysostom, "leave, as it were, something of their personality in those places where we have been with them, and when they are departed, we are sensible, with a tender sadness, of the perfume of their presence."

With this perfume, this tender sadness, the good Mother's heart was full, and she goes on to say : "Alas! all passes away with time : your remembrance alone remains to me, for an immense distance, the ocean itself, rolls between us !"

"Whatever the world may think," writes Mgr. Gay, "the heart grows but the warmer by self-purification : more elevated ideas produce greater sincerity of feeling, and it is a property of the religious life, thoroughly understood and holily practised, to develop considerably the power of affection. To love less would be a strange effect of a closer union with God !"[1]

Ah, no ! one loves not less but more ; one loves not for time, but forever, for eternity ! And full of this thought, the Mother continues : "But if the ocean part us here below, we shall meet again in eternity. Oh, that I could better express what this thought, 'We shall meet in eternity,' means to me, what consolation it gives me ! What a joy shall be our first meeting in Heaven ! We shall be reunited, never, never again to part. Yes ; I confidently believe our good God will receive us all into His bosom,

---

[1] *The Christian Life,* by Mgr. Gay.

granting us mercy by the merits of our Lord Jesus Christ.

"Let us implore the Blessed Virgin, our good Mother, and our glorious Patron St. Joseph, to obtain this grace for us all, my beloved daughters."

After giving them details about herself, the dear Mother House, and the Sisters who were around her, she concludes her letter thus: "Write to me, I beg you, on the first occasion; tell me everything that you do, all that you suffer; pour into the heart of a mother who loves you tenderly, your trials, your cares, your anxieties, your joys, if you have any; I shall share in all . . . . . . Let me not think that America makes you forget your old Mother, who embraces you each and all in our Lord Jesus Christ."

On the 22d of February of the same year, after informing them that Rev. Father Cholleton had become a Marist, and had been replaced as Superior of the Congregation, by the Abbé Grange, she speaks of the necessity of absolute confidence in God under trials and difficulties. "This," she says, "has been my only resource in all the trials, sorrows, and tribulations of my long life. God can do all; without Him we can effect nothing; we must, like little children, cast ourselves into His arms. Whether we be in the height of misery or in the depth of the abyss, His almighty arm can restore us. Whatsoever this arm upholds, nothing shall put down, and what it abases, nothing can raise up."

Encouraging them to live in the Divine Presence, she reminds them that "No matter where on this lower earth we may be, we are never exiled, never far from the eyes of our Heavenly Father. Whether we be on one side of the world or the other, in America or in Europe, everywhere He is the witness of our labors and our conflicts. When I think that you are in a different world from me, I am consoled by the reflection that we are all in the bosom of our God."

Thus, like Saint Basil the Great, she thought no place on earth more of an exile than another, as "the earth is the Lord's," in whom "we live and move and have our being."

She recommends her children to do everything perfectly, everything for God, that their actions may be worthy of eternal recompense. She wishes them to be good, kind and patient, and to reprove others with sweetness. "All my desire," she concludes, "is that you become Saints, and that your little communities be truly regular and edifying. . . . I conjure our Lord to shed on you, more and more copiously, His benedictions and to assist you ever with His grace."

Mme. de la Rochejacquelin, united in affection with Mother St. John, shared her solicitude in regard to the missions so largely indebted to her zeal and charity.

Writing to Mother Febronia on the 12th of November, 1836, the noble Countess says : " I am most eager to receive details of your establishment at Cahokia. What kind of a house do you live in ? Have you any grounds ? How many pupils have you? Tell me how many pay, how many are free ? Shall you soon know English ? Have you any postulants ? Has Divine Providence granted you any resources ? In a word, my dear Mother, what do you live on ? . . . Answer me as soon as possible, because I want to send you some things. Tell me what you most need. . . . I am anxious that you should attend the poor, the sick, and that you should open a little dispensary. You must learn from a doctor the medicinal properties of American plants. I shall try myself to procure for you a work on that subject.

" Your venerable aunt is made happy at the thought of your devotedness, which fears neither distance, climate, nor difficulty, when there is question of winning souls to Jesus Christ. Europe does not suffice for the ardent charity of the Sisters of St. Joseph. They have undertaken to teach in foreign lands the truths of our holy religion to minds and hearts hitherto uncultivated. Those are sheep without a pastor whom you are to lead into the fold of the Church. It is a difficult task, but the Crib and the Cross have triumphed over everything. Oh, may you be Saints! . . . Pray for me that I may serve God as I should, after all the graces He has lavished on me and which I have so greatly abused. . . . Adieu, my dear little Mother; be so kind as to present my respects to your Bishop and recommend me to his good prayers, to those of your community, your brother, and Mother Mary Delphine, your sister in a double sense. I offer a thousand wishes and prayers for you."

In a letter of July 28th, 1841, the Countess expresses the pleasure she had felt on hearing from Mother Febronia: "Your letter of April 24th has been received with much delight. Numerous occupations have prevented my acknowledging it sooner, but I have also delayed in the hope of being able in a short time to send some money in my letter, so as to prove to you that the work you are engaged in is and ever shall be very dear to me. I arrange all that with Rev. Mother St. John, your dear aunt.

"I am happy to learn that your sister, Mother Delphine, has opened several establishments, and that you have received many subjects. You have made yourselves all to all; you have put your trust in God and He has blessed you.

"In your answer tell me all that concerns your Houses: their situation, their work, their object; tell me the good they do; the resources opened to you. May the little assistance I am able to send you be a consolation, an encouragement. Rely upon God who can do all things, and that most effectually where creatures can do nothing. You are the mustard-seed; you will become a great tree whose branches shall extend over that immense land whose time of civilization has arrived.

" I am not worthy, my dear Mother, my beloved Sisters, to address to you such language ; but since God has put these thoughts at the end of my pen, I beg Him to realize them, to bless you, and to cement between you and your poor benefactress those links of charity which never shall be broken. I count much on the succor of your prayers for myself, my relatives, and friends.

" The number of your Sisters in La Vendée, Touraine, Saint-Aubin and Ussé is increased. The foundation of Annecy has been very prosperous ; it has already sent forth several *swarms.*

" Implore God to bless these establishments, so that new convents may be opened, especially in the west of France, and that we may be enabled soon to open a novitiate there for the American Houses. This is both Mother St. John's hope and mine."

These letters reveal the ardent faith and apostolic zeal of the noble Vendean, and what a conformitiy of ideas existed between herself and Mother St. John. Can we wonder that they encouraged the Sisters to whom they were addressed, since they were enforced by the more eloquent voice of example ? Well might the descendant of martyred heroes, and the religious who had herself confronted martyrdom, inculcate heroism of faith to others !

The establishment of the American missions may be considered a fitting consummation of Mother St. John's long and blessed administration. As the glow of the setting sun illumines the decline of day, so we may say the close of her earthly pilgrimage was rendered brighter by the light reflected on it from the western world. For the love of God she had sacrificed her most legitimate affections, and with the confidence of St. Peter she could say : " I have left all things to follow Thee." Our Lord did, then, but accomplish His Divine promise by giving her " the hundred fold " in this life, " ere He called her unto life everlasting."

*   *   *   *

As this, the Third Book of Mother St. John's Life, has been mainly devoted to information regarding the foundations of the Sisters of St. Joseph in different parts of the world, a statistical table of the various communities, convents, etc., of the Congregation will be a fitting supplement thereto.

This information having been received directly from the majority of the Mother Houses themselves, the record is substantially correct, but from many houses in France and Italy we have been unable to obtain the desired data in time for publication. For the former we can partially supply by extracts from documents drawn up for the Government in 1878, which, however, give but the number of the Sisters and the *schools* under their care in the various Departments, without direct reference to the asylums and hospitals, which are, frequently, under the direction of one Community.

From the subjoined record, incomplete as it is, it will be seen that the Congregation of St. Joseph, outgrowth of the little seed sown and cultivated in the retirement of Le Puy, has renewed in its extension and development the history of the devotion to St. Joseph, a devotion which, having for centuries " lain, as it were. dormant in the bosom of the Church," has, in later times, through the impetus received from the infallible voice of Peter, become as universal as the Church herself.[1]

---

[1] " It rose from a Confraternity in the white City of Avignon, and was cradled by the swift Rhone, that river of martyr memories that runs by Lyons, Orange, Vienne, and Arles, and flows into the same sea that laves the shores of Palestine. . . . . . . When it had filled Europe with its odor, it went over the Atlantic, plunged into the umbrage of the back-woods, embraced all Canada, became a mighty missionary power, and tens of thousands of savages filled the forests and the rolling prairies with the praises of St. Joseph." (Faber.)

So, too, from Scandinavia to Madagascar, from the Eastern shores of the Pacific to where, through the Golden Gate, its mighty waters roll to the feet of San Francisco, the Daughters of St. Joseph " are to be found in the hospitals of the poor, the asylums of the fallen, the cell of the prisoner, and the halls of the academy. . . . diffusing on every side the blessings of peace, consolation, and instruction." [1]

------

[1] Catholicity in the United States, Murray.

Congregation of the Sisters of St. Joseph

In the Eastern Hemisphere and South America.

Congregation.	Central or Mother-House.	Founded.	No. in Com.	Schools.	Char. Inst.
Lyons (1812) [1]	Le Chartreux (Lyons) [2]	17—	3000	431 [3]	48
Le Puy (1815) [1]	Le Puy	1650	748	72	12
Clermont (1809) [1]	Le Bon Pasteur (Cler't)	1723	560	80	15
Bourg	Belley	1819	1625	223 [5]	
Gap (1837) [1]	Gap	1671	130	31 [5]	
Alby	Oulias	1824	300	64 [5]	
Bordeaux	Bordeaux	1840	360	40 [5]	
St. Gervais-sur-Marc	St. Gervais	*	552	156 [5]	
Dep't of Ardèche [4]	Aux Vaus, etc.,	*	1445	395 [5]	
" " Aveyron [4]	Clairveaux, etc.,	*	645	119 [5]	
" " Jura [4]	Champagnole, etc.,	*	89	25 [5]	
" " Drôme [4]	St. Vallier, etc.,	*	115	16 [5]	
" " Cantal, Tarn, etc. [4]	. . . .	*	102	* [5]	
" " H'te Pyrenees [4]	Turbes, etc.,	*	234	140 [5]	
" " Mayenne [4]	Laval, etc..	*	69	*	
" " Maine-et-Loire [4]	Bauge, etc.,	*	78	*	
Cong. of Chambéry. — Chambéry	Chambéry	1812		45	12
Roman	Rome	1839		5	3
Bourbonnais	Cusset	1854		12	1
Danish	Copenhagen	1856	800	8	2
Brazilian	Itu	1858		6	6
Scandinavian	Stockholm	1862		5	2
Russian	St. Petersburg	1863		2	1
Cong. of Annecy. — Annecy	Annecy	1833	363	*	7
India	Vizagapatam	1852	78	10	2
England	Newport	1864	33	4	2
Cong. of St. Jean de M. — St. Jean de Maurienne	St. J. de M.	1822	. . . . . .	*	*
India	Vizianagram	1852	100		
Africa	*	1884	. . . . . .	*	*
S. America	Buenos Ayres	1884	. . . . . .	*	*
Moutiers	Moutiers	1825	150	20 [5]	
Turin	Turin	1821	*	*	*
Pignerol	Pignerol	1825	*	*	*
			11576		

[1] Date of Restoration after the Revolution.

[2] The Congregation of Lyons extends over eighteen dioceses of France.

[3] The statistics for schools include Communal Schools, Pensionnats, Externats, and Salles d'Asile to the great majority of which are attached Dispensaries for the poor and sick.

[4] For the sake of brevity, we here include all the Sisters of St. Joseph in the Department.   [5] Probably, the number of Convents.   * Not given.

STATISTICS

— OF THE —

Congregation of the Sisters of St. Joseph

In North America, in 1886.

Diocese or Province.	Provincial or Mother House.	Founded.	No. of Community.	Acad.	Parochial Schools.	No. of Pupils.	Char. Inst.
St. Louis. St. Louis, Mo.	Mother House, Carondelet	1836	500	3	45	10933	6
St. Paul, Minn.	St. Joseph's Convent,	1851	125	2	19	1965	3
Troy, N. Y.	"	1851	125	3	20	6017	1
Arizona Ty.	" Tucson.	1869	95	—	7	750	2
Phila. Phila., Pa.	Mt. St. Joseph, Chestnut Hill.	1847	274	12	15	8845	3
Baltimore, Md.	" "	1875	18	—	8	818	—
Newark, N. J.	" "	1872	28	2	3	1105	—
Wheeling, W. Va.	St. Joseph's Convent,	1853	76	1	11	1200	2
Buffalo, N. Y.	Mt. St. Joseph.	1854	133	2	15	2970	3
Rochester, N. Y.	Nazareth Convent.	1854	180	3	16	5018	5
Brooklyn, N. Y.	St. Jos. Convent, Flushing.	1856	250	6	20	9588	2
Erie, Pa.	"	1852	65	4	8	2890	4
McSherrystown, Pa.	"	1868	40	3	6	484	2
Ebensburg. Ebensburg, Pa.	Mt. Gallitzin.	1869	51	1	3	1045	—
Columbus, O.	"	1877	14	1	3	500	—
Boston, Mass.	Mt. St. Joseph, Cambridge.	1873	69	1	4	1626	—
Rutland, Vt.	"	1876	24	1	3	704	—
Springfield, Mass.	St. Michael's Convent.	1880	42	—	4	1950	—
St. Augustine, Fla.	St. Joseph's Convent.	1866	70	6	8	*	—
Savannah, Ga.	" Washington.	1867	34	2	3	115	1
CANADA.							
Toronto. Toronto.	St. Jos. Convent, Toronto.	1851	157	5	15	1907	5
Peterborough.	" "	"	19	2	3	390	2
Hamilton.	" Hamilton.	1852	100	—	11	2450	6
London.	Mt. Hope, London.	1868	54	—	4	775	3
Total.			2543	60	249	64075	50

Fourth Book.

Closing Years of Mother St. John's Life.

CHAPTER I.

Mother St. John's desire to secure a suitable successor.—Mother Sacred Heart of Jesus is appointed Assistant Superior General.—The Mother General's greatness of soul.—Her re-election.

ARRIVED at the limits of human life, and convinced that death could not be far distant, the Mother General made it her fervent petition to God that He would make known to her a soul capable of aiding her in her endeavors for the perfection and consolidation of the Congregation, one who could assume the burden she had so long borne. He who has said, " Seek and you shall find," deigned, ere long, to reveal to her the priceless treasure her Congregation possessed in a soul whose only desire was to live hidden in God, and dead to the world. Being on her visitation of one of her convents, Mother St. John was suddenly enlightened as to the designs of God, and joyfully exclaimed: " At last have I found her whom I needed for our dear Congregation." This chosen soul was Mother Sacred Heart of Jesus, known in the world as Virginia Tézénas du Montcel, a religious to whose nobility of birth were added gifts of nature and of grace which have made her the glory of her Congregation, the admiration of her contemporaries.[1] Mgr. Plantier, the famous

---

[1] See her Life, by l'Abbé Rivaux.

Bishop of Nismes. speaking of her, has said : "Mother St. John re-created the Congregation of St. Joseph ; Mother Sacred Heart has a second time restored it: the latter act, it seems to me, is equally as great as the former."

Having for several years been Mistress of Novices at Mi-Carême,—that blessed community of Saint-Etienne whose religious have been chosen by God for so many important works,—Mother Sacred Heart was appointed Superior of that House, which office she filled at the time of which we write.

Mother St. John had long known and appreciated her worth, but it was only on the occasion of her last visitation that she received the mysterious intimation, which, indeed, proved prophetic.

The great age and failing strength of the Mother-General convinced Mgr. de Pins that a co-operatrix in the government of the Congregation was necessary ; and, by virtue of his authority as Superior, he named for that office Mother Sacred Heart, Superior of Saint-Etienne. Her parents, however, who had never become fully reconciled to Virginia's vocation, raised great opposition, and by every means in their power tried to retain her at Saint-Etienne, which was but a short distance from the family domain of Montcel.

But it was the will of Divine Providence that the inspiration and hope given to Mother St. John should be accomplished. Mother Sacred Heart was accordingly summoned to Le Chartreux, and formally installed as Assistant-General. Here she found herself, for a time, placed in a very delicate position. God, who had so great a future in reserve for her, permitted that the path of office should at first prove a thorny one, and that by the difficulties she had to encounter, the depth and solidity of her virtue, of which her Superior was fully cognizant, should be proved to the community in general.

The majority of the Sisters of the Mother House of Lyons most ardently desired that Mother St. John, the restorer of their Congregation, should retain its government until the end of her life. Others, sensible that, on account of her great age, they could not hope to keep her very long in their midst, had cast their eyes on Sister Antoinette Louis, as being the religious most capable of aiding the Mother by whom she had been trained to the religious life, and with whom her office of Secretary had for years brought her into the closest relations. Both these classes, into whose affection for the Superior human feeling and sentiment had crept, resented the appointment of Mother Sacred Heart, of whose virtues and qualifications they had no knowledge. Judging that the Archbishop's action was but the preparatory step to the Mother General's deposition, they were not slow to show their feelings and express their prejudices, forgetting that the voice of authority is the voice of God, and that judgments grounded on passion must necessarily be false. Mother Sacred Heart was not ignorant of the suspicions entertained in regard to her by some of her Sisters, and the knowledge added not a little to the weight of a cross she had felt almost beyond her strength. She who, on her appointment as local Superior, fourteen years previously, had felt such anguish as turned her hair white in one night, could not. but with extreme grief, behold herself called to the exalted and responsible position of Assistant-General. Wisely dissembling, however, she met coldness only with kindness, and made the Sacred Heart of Jesus the sole Depositary of her loneliness and sorrow. " Patience had its perfect work;" it was not long ere those who had distrusted her most became her warmest admirers and most devoted children.

The Mother General, as we may well believe, had had no share in the feelings to which we have just alluded. Accustomed, in all the occurrences of life, to look first to the Divine will, and endowed with that gift which the Holy Spirit calls *latitudinem cordis*, she rose superior to those littlenesses which are but too frequently to be found in ordinary souls. Hence she received with maternal tenderness the dear Sister whom God had sent to be the stay and support of her declining years ; she lavished on her tokens of affectionate and delicate attention, seeming by every act to repeat with St. John : She " must increase but I must decrease." Making her great age the cloak of her humility, she tried to put Mother Sacred Heart forward on every occasion. This feeling of humble and exquisite delicacy she carried almost to extremes, for on the approach of the time for election, she secretly withdrew from the Mother House and set out for Paris, where she intended to lodge at the monastery of the Visitandines, whose Superior was her intimate friend. As the election was to take place after the annual retreat, Mother St. John's excuse was that she wished to make hers at a distance, so as to be free from business and preoccupation ; but in reality, her intention was to efface herself, as it were, from the minds of the Sisters, and to make them feel more free in their choice. From her first stopping-place on her journey she wrote to the Father Superior, entreating him not to recall her until after the election. To this M. Cholleton agreed, not without reproaching her for having undertaken so uncalled-for a journey.

The Sisters, however, were not so easily pacified, for on the morning that followed her departure, they noticed her absence from Mass and the community breakfast, and hastened to her cell to find it untenanted, their feelings almost overpowered them. Inquiry elicited no information : the Portress had not opened or heard any one open the door. Only one thing was certain,—their Mother had gone ; why, they fully understood ; whither, they were not so sure. By Mother Sacred Heart's direction, one of the religious deeply devoted to her Superior set out to trace the steps of the would-be absentee.

Examination of the lists at the Diligence Office disclosed that *Mme. Fontbonne* had been one of the passengers; and calling a carriage, Sister Delphine set off in her filial pursuit. Two hours' rapid driving brought her up to the diligence, which had stopped for a relay of horses; and there, calmly seated in the coach, she beheld her runaway Mother, whom she hastened to embrace with all the effusion of her heart, speaking more by tears than by words. Amazed at the sight of one whom she had thought in Lyons, engaged in the holy exercises of retreat, Mother St. John exclaimed : "What, my dear child ! you here ? But who told you where I was ? What has brought you so far from home ?" "O Mother," she replied, "we guessed everything. We had only to follow your traces, and I have done so in the greatest anxiety of mind. Now I have found you, I shall not leave you again. How could you leave us just when we had most need of you ? How could you, who are so good, subject your children to such alarm and sadness ?" Tenderly sensible of her Sisters' affection, the Mother could not restrain her tears at the recital of their emotion. Nevertheless, she urged Sister Delphine to return at once to Lyons, saying that God would watch over her during her journey to Paris, and that she would arrive there in good health. "No, no, Mother," replied Sister Dephine; "I will not leave you ; like Ruth the Moabite, I shall be where you will be. I repeat it, I will not go; I am here by the wish of your spiritual family."

"But, my dear child," answered Mother St. John with that simple *naïvete* habitual to her, " it is impossible for me to take you with me. I have only enough to pay my own fare." " Oh, you need not be anxious on that point," replied Sister Delphine. "The diligence is to stop at Roanne; and I can there draw on my father's banker. He will only be too happy to give me the means of accompanying you."

At Roanne, accordingly, Sister Delphine drew five hundred francs and wrote to that effect to her father, who, as she had foreseen, was pleased to be of some service to the Mother General, whom he venerated as a Saint.

Mother St. John could not but be grateful for the tender attentions of her beloved child, and with a look of maternal affection, she exclaimed: "You are the guardian angel of your old Mother; may our Lord recompense your filial devotedness!"

On arriving at Paris she was most cordially and affectionately received by the Daughters of St. Francis de Sales, and, as soon as possible, she entered on her spiritual retreat, which she made with all the fervor of her soul. Entire days she spent in the chapel, so absorbed in the presence of her Beloved, so dead to all external things, that it became necessary, at certain times, to recall her to herself. Having, on one occasion, by this means, been the cause of an hour's delay to the community, she was overwhelmed with confusion, most humbly begged pardon, and begged Sister Delphine, as her *guardian angel*, to prevent the recurrence of so great a fault.

In the meantime, the retreat at Lyons had been closed and the general elections held, with the result that Mother St. John was unanimously re-elected Superior General, with Mother Sacred Heart as Assistant. Father Cholleton wrote to Paris to apprize her of the result and order her to return immediately "to that spiritual family who were so eager to greet her again." The news was far from joyful to her who had hoped for a respite from labor, but she, in all simplicity, obeyed the summons, and returned to the Mother House, where, in her honor, they held a veritable feast, a triumph. The bells were rung in token of the joy felt by the community, the *Te Deum* was solemnly chanted in the chapel, and every one insisted on seeing her, speaking to her, and embracing her. Mingling reproaches with their welcome, the Sisters exclaimed : " Why, Mother, did you leave us in such a way?" "Ah, well," she replied, pleasantly, " was it not better that I should ? If I had stayed here in some little corner of the chapel, some of you might have thought : 'There is that good old woman ; we must nominate her ; it won't do to give her up.' But when I wasn't here, nobody could see me." Ah, how beautiful is childlike humility ! How sweet, how edifying is Christian union !

Finding themselves again, by the voice of God, placed conjointly at the head of the Congregation of St. Joseph, Mother St. John and Mother Sacred Heart governed it with perfect unanimity of spirit and action. Their sincere affection, mutual respect, deference, and veneration were a most edifying spectacle to all who beheld them. Mother Sacred Heart rejoiced that her duties brought her into daily contact with one whose life was a living reproduction of her Rule, and whose example was that of a Saint. She did nothing but by her advice and consent, showing the most absolute and filial obedience. On her part, Mother St. John, whose age, infirmities, and deep humility, more than all, made her sigh to be released from the burden of superiority, labored assiduously to initiate her Assistant into the duties of the office, to instruct her on its requirements, and to win for her the affections of the other Sisters. The humble and charitable struggle carried on between those two venerable Mothers in the delicate circumstances by which they were surrounded was a living reproduction of the touching records of the Saints. Mother St. John, so pure, peaceful, and majestic, was, as it were, a planet tending towards its decline ; Mother Sacred Heart, as a bright and beautiful morning-star, called by the voice of God to shine for awhile in union with her, and later, to illumine alone the religious firmament.

God willed, however, that the close of that long and eventful life should bear, in a special manner, the seal of salvation, the sign of the holy Cross; and a cross all the heavier because it came from the hands of her Superiors.

This cross, with which God has so often crowned the summit of His servants' perfection, is the desolation, the abandonment of Calvary, which forces them to cry out, with their Divine Prototype, " My God, my God, why hast Thou forsaken me?" [1]

But, as we shall see, the grand soul of the Superior General accepted, with edifying resignation and generosity, the final trial, for it is the storms of life that reveal the difference between the good and the bad. Agitate a stagnant pool, says a great master of the spiritual life, and it will spread abroad infection; disturb, on the contrary, perfumed waters, and the air becomes odorous.

---

[1] Mark xv. 34.

CHAPTER II.

Mgr. de Pins demands Mother St. John's resignation.—Election of
Mother Sacred Heart.—Mother St. John obeys like a novice.—
Last years of the Venerable Mother.—Her edifying patience.—
Her holy death.—Circular letters to the Congregation.—Grati-
tude due to religious founders.

 E have already shown that Mother St. John, sensi-
sible of her declining strength, would have been
glad to retire from office. Scarcely, however,
had she been reinstated by the choice of the Sisters, when,
suddenly, without any previous notification or warning,
without any of those little acts of consideration which
might have seemed due to a Foundress, to a religious of
half a century, the Archbishop of Lyons called on her to resign. It would seem, from some documents, that his Grace
had been prejudiced against the Venerable Mother, and
hence resulted a course of action which could not but be
deemed somewhat severe.[1] However this may be, whether
simply demanded, or harshly imposed, Mother St. John immediately gave in her resignation, not only with humility,
but with eagerness and joy; asking only permission to spend
in retreat, under the saintly Curé of Ars, the first days of
her private life and her immediate preparation for eternity.
There, in recollection and prayer, she conjured the Lord
to bless her cherished daughters then engaged on their re-

---

[1] Among the Notes sent for this Life we find the following: Mother St. John had
received from the Sovereign Pontiff, Pius VII., a Brief by which she was named
Superior General for life of the Sisters of St. Joseph.—Yet she never revealed it.

treat, at the close of which the new Superior-General was to be elected.

The unanimous choice of the community fell on Rev. Mother Sacred Heart, Mother St. John's second self; and the latter, on receiving the news, hastened her return from Ars. Great was the joy and edification of the community on beholding the late Superior again in their midst, and as she knelt, with the humility of the youngest novice, to kiss the hand of Mother Sacred Heart and promise obedience to her, the Sisters were all moved to tears.

Thenceforth the lowest place became the sole object of her ambition, and she studied by every means to profit by the occasions of humiliation which the religious life affords. Mother Sacred Heart would fain have interfered to prevent it, but Mother St. John earnestly begged her not to do so. "Allow me, Mother, to act in this way," she used to say; "I am so happy to obey! Our dear Lord is so good in granting me this time wherein to think of my eternity; and in affording me, for my greater merit, the means and opportunity of imitating Him."

The same sentiments she expresses in her letters to her American children. "Never have I been more joyous or contented," writes she, "as since I have had the happiness of being freed from the burden of superiority. . . . . Every day I thank God for having given me some time in which to think only of my salvation. My only regret is that I do not profit sufficiently by it."

A scrupulous observer of holy poverty, she would not suffer the Divine Master to find her standing idle, and she was continually employed in some kind of work. "Do not be uneasy," we read in another of her letters to her beloved missionaries; "thanks be to God, I enjoy all my faculties as well as when I was fifty years old, and now I am eighty-four. I rise with the community and am present at all the exercises. I write, I sew, I crochet, yet do not need spectacles. . . . . Help me to bless my God for granting me time and strength to lay up treasures for eternity." This is ever the refrain of her ardent faith.

In view of this eternity she thought only of realizing that sublime maxim of her Rule : " Regret that the world thinks of you. . . Believe this truth, that its thoughts and affections are uselessly bestowed on persons who so little merit them." " Ah, might I ask but one favor of you," said she to the Superior General, " it would be to let me occupy the little room on the passage-way, at the end of the court. There I should be more retired. That little solitude would help me to be more recollected ; I should have more freedom to speak heart to heart with my God ; and the Sisters would be freer in their relations with you." Mother Sacred Heart, however, anxious to keep her near herself, begged her to retain the same room as formerly, and to make no change in her accustomed habits. Filial delicacy and love on the one side, profound humility and self-abnegation on the other, struggled for the mastery, each being emulous of the better gifts, according to the expression of the Apostle.

Mother St. John carried her point for the moment, but His Eminence Cardinal de Bonald interfered later on, and robbed her of her dearly loved " little corner." Still she continued to keep ever as her Model, Him who, for thirty-three years, set us the lesson of silence, retirement, humiliation, and the hidden life, and with the Apostle she might have exclaimed : My " life is hid with Christ in God.' . . . . I know both how to be brought low, and I know how to abound: (everywhere, and in all things I am instructed ").[2]

Oh, what an edifying spectacle was it to the Sisters, young and old, to see that Mother, doubly venerable for her four-

---

[1] Colossians iii. 3.   [2] Philippians iii. 12.

score years of life and her more than half a century of religious profession, prostrating herself at the feet of her whom she had received to the Congregation, to beg her permission for Communion and the other daily acts of her conventual life! And that beloved daughter, who then, by the will of God, held His place and acted by His authority, would, while granting the permission, tenderly raise up her aged Mother, to cast herself in turn before her to beg her maternal blessing! O blessed struggle of humility! holy contest for self-abasement, wherein while one gloried in being the last, the other grieved at beholding herself the first!

It was Mother St. John's delight and joy to notice how, under the leadership of her successor, the Congregation continued to increase and enlarge its field of action; and Mother Sacred Heart's loving attention to the Sisters' wants, her tender sympathy in their sickness and suffering, were received by the aged Mother as personal benefactions. Unable longer to walk unaided, she yet would not permit that a Sister should be detailed to help her, and in going to and from the chapel, she made use of a stick to support her tottering limbs. "I am come to serve, not to be served," were the words of her Divine Master, an imitation of whom she desired her every action to be; and on this account she insisted on attending herself to providing the water, etc., for her cell, though her children lovingly desired and endeavored to forestall her. Thus gradually was her life tending to its peaceful close, when God willed to lay her on a bed of suffering, whereon she might become more conformable to His Divine Son. One winter's day, while crossing the yard, her stick slipped and she fell heavily to the ground. She was unable to rise, but her children ran to her in all haste, tenderly lifted and carried her to her room. The physicians, upon examination, declared that her shoulder was dislocated, and, on account of her great age and infirmity, they were fearful for the consequences of the necessary operation. The head physicians of the Hotel-Dieu were called, and while the operation was being performed, the whole community, in a state of agonizing suspense, united in fervent supplications for its success. Mother Sacred Heart never left the side of the beloved sufferer, from whom there came not the least moan or the slightest complaint. At the sight of such angelic patience, Doctor Bonnet could not restrain the expression of his admiration. " It is very good when one has to deal with saintly people," said he; " we can do with them whatever we wish. This good Mother, in the midst of her extraordinary sufferings, sets us an example of heroic patience and sublime resignation." God deigned to bless the filial attentions and prayers of the Sisters by granting to the operation a success they could scarcely have hoped for, and the rapid convalescence of the beloved patient gave the Congregation hopes of possessing her for some time longer. The respite was, nevertheless, but a brief one, and Mother Sacred Heart, in a circular letter to her children, writes, but a short time later : " I regret to be obliged to say that the state of our Rev. Mother St. John's health causes us grave uneasiness." And again: " Since our last circular, the suffering state of our venerable Mother St. John has more than once alarmed us ; at present, however, she is somewhat better. Continue to unite your prayers with ours for the prolongation of that life dear to us on so many titles."

The improvement thus noted was of brief continuance, for in the next circular we read : " The life of our venerated and beloved Mother St. John has, for the past few days, been seriously threatened. We have all the more reason to dread the disease, as her great age has deprived her of strength to struggle against it. Our sole reliance now is on God ; let us redouble our prayers for her restoration. You know how many titles she has to our filial love. In a certain sense she has created our Congregation; her long administration was equally remarkable for the prudence of her acts, the wisdom of her counsels, the fecundity of her works. There is scarcely one amongst us whom she has not received to her holy vows : scarcely one in whose regard she has not fulfilled the office of a mother. Her goodness, her high perfection, her admirable regularity, have ever made her the model for all, and make her so still, despite her eighty-four years. Ah, how ardent a desire for her re-establishment in health should such remembrances, such a spectacle excite within us ! With what fervor should we not unite in imploring God to spare to our imitation, our gratitude, and our love, a soul so rich in experience, virtue, and merit !" This letter is dated March 11th, 1843.

For several months Mother St. John lingered on in the same suffering condition, preaching still more eloquently to her children by her fervent prayer, calm and holy resignation to the Divine will, than she had ever done by words. With humble and child-like confidence she spoke of her last hour, and it was only the thought that such was the will of her Beloved that enabled her to restrain her holy longing for the termination of her exile. "Ah, have I still much longer to live ?" was the cry that burst from her lips but a few moments before her happy release. When answered that her chains would soon be broken, a smile of ineffable happiness beamed on her countenance ; then calmly, almost imperceptibly, she sank into the slumber of death : with her lamp illumined with the light of heroic faith and filled with the good works that had adorned her almost eighty-five years, she entered into the eternal feast of the Heavenly Bridegroom.

Communicating to the Houses of the Congregation the news of their loss, Mother Sacred Heart writes : "Our

Rev. Mother St. John is no more. After sixty-three and a half years of religious profession, God called her to Himself on the morning of November 22d, 1843, she being eighty-four years and eight months old. Her last moments on earth were not less beautiful than the preceding years of her life. With her usual peaceful calm and untroubled sweetness, she sank to sleep as sink the just, after a long life of glorious labor and extraordinary virtue.

" Her obsequies were celebrated on the 23d with a religious pomp worthy of her who was its object. All our Sisters who could, came to the ceremony, lovingly desirous to aid us in paying, in the name of the whole Congregation, the last tribute of regard and affection to her whom we have so long admired as the most perfect of religious, the most prudent and enlightened of Superiors, and the tenderest of Mothers. We take this opportunity of expressing our gratitude to them.

" Continue to recommend to God in your prayers the soul of our beloved Mother ; and let the ardor of our supplications bear some proportion to the extent of the benefits we have received from her, and that wealth of sweet and holy memories which she has left us as our heritage."

" After the Holy Scriptures," says a zealous prelate, "there is nothing so attractive to me as the Lives of the Saints. I know of nothing more useful to souls. In my opinion, nothing is better calculated, not only to animate the soul and strengthen the faint-hearted, but yet more to lead back to God and religion those whom the temptations of the world have led astray. ' Though dead, the Saints still speak,' writes the Apostle, and, we may add, more eloquently in death than in life."

This is especially true of Saints who have been founders or restorers of religious orders, and who have left after them a numerous posterity of servants of God, wholly devoted to His service and that of their neighbor. For they live not alone by the perfume of the example they have left behind them ; they continue to act, to speak, in the persons of their spiritual children, and their work is perpetuated, extended, multiplied ; the world, meanwhile, forgetful or contemptuous in regard to those to whom it owes such incalculable benefits.

To this class of the holy ones of God, Mother St. John belongs ; angelic legions, who, to her, under God, can trace their religious life, combat in two hemispheres either the dangers of mental ignorance, or the innumerable host of miseries that are the heritage of humanity from the cradle to the tomb.

Blessed, then, forever blessed, be the founders of those holy nurseries whence issue forth the glorious militia of faithful teachers and guardians of youth. " The highest interest of modern times and of society in its actual state is Christian education," says Cardinal Guibert. And, adds M. Chesnelong, " Of all the creations of Catholic devotedness, there is none more beautiful, none more fruitful, none more popular, in the best and highest sense of the word, than those congregations of Brothers and Sisters devoted to education."

While free-thinkers and atheists are prodigal only of the speeches—as high-sounding as they are deceitful and poisonous—in which they laud *popular education*, which to them means the ignoring or the denial of God, the religious orders of teachers devote, unreservedly, talents, time, labor, nay, even life itself to the diffusion of true knowledge, the advancement of that education alone worthy of the name, because it gives the first place to that science which ennobles all the others, the knowledge of God and the religious obligations of man.

Science, properly so called, must ever be the possession of the few, but with religion one is instructed though he may not become learned. She teaches necessary duties, she reveals useful truths to the vast multitudes who have neither talent, time, nor opportunity for painful research.

Woe, then, to those who seek to destroy that source of sacred instruction which sows good maxims everywhere, renders them living, present realities, perpetuates them by linking them with durable and permanent establishments, and communicates to them that character of authority and popularity, wanting which they would remain foreign to the people, that is, to the far greater majority of men !

CHAPTER III.

IN the course of this history we have endeavored to
give, as far as lay in our power, the moral and
mental portrait of the holy Foundress of the
Congregation of St. Joseph in Lyons ; realizing, meanwhile, how difficult, nay, how impossible it would be to
give a complete picture of the life of one whose most earnest endeavor was to realize in herself that maxim of her holy
rule : "Let your good actions be hidden in time and
known only to God, that they may appear in eternity, or
never appear, if such be the will of God." The inner life
of His Saints God generally keeps in the secret of His Divine counsels, allowing it to reveal itself on earth only by
the aroma of sanctity, which, like the perfume of a concealed exotic, diffuses itself on all sides, intangible, im-
palpable, but sensibly and powerfully beneficent to all who
come within the sphere of its influence.

Agreeing with Chateaubriand, "that the most beautiful eulogy one could write on the life of a religious would
be to present a list of the labors to which it has been consecrated," we have spoken of the noble work inaugurated by her, or by those acting under her direction, and
of foundations even "to the uttermost bounds of the
earth," which are but branches of the glorious tree planted
by her hand.

We can imagine how earnestly the Sisters must have
desired to obtain for themselves and succeeding genera-

tions the pictured lineaments of her with whom the sweet
and blessed memories of the restoration of the Institute
were inseparably connected : but on this point she was inex-
orable. The most pressing entreaties met with a gentle yet
firm refusal : her humility was alarmed at the very thought
that her picture might be handed down as that of the
Foundress and Restorer. Nevertheless, her children were
not to be robbed of their natural right ; and the possession
of a portrait of their venerable Mother, as true and striking
in resemblance as perfect in execution, is due to the talent
and affection of the Countess de Virieu, the foundress of
the establishment of the Sisters of St. Joseph in Grand-
Lemps. Taking advantage of a visit of gratitude which
the Rev. Mother made her in 1836, the noble lady availed
herself of every favorable moment to obtain what she so
ardently longed for. When her religious guest finally perceived on what work the Countess was engaged, she desired to withdraw, but the delicacy of the circumstances in
which she was placed, and the affectionate earnestness of
her hostess, won the victory.

The Houses of the Congregation were not slow to obtain
copies of the stolen portrait, for such we may call it ; and
when, on her visitations, she saw such pictures and recognized how futile had been her long resistance, the Mother
used, with simple *naïveté*, to deplore the tender deception
that had been practised on her.

Mother St. John's countenance, as revealed in this picture, is all that our imagination would have led us to suppose the fitting accompaniment of the beautiful soul within. There is in it such an air of blended majesty and
sweetness, that one is at no loss to understand the charm
which attracted souls to her at first sight : and while it
images forth that high and magnanimous spirit which,
with the great Apostle, dared to say. " I can do all things
in Him who strengtheneth me," speaks no less eloquently of

a maternal love, an unfailing charity, that made itself "all to all, to gain all to Christ."

The power of Mother St. John's intercession with God has been several times manifested, both before and after her death. In 1838, one of the postulants in the Novitiate of Lyons was attacked by a brain fever so violent that four persons could not restrain her convulsive movements. The moment of dissolution seemed at hand, yet there was no possibility of administering the last Sacraments. In this extremity, Mother St. John drew near the bed and said: "In the name of God, my child, calm yourself;" then taking holy water, she made the sign of the cross on the closed eyelids of the patient. At that moment the fever and convulsions ceased, the young girl recovered the full use of her senses, and remained calm for one hour, during which time she received, with edifying dispositions, the last rites of the Church. Everybody attributed this precious favor to the virtue and prayers of the Rev. Mother.

During a very rigorous winter, the supply of coal in her convent was exhausted, and owing to her poverty, she was unable to purchase more ; she endeavored, however, to inspire the Sisters with a more fervent spirit of prayer and unwavering confidence in Divine Providence. Full of this holy spirit, Sister St. Ursula, who had charge of attending the fires, used, day after day, as she took what seemed to be almost the last shovelful of coal, fall on her knees before the little remnant, and with tears implore of God to have pity on the poor Rev. Mother, whose only reliance was on Him, and to save her from distress. Every day there was a repetition of the same fear, the same prayer, with the result that what had seemed insufficient for the coming day lasted until the close of that long and severe winter. The Sisters attributed this prodigy to the faith and trust of their venerable Superior.

After the decease of this holy Mother, a young religious, occupied by obedience in transcribing some details of her life, received news that her uncle, a holy religious who had been a second father to her, had been attacked by a violent epidemic and lay at the point of death. "O my good Mother St. John!" cried she with faith and simplicity, "I am laboring for you. If you are in Heaven, obtain from God the preservation of my dear uncle." Almost on the instant she received word that the beloved invalid was better; and but a short time later, was advised of his perfect recovery, which, on account of his great age, exhausted strength, and the virulence of the malady, could hardly have been expected.

Another religious who was attacked by a temptation of extreme antipathy against her Superior, which she had labored in vain to overcome, felt an inspiration, after an unusually long and violent struggle, to have recourse to Mother St. John and to go and pray at her tomb. Following the attraction of grace, she said to her in all simplicity: "O my Mother, you who were so good; you who knew so well how to love us all; you who have borne with such sweet and maternal patience the contrarieties of various characters and dispositions, you see my difficulty. You see that I suffer, that I make others suffer: help me to come forth victorious from the conflict. I have confidence in you, for I know you are in Heaven, and are all-powerful in the presence of God." So humble and filial a prayer could not fail of being heard; the Sister's sentiments underwent a wonderful change, and that soul that had been so anxious and unhappy was strengthened and encouraged; her dislike and ill-feeling gave place to the sweetest confidence and charity.

Two Sisters of St. Joseph from a distance, being on a visit to Lyons, were anxious to see the tomb of Mother St. John, for whose memory they had the greatest veneration. But for want of exact information, they were unable to find her grave among the hosts that filled the immense necropolis of Loyasse. Wearied and disheartened, after hours of useless search, they fell on their knees and with tears besought their Mother, in the words of the Spouse of the Canticles, " to show them the place of her repose." " My Sisters, I am here," answered a sweet voice, distinctly heard and recognized by each of the petitioners. Turning to where it indicated, they found themselves at the sacred spot they had so long and vainly sought. We can judge what then must have been the fervor of their supplications, how deep must have been their feelings of gratitude and filial love! Their souls were inundated with grace at the hallowed spot whence their Mother had deigned to speak to them.

About three months after the Rev. Mother's death, one of her children went to the Curé of Ars to offer an *honorarium* for Masses for the repose of her soul. But the holy priest refused to say them for that intention, adding decidedly: " Your Rev. Mother does not need them. She is high in glory; I know it." If these words were not the expression of a particular revelation, they, at least, prove what an exalted opinion the Thaumaturgus of Ars had of the sanctity of the deceased, whom he had known long and intimately. Thus of two Sisters of St. Joseph, Mother St. Joseph of Bordeaux and Mother St. John of Lyons, the Saint of Ars has rendered the consoling testimony of their eternal beatitude.

In the Life of Rev. Mother Sacred Heart of Jesus we read that she would never allow any one to speak in the presence of a sick Sister of her virtues and good qualities, and that the wisdom of this precaution was fully proved by the following occurrence, which took place in one of the communities of St. Joseph in Lyons, some years after Mother St. John's death. One of the religious, at the point of death, had lost her speech and become, apparently, wholly unconscious. Nevertheless, she still had the power of hearing, of which those around her were ignorant.

The Sisters, who deeply regretted her loss, expressed their grief aloud, eulogizing her virtues and good qualities. The devil, who is especially eager for his prey in the last struggle, tempted the poor Sister to vain complacency, and she entertained the thought with pleasure. She felt herself immediately transported before the throne of the Sovereign Judge and condemned. Then she thought she saw Mother St. John prostrate herself at the feet of our Lord, crying : "Mercy, O my God ! she is one of my children. Give her time and strength to confess !" Her prayer was granted, and the Sister, returning to herself, cried aloud, "A priest ! quick ! a priest !" The minister of God arrived, heard the confession of the agonizing Sister, who immediately expired after having received absolution. She had authorized the confessor to reveal to her Sisters what had occurred, which he did, strongly warning them against ever speaking in praise of the dying in their presence.

* * * *

"The just that walketh in simplicity," says Solomon, "shall leave behind him blessed children," and in the children through whom Mother St. John founded the Institute of St. Joseph in America, the promise has been fully verified. Lovers of their holy Superior with the love that impels to imitation, they were, according to the testimony rendered by their Sisters and others to whom they were intimately known, disciples, who, like Eliseus, merited to inherit the spirit and mantle of their teacher, whose work they were to perpetuate and extend.

The first of this little band to rejoin her Mother where "parting shall be no more," was Mother Delphine Fontbonne, to whose life and labors we have had occasion, during the course of this work, frequently to advert. After having established the Congregation in Toronto and Hamilton, and inspired the Sisters with the true spirit of the Institute, it pleased God to crown her life by the glorious death of a martyr of charity.

About the beginning of the year 1856, a patient was admitted into the common ward of the Sisters' Hospital, who, as was discovered when too late, was attacked by a virulent and contagious fever. The disease spread rapidly among the inmates, and nine of the Sisters fell victims to its ravages. During this period of sorrow and trial, Mother Delphine's courage never failed, and although it is known that she had a great natural dread of fever, she was devoted and unwearied in her attendance on the sick. After having assisted at the death-beds of two of her Sisters, she herself succumbed to the disease ; and having taught her children, by her example, how the Spouse of a crucified God should suffer, she calmly passed to her eternal rest.

In a letter addressed to Rev. M. Denavit, Director of the Grand Seminary of Lyons, to be communicated to Rev. Fr. Fontbonne, Mother Delphine's brother, Rt. Rev. Mgr. de Charbonnel, Bishop of Toronto, thus expresses himself :—

"My DEAR FRIEND:

"It will be easier for you than for me to find the Abbé Fontbonne, formerly a missionary in America, and at present stationed in the diocese of Lyons, somewhere about Verrières, if I am not mistaken.

"It is my sad duty to announce to him that his sister, Mother Delphine Fontbonne, foundress and Superioress of the Religious of St. Joseph in Toronto, entered into her eternal reward, February 7, 1856, one hour after midnight, holily fortified with all the rites of the Church, and surrounded by the most devoted attentions.

"This excellent and worthy niece of the saintly Mother St. John, had, in five years, established in Toronto a novitiate, an orphan asylum, a House of Providence, which affords to the poor every spiritual and temporal succor, and several other houses in the diocese. Endowed with great wisdom and experience, this holy Superior enforced the Rule with sweetness and firmness. Her judgment was solid, her mind clear and penetrating, her prudence enlightened and far-seeing. She was laborious, energetic, active, and provident.

"At the age of twenty-one she was appointed Superior of the first colony of Sisters sent from France to St. Louis, and now she is dead at the early age of forty-two. Her robust health promised her a long life, but she has fallen a victim to her charity, while attending some of her Sisters and novices stricken with fever.

"Will you be so kind as to transmit this communication to her Reverend brother, and inform, also, the Rev. Superior General of the Mother House of Lyons that the suffrages of the community may be given our dear deceased Sister, although I feel assured she has entered into beatitude. . . . .

"We are now somewhat in distress, but have written to Rev. Mother Celestine of Carondelet, begging her to come to our aid. . . .

"I hope when I go to Europe to be able to get a considerable number of Sisters and novices. We have work here for a hundred at present, if we could get them. . . . . The religious are called to do immense good here, and, as I sometimes tell them, they can do everything but give absolution ; they can, however, give, instead, perfect contrition and charity."

* * * *

But Mother Celestine herself was, in the inscrutable designs of God, to be called to her reward about one year later, at a time when, humanly speaking, circumstances conspired to render her presence more than ever necessary to the rapidly developing communities of St. Joseph in America.

This saintly religious was born in 1814, at Tellien, in Burgundy, and was early confided by her parents to the care of the Sisters of St. Charles at Macon. By her ardent piety and purity of life, she merited to receive that invitation of the Spouse: "Hearken, O daughter, and see, and incline thine ear: and forget thy people and thy father's house, and the king shall greatly desire thy beauty."

The better to free herself from the importunities of her family and the endearments of home, she, with the advice of her confessor, decided to enter a community at some distance; and accordingly, at the age of fifteen, she was received into the Novitiate of the Sisters of St. Joseph at Lyons, where she made her profession, October 15, 1832. During her novitiate she had made known to her Superiors her wish to devote her life to the propagation of the faith in foreign countries, and when there was question of selecting subjects for the American Mission, Mother St. John remembered the wish of her fervent disciple. Sister Celestine had, in the meantime, been sent to the Diocese of Chambéry, but she was summoned thence to sail with the first band of missionaries. It would seem, however, that the Superiors of Chambéry hoped, by delay, to keep with them so valuable a subject, and her letter of obedience was handed to her too late; she arrived in Lyons to find, to her intense disappointment, that the vessel on which she was to have sailed to her "land of promise" was far out at sea.

Her family, when made aware of her resolve, exhausted every means in their power to retain her in France; and her Superiors were obliged, in view of the difficulties raised by them, to leave to herself the decision of the painful and delicate question. But He who had given her the strength and zeal of an apostle, enabled her to put flesh and blood out of the question, and seek, solely, the accomplishment of that Divine Will, which, from her earliest years, she had made the touchstone of her actions. Deprived in this conjuncture of the infallible guide of obedience, she, in fervent prayer and holy retirement, sought light from the Holy Spirit as to what was her duty to God and her Congregation. The guidance she implored was not denied her ; and convinced that her wish had been inspired by Heaven, she, in April, 1837, accompanied by one fervent companion, left forever the shores of her native land, to follow her Sisters to what might then be fitly termed " the wilds of the West." We have spoken heretofore of the arrival of the two Sisters at St. Louis, and of their reception by the Bishop. It was not long before the Prelate recognized the sanctity, prudence, and talents of Sister Celestine, and, in 1839, she was appointed Superior of the Sisters of St. Joseph in St. Louis. This is no fitting place to enter into an extended account of Mother Celestine's religious life and laborious administration, the fruits of which the later generations of the Institute have been privileged to reap, and a worthy relation of which, we trust, her children of Carondelet may yet present to us.

Belonging to that third class of the really great of whom Paschal says: " They are those who by their wisdom, ardent piety, and true religion, subdue themselves, and teach others to submit to the yoke of Christ," she attracted to God all those with whom she came in contact, by that sweet charm of meekness to which God Himself has promised empire. Tender as a mother even when firmest as a Superior, her words of counsel, admonition, and reproof were most potent for good, and it has been beautifully said that in their errors and delinquencies, her Sisters most frequently found their place of penance on the heart of their Mother. Thus " all loving, loved by all, but loving best and best beloved of Christ," she spent the twenty years of her religious life in America: and having been tried in the crucible of long and painful suffering, she, at last, was called to the nuptials of the Lamb on the 7th of June, 1857, at the Mother House of Carondelet. "Our grief at her loss," write her Sisters, "it is impossible for you to imagine or for us to describe. It is a terrible blow to the communities of St. Joseph. Her memory shall live eternally with us."

That blessed memory has, in truth, been zealously kept alive, and the revered name of Mother Celestine is held by the Sisters, even those to whom personal knowledge of her has been denied, as synonymous with all that the title, "a perfect religious," conveys and implies.

*   *   *   *

Mother St. John, the religious who, as above mentioned, accompanied Mother Celestine from France in 1837, and who was known in the world as Julia Alexia Fournier, was born at Arbois, France, November 11, 1814; and in the fourteenth year of her age, ere the world had claimed her heart or sullied the purity of her affections, she devoted herself to the Divine service in the religious state. Feeling within herself a supernatural attraction to the work of the missions in North America,—an attraction no doubt intensified by her study of the *Annals of the Propagation of the Faith*, which at that time aroused to enthusiasm the zeal of so many holy souls in France,—she consulted on the subject Rev. Father Cholleton, Vicar-General of Lyons and Superior of the Sisters of St. Joseph, by whose advice she made known her wish to Rev. Mother St. John. Her sacrifice was accepted; but while awaiting the time assigned for Mother Celestine's departure, she was sent with her to study at Saint-Etienne the deaf-mute language, as the Bishop of St. Louis contemplated opening a school or asylum for that class of the afflicted.

After her arrival in St. Louis, Mother St. John was assigned to different positions, both as teacher and Superior, in all of which she labored earnestly and successfully under the influence of that zeal which was so potent a factor in her character.

But the establishment of the Institute of St. Joseph in Philadelphia and adjacent dioceses seems to have been the great life-work allotted her by God, for the furtherance of which He endowed her with so many and such great gifts of nature and of grace.

Having, by a special Providence, been restored to that diocese in 1853, she, for twenty-two years, with a generosity that counted no sacrifice, an intensity of purpose that overcame almost insuperable obstacles, labored to organize and definitely established those institutions of religion, charity, and Christian education which are, to-day, her imperishable monument. "Her labors have not been without fruit, nor her works unprofitable," because their impelling principal was that spirit of simple, earnest, God-seeking faith with which she was so wonderfully endowed, that, frequently, holy and distinguished ecclesiastics, after hearing her speak of the things of God, have been heard to exclaim, in the words of the Gospel: " O woman, great is thy faith ! " Thence proceeded her intense, absorbing reverence for the Adorable Sacrament, " the grand and royal devotion of faith," and for all that appertained to the Divine worship.

Who that has heard her speak in the community conferences of the demeanor that a Spouse of Christ should maintain in presence of her Sacramental Lord, and has seen her words enforced by the eloquent preaching of her own example, can ever forget the lessons she taught, the impressions she produced?

It was this devotion, also, that inspired her with such veneration for the sacerdotal character, that any slighting word of a minister of God, any expression regarding his faults or eccentricities, was looked upon by her as little less than a sacrilege. This characteristic, so noticeable under a variety of circumstances, throughout her life, was emphasized particularly by her dying injunctions to the local Superiors of the Congregation.

Another revelation of her faith was that supernatural loyalty to the Church which Faber notes as a necessary element of sanctity, especially under times of persecution, such as at present. The sorrows and trials of the Pope, the " visible shadow of the Invisible Head of the Church in the Blessed Sacrament," weighed heavily on her heart ; and from the time of the occupation of Rome until her death, she never ceased urging her Sisters to prayer, penance, and self-immolation for the deliverance of the Holy See. These sentiments she sought to perpetuate by establishing in the Mother House the Midnight Hour of Adoration for this intention, an exercise which she never failed to conduct herself, unless prevented by sheer physical inability.

A soul so deeply imbued with a sense of the Divine Majesty could not but be an ardent lover of humility : indeed, that one word might well epitomize Mother St. John's spiritual temperament. In private direction as in public instruction, to professed Sisters as to novices, " in season and out of season," the exhortation to humility was ever on her lips; and one of her most frequent sayings, uttered archly but with a depth of meaning, was that, " A Sister of St. Joseph should love to keep in her little corner."

Of lively and impetuous disposition and most energetic character, no heavier cross, one would suppose, could have been given her by God than the twelve years of forced inaction which preceded her death. Yet we doubt if ever even those most closely in companionship with her heard the slightest complaint, or perceived any trace of want of conformity with the Divine Will in this regard; and although the excruciating attacks to which she was fre-

quently subjected, drew from her, at times, some expression
of suffering, it was always joined with the wish that God's
holy will might be fully accomplished in her, in that as in
all else. Solace in pain she found in prayer and labor;
and, incapacitated as she was by disease from the active external duties of her vocation, she conceived the design of
promoting the glory of God by the translation of works
that should tend to make Him better known and served.
The principal of these were Barthé's "Meditations on the
Litany of the Blessed Virgin"; Martinet's "Ark of the
People"; "The Sign of the Cross"; "Daily Life of the
Sick"; "Life of St. Benedict the Moor"; and "Madame
de Lavalle's Bequest"; to which we may add several books
for the amusement and instruction of the young.

Strong, vigorous, prudent, and far-seeing as to all the details of her government of the community, Mother St. John
was what we may call "an old-fashioned religious" in
her interpretation of the Rule, and her keen sense of the
sublimity of the religious vocation and the obligations contracted by those who embraced it. Softness, effeminacy,
half-hearted service of God found her a strict and, at times,
a severe judge, but her reproofs were always rendered
acceptable by the conviction that they proceeded from the
purest motives. In her personal intercourse there was an
irresistible charm; and her intimate knowledge of the character, disposition, trials, and wants of her religious, enabled her to reach what was best in them, even while, with
unsparing hand, she tried to uproot what was defective.
Seldom, if ever, has a Superior been more tenderly loved,
more deeply venerated; her slightest word was law, and
even though the silence of death has fallen on her, it has
not stilled the voice whose words and counsels, treasured
in faithful, filial hearts, are blessed, potent traditions to
the rising generations.

She had, indeed, "fought the good fight;" it was time

she should return to Him who had sent her to do His work; there was "laid up for her the crown of justice," with which our Lord delights to adorn the faithful soul. On the 15th of October, 1875, the anniversary of the foundation of St. Joseph's Institute, Mother St. John entered into her eternal rest, after having, by her sublime patience during her illness, her loving thoughtfulness for the future of those whom she promised to bear in her heart to Heaven, and her never-to-be-forgotten dying instructions to her community, fitly consummated her life of edification.

> " How Saints have lived that blessed life had taught us;
>   Woe for the days gone by!
> The sacred seal upon her life-work setting,
>   She taught us how they die."

Many and beautiful were the tributes rendered to her memory by prelates and distinguished ecclesiastics, by religious and laymen : but the memento made of her by the Holy Father Pius IX., to whom in life she had been so devoted, was to her Sisters a consolation precious beyond all price.

Her love for the Sacrament of the Altar had led her to spend much of the time of her illness in making lace for the use of the sanctuary, and she had earnestly cherished the hope of being allowed to present to the Holy Father a rochet made by herself and her Sisters. The visit to the Eternal City of a highly valued friend, whose influence there rendered the desired presentation practicable, enabled her to realize the wish of her heart. Her death, however, happening in the meantime, the kind bearer of the offering touchingly alluded to the fact in the beautiful letter of presentation. When his Holiness had read that part of the document he raised his eyes to Heaven, and murmured a fervent *Requiescat in pace.* Then taking his pen, he deigned to append to the Letter of Presentation the following words of consolation to her bereaved children:—

"23d of November, 1875.

"May God bless you and your good works, and may He grant peace to her that has departed.

"POPE PIUS IX."

It is unnecessary to add that this doubly precious document is religiously preserved in the archives of the Congregation of Philadelphia, to be handed down to future generations of its religious as a proof that our Lord recompensed, even in time, the devotion of this true daughter of the Church.

*   *   *   *

Mother St. John Fournier had been preceded in death by another of the American Foundresses, concerning whom we find the following notice in the Necrology of the Congregation, published at Lyons in 1861 :

"Sister St. Philomene, *née Devilaine*, aged fifty-one years, professed twenty-four years, died in our Community of Carondelet, America, on the 11th of November, 1861.

"This holy religious was one of the six Sisters who left us, in 1835, to devote themselves in far-distant lands to the promotion of God's glory, exercising their religious zeal at the cost of all they held dearest in the world. Alas ! in that laborious and painful mission, what privations had to be endured, what trials undergone ! . . . . . These, however, our beloved Sister accepted for the love of Jesus Christ. Firm as a rock amidst the raging billows, she was ever calm, tranquil, nay, even joyous in the midst of tribulation. She put all her trust in our Lord, and renewed her strength by the accomplishment of those religious virtues, of which she gave us such a brilliant example even to the last moment of her life."

Mother M. Félicité Bouté, whose first religious name of Sister Marguerite had been changed as heretofore noted, in compliment to the Countess de la Rochejacquelin, died also at the Mother House of Carondelet, September 23, 1881, at the age of seventy.

Her " old age was, in truth, a crown of dignity," because " it was found in the ways of justice." The sacrifice of health, talents, strength, and life, which in early years she had made to God, was not revoked when the weakness of exhaustion and the infirmities of later years came upon her. Eager to lay up treasures in Heaven before the coming of that " night wherein no man can work," she diligently employed herself in such labor as she was capable of when dispensed from the onerous duties of superiorship, keeping her heart meanwhile centered in God, walking daily in His holy presence. Humbling herself as a little child, she merited to sink to her eternal rest lovingly cradled in the arms of her Heavenly Father; and her soul, we confidently trust, was borne to Heaven by the angels of the countless little ones whom she had received, loved, and cared for with a supernatural maternal affection.

But *one* of the dear missionary Sisters of 1836 has been spared to witness the fiftieth year of her American apostolate, and to behold the fruitful harvest given by God in recompense of the laborious planting and tillage of earlier years. Yet Sister St. Protais, forgetful, like the great Apostle, " of the things that are behind and stretching forth to those that are before," continues, even at the present day, to work at the Indian mission of Baraga, Mich., for the love of that Divine Master from whose sweet lips she will, assuredly, one day hear the glorious commendation : " Well done, good and faithful servant; enter into the joy of thy Lord."

Ah, how eloquent, continues the Abbè Rivaux (whose narration we have interrupted to give a more extended notice of the American foundresses than he was able to obtain), how eloquent is the voice that issues from those far-distant tombs, inviting the whole Congregation of St. Joseph to venerate and imitate Rev. Mother St. John! The Sisters of America, worthy daughters of the Mothers she gave them, have often asked that her life might be written. We now offer it to them, as well as to their Sisters in the Old World, in all its simplicity. Fuller in details, more interesting in style it might have been, but such as it is, they will value it as a monument to one whom they would fain have held " in everlasting remembrance." The lives of religious have, for the members of their Order, an interest out of all proportion to their literary value. It is this salutary interest and reverence which Mother M. Alphonse de Ligouri, one of the Superiors General of the Congregation of Lyons, has recommended to her spiritual children in the following pious and touching words :

" Believe me that since I have become wholly yours, I have had only one desire, viz., that the Rev. Mother, Mothers Counsellors, Mother Superiors or Daughters of our Congregations should, by the most tender unanimity, form that beautiful fraternal crown of which the Holy Scripture speaks. Shall we not give this joy, my beloved children, to our ever-to-be-regretted Rev. Mothers? Let us not forget that we have all been formed and trained under the beneficent influence of their love. Oh! blessed forever shall be the precious and fruitful years of the government of our Rev. Mother Sacred Heart of Jesus, and the gentle and maternal administration of our beloved Rev. Mother Marie-Louise! God alone knows how ardent is my desire to profit by their lessons and example, forgetting not, in the meanwhile, her whose name must be forever blessed, our worthy Rev. Mother St. John. What perfect models our glorious Patriarch has successively chosen to set before his children the way of religious virtues! What a spirit of practical faith! What wisdom in their communications! What abnegation of self ! O my beloved daughters, what beautiful actions we could admire together, did the limits of our Circular admit of our giving free vent to our memories and our sentiments ! But to Him who crowns them this day we confide the effusions of our gratitude ; it is He, also, whom you will implore to grant me the grace of reproducing some of their characteristics, of renewing some of their glorious virtues."

On the receipt of this circular the Superior of the Sisters of St. Joseph of Philadelphia wrote to Mother Alphonse a letter of filial congratulation and holy delight. "Our hearts," she writes, "rejoice with yours at the remembrance which you so touchingly recall of those three incomparable Rev. Mothers, Mother St. John, Mother Sacred Heart of Jesus, and Mother Marie-Louise. Their saintly example, their great faith and rare virtues have established, edified, and embalmed the whole Congregation of St. Joseph. Although so widely separated from you, be assured the heart of each of our Sisters throbs in unison with yours at the names of those holy Mothers. We have been their children, we shall be yours. Our hearts exult with joy at the thought that one day, in our heavenly country, we shall all meet together with our blessed and venerated Mothers."

"The Church," says Mgr. Plantier, "living by the traditions preserved within her own bosom, loves to see religious congregations living and acting according to their traditional spirits ; and—while not rejecting salutary innovations—making as far as possible, both as regards persons and things, the present but a prolongation of the past."

Frederic Ozanam, the Vincent de Paul of laymen, has said : "The benediction of the Lord is upon those houses that remember their ancestors. It is under the shadow of those whom the grace of God and their own merits make so much greater than we, that we must shelter ourselves.

The beneficent shadow cast upon us by the story of their lives and our own meditations on their works will strengthen and vivify those virtues that should be born within us. Thus it is that, from this nest, formed, so to say, from the relics of their life, shall fly forth a glorious brood of souls worthy of their ancestors."

We leave to the pious Congregation of St. Joseph these eloquent invitations and recommendations regarding the remembrance of their early Mothers, virgins of exquisite moral beauty, whose immaculate and august prototype was the Virgin Mother of God. Virgins and Mothers themselves, they, conjointly with their religious family, have honored, rejoiced, enlarged, and adorned the Church. By their religious method of instruction and education, by their exercise of evangelical charity and the edification of their lives, the Sisters of St. Joseph are destined to take a great and glorious part in the struggle of good against evil, of truth against error and falsehood.

In this conflict they, after the example of their foundresses, teach and contend, according to the expression of the Imitation, " without noise of words, without confusion of opinions, without ambition of honor, without contention of arguments,"[1] rather after the manner of the stars. For the Scripture says, the stars have combated : *stellæ dimicaverunt,* which they do, however, only by shining, scintillating, enlightening, and thus sweetly overcoming the shadows of darkness. The Congregation of St. Joseph is a beautiful constellation in the starry firmament of the Church, diffusing its light amidst the darkness of pagan lands, and shedding on thousands of souls those beneficent rays which dissipate the clouds of error. God alone knows, for He alone could number, the multitude of souls whom it has formed to virtue and elevated to eternal happi-

---

[1] Bk. III., 43.

ness and the intuitive vision, since, restored by the venerable Mother St. John it has taken its place beside its illustrious and admirable sisters, the various religious Congregations.

May those blessed luminaries, conjointly, by the sweet brilliancy of their faith, hope, charity, and religious perfection, wage, successfully, their peaceful war against the powers of darkness, which, in our day especially, have been able to impregnate the minds even of many well-intentioned persons with the poisonous miasma of secular education, that satanic device for robbing the soul of the helps of religion, the knowledge of God. The combat is unequal as regards material resources, but that only renders it more imperative on religious to bring all the strength of their zeal and devotedness to the task of their own intellectual development, the elevation and perfection of their system of instruction, and the devising of effectual means for drawing to our Catholic schools and retaining therein, the children for whose benefit they have been organized. There is no means so potent as this for withdrawing the young from impiety at present, and for raising up, in the future, strong generations, who shall derive their being from parents firmly grounded in the love and practice of their holy religion. Society can be purified and elevated only by the purification and elevation of individual minds and characters, which, in turn, will react on families and communities. How grand, then, the work of re-edification to which the religious-teaching bodies are called, since, by the influence of religion alone, can this blessed end be reached! But how ardent, also, must be the faith and confidence that will animate those God-chosen instruments, how deep and solid that spirit of sanctity which will render them the living embodiment of the lessons of virtue they daily inculcate! Of such it shall be said in the words of Holy Writ : the stars have combated, and they have vanquished, *dimicaverunt stellæ et vicerunt.*

The religious orders, whose direct end is to make Saints, shall then be seen to have saved the world, not by remembering the attacks directed against God and themselves, but by having expiated them by prayers and tears, by generous forgiveness, by the merits of their sacrifices, and the heroism of their devotion.

The Cheapest and Best Book for Missions.

Catholic Belief:

or, A Short and Simple Exposition of Catholic Doctrine.

By the **Very Rev. Joseph Faà di Bruno, D.D.** Author's American edition edited by **Rev. Louis A. Lambert,** author of "Notes on Ingersoll," etc.

With the Imprimatur of Their Eminences the Cardinal, Archbishop of New York, and the Cardinal, Archbishop of Westminster, and an Introduction by the Right Rev. S. V. Ryan, Bishop of Buffalo.

16mo, flexible cloth, ... 40 cents.

10 copies, $2.65 ;   **50 copies, $12.00 ;**   **100 copies, $20.00.**

Extra cloth, red edges, 75 cents.

This is an admirable book of instruction on Christian Doctrine for both Catholics and Protestants.

Short, clear, simple and concise it meets the needs of a numerous class of non-Catholics, who yearning after Truth, unsettled in their convictions, sincere in their inquiries, and curious to know **just what Catholics do believe,** have neither leisure nor inclination to pore over large volumes or study elaborate dogmatical treatises.

The author evinces rare ability and tact in setting forth **Catholic principles in a few words, with winning** simplicity and yet scholastic **accuracy.** He treats of all **the leading dogmas of the Church,** yet as his aim is to remove "from minds otherwise well disposed, misconceptions of our holy religion, and still deep-rooted prejudices against Catholic faith," he naturally addresses himself more particularly to, and dwells more lengthily on, those doctrines which Protestantism has rejected. Another feature of the work is its **entire freedom from anything which might give offence** to any one, without, however, compromising or disguising the truth. He shows throughout a delicate consideration for those in error, and a just appreciation of the difficulties, intellectual, moral, and social, which converts to the Faith must encounter and overcome.

There is another feature of the book which is rarely found in controversial works : Though entirely master of the situation as regards the principles, the arguments, and facts at issue, the author does not rely wholly on these. The grace of God is essential to a true conversion, and hence this little book treats of grace and the means of obtaining it. Prayer is the primary means of grace, and hence **a spirit of prayer pervades the whole work, and the second part is specially devoted to this subject.**

The book is just the one to put in the hands of a Protestant friend, confident that Catholic faith will more readily reach the soul and bring conviction to the understanding, when Catholic charity has won the heart and favorably predisposed the will.

Over 80,000 copies of the book have been sold in England, and it has perhaps more than any other work been the means of bringing very many into the Church.

A Great Success! Over 65,000 sold!

The Right Rev. Bishop of Erie writes: "These books must and should receive the name of

"The Catholic Family Library."

The Christian Father;

What he should be, and what he should do. With Prayers suitable to his condition. From the German by Rev. L. A. Lambert, Waterloo, N. Y. With an Introduction, by Rt. Rev. S. V. RYAN, D.D., C.M., Bishop of Buffalo.

Paper,..................25 cents	Cloth,.......................50 cents
Maroquette, ...35 "	French Mor., flex., red edges, $1.00

The Christian Mother;

The Education of her Children and her Prayer. Translated by a Father of the Society of Jesus. With an Introduction by the Most Rev. JAMES GIBBONS, D.D., Archbishop of Baltimore.

Paper,..................25 cents	Cloth,......................... 50 cents
Maroquette, ...35 "	Calf, padded, red and gilt edges,..$2.50

A Sure Way to a Happy Marriage.

A Book of Instructions for those Betrothed and for Married People. Translated by Rev. Edward I. Taylor.

Paper,..................30 cents	Cloth ....60 cents
Maroquette,...........40 "	White Mar., gilt side and edges,..$1.25

In token of my appreciation, I request you to forward me **A thousand (1000) copies** of each of the two former books, and **five hundred (500)** of the third for distribution among my people.

Yours faithfully in Christ,

✠ JAMES VINCENT CLEARY, *Bishop of Kingston.*

From the Pastoral Letters of Rt. Rev. M. J. O'FARRELL, D.D., Bishop of Trenton.

"For Parents we recommend 'THE CHRISTIAN FATHER' and 'THE CHRISTIAN MOTHER,' in which they will fully learn all their duties to their children."—*Pastoral,* 1883.

"We **strongly recommend for your perusal and serious consideration** two little books lately published; one is entitled 'A SURE WAY TO A HAPPY MARRIAGE,' and the other 'An Instruction on Mixed Marriages,' by the Rt. Rev. Dr. Ullathorne.—*Pastoral,* 1882.

Warmly recommended and approved by **Five (5) Archbishops** and **Twenty-one (21) Bishops,** as follows:

The Most Rev. Archbishops of

BALTIMORE, CINCINNATI, OREGON, TORONTO, Can., TUAM, Ireland.

The Right Rev. Bishops of

ALTON,	GRASS VALLEY,	LONDON, Can.,	NEWARK,	ST. PAUL,
BUFFALO,	KINGSTON, Can.,	MARQUETTE,	OGDENSBURG,	SAVANNAH,
COVINGTON,	LA CROSSE,	NATCHEZ,	ST. CLOUD,	TRENTON,
ERIE,	LITTLE ROCK,	NESQUALLY,	ST. JOHN, N.B.	VINCENNES,
		WILMINGTON.		

A Most Liberal Discount to those who order in Quantities

BENZIGER BROTHERS, NEW YORK, CINCINNATI, AND CHICAGO.

www.ingramcontent.com/pod-product-compliance
Lightning Source LLC
Chambersburg PA
CBHW020943120726
47905CB00008B/2655